Theatre Matters
Performance and Culture on the World Stage

Theatre, in a variety of forms and contexts, can make, and indeed
has made, positive political and social interventions in a range of
developing cultures across the world. In this book a distinguished
team of theatre historians, practitioners and dramatists explores how
theatre has a dynamic and often difficult relationship with societies
and states, arguing positively that theatrical activity can make a
difference.

The collection begins with a foreword by Wole Soyinka and,
through the volume, specially chosen plays, projects and movements
are examined, embracing a variety of theatrical forms from
conventional text to on-site developmental work. The communities
addressed range from the national to the local, from middle-class
elites to the economically dispossessed in countries such as Brazil
and Argentina, Nigeria, Eritrea and South Africa, and India and the
Caribbean countries.

# CAMBRIDGE STUDIES IN MODERN THEATRE

Volumes for Cambridge Studies in Modern Theatre explore the political, social and cultural functions of theatre while also paying careful attention to detailed performance analysis. The focus of the series is on political approaches to the modern theatre with attention also being paid to theatres of earlier periods and their influence on contemporary drama. Topics in the series are chosen to investigate this relationship and include both playwrights (their aims and intentions set against the effects of their work) and process (with emphasis on rehearsal and production methods, the political structure within theatre companies, and their choice of audiences or performance venues). Further topics will include devised theatre, agitprop, community theatre, para-theatre and performance art. In all cases the series will be alive to the special cultural and political factors operating in the theatres they examine.

# Theatre Matters

Performance and Culture on the World Stage

edited by
Richard Boon and Jane Plastow

CAMBRIDGE
UNIVERSITY PRESS

PUBLISHED BY THE PRESS SYNDICATE OF THE UNIVERSITY OF CAMBRIDGE
The Pitt Building, Trumpington Street, Cambridge CB2 1RP, United Kingdom

CAMBRIDGE UNIVERSITY PRESS
The Edinburgh Building, Cambridge CB2 2RU, United Kingdom
40 West 20th Street, New York, NY 10011–4211, USA
10 Stamford Road, Oakleigh, Melbourne 3166, Australia

First published 1998

Printed in the United Kingdom at the University Press, Cambridge

Typeset in Trump Mediaeval and Schadow BT, in QuarkXPress™ GC

*A catalogue record for this book is available from the British Library*

*Library of Congress cataloguing in publication data*

Theatre matters: performance and culture on the world stage / edited by
Richard Boon and Jane Plastow.
    p.   cm. – (Cambridge studies in modern theatre)
Includes bibliographical references and index.
ISBN 0 521 63054 1 (hardback) 0 521 63443 1 (paperback)
1. Theatre – Political aspects.   2. Theatre – Social aspects.
I. Plastow, Jane.   II. Boon, Richard.   III. Series.
PN2049.T44   1998
792 – dc21   97-46774   CIP

ISBN 0 521 63054 1 hardback
ISBN 0 521 63443 1 paperback

# Contents

*Notes on contributors* ix

*Foreword: A letter from Kingston* xi
WOLE SOYINKA

*Preface* xix

*Acknowledgements* xxii

1 Introduction *1*
JANE PLASTOW

2 'The Revolution as Muse': drama as surreptitious insurrection in a post-colonial, military state *11*
FEMI OSOFISAN

3 Making theatre for a change: two plays of the Eritrean liberation struggle *36*
JANE PLASTOW AND SOLOMON TSEHAYE

4 Race matters in South African theatre *55*
IAN STEADMAN

5 Dreams of violence: moving beyond colonialism in Canadian and Caribbean drama *76*
CHRISTOPHER INNES

6 The French-speaking Caribbean: journeying from the native land *97*
CAROLE-ANNE UPTON

7 'Binglishing' the stage: a generation of Asian theatre in England *126*
JATINDER VERMA

*Contents*

8 Popular theatre for the building of social awareness: the
  Indian experience  *135*
  JACOB SRAMPICKAL SJ AND RICHARD BOON

9 The promise of performance: True Love/Real Love  *154*
  PAUL HERITAGE

10 Making America or making revolution: the theatre of Ricardo
   Halac in Argentina  *177*
   GEORGE WOODYARD

Index  *199*

# Notes on contributors

RICHARD BOON is the Deputy Director of the Workshop Theatre at the University of Leeds, UK, and the Course Director of the MA in Theatre Studies founded by Martin Banham in 1969. His teaching and research interests lie primarily in political theatre of all kinds, in directing for the stage and in multi-cultural theatre. He is author of *Brenton the Playwright* and of a number of articles, mainly in the area of political theatre in Britain.

PAUL HERITAGE is head of the Drama Department at Queen Mary and Westfield College, University of London, UK, and Associate Professor at the University of Rio de Janeiro, Brazil. He has worked extensively in Brazil using Boalian techniques, and has made a major contribution to the development of work with theatre in prisons in both the UK and Brazil.

CHRISTOPHER INNES is Professor of Theatre at York University, Ontario, Canada. He has published very widely, his interests including avant-garde theatre and African and Caribbean theatre. He is a member of the Advisory Editorial Board of the *Cambridge Guide to Theatre*.

FEMI OSOFISAN is Professor of Drama at the University of Ibadan, Nigeria, and a prolific playwright whose fame is second only to that of Wole Soyinka in their home country. He writes pungently political theatre from a broadly Marxist point of view.

JANE PLASTOW is Lecturer in Theatre Studies at the Workshop Theatre, University of Leeds, UK, where she teaches primarily in the areas of African theatre and gender in the theatre. She has worked on a variety of theatre projects in Africa since the 1980s, primarily in Ethiopia, Tanzania and Zimbabwe, and at present is closely involved in developing Eritrean theatre in the post-liberation period. She has written widely on emergent Eritrean theatre and is the author of *African Theatre and Politics*.

WOLE SOYINKA is a graduate of the University of Leeds, UK, and winner of the Nobel Prize for Literature in 1986. Playwright, poet, novelist, essayist and critic, he is generally recognised as Africa's greatest living playwright and one of the foremost writers of his generation. His most recent play is *The Beatification of Area Boy*.

JACOB SRAMPICKAL is a member of the Society of Jesus, and a doctoral graduate of the University of Leeds, UK. He has worked extensively in rural India using developmental theatre techniques, and is currently involved in the establishment of the National Institute of Social Communications, Research and Training in India.

IAN STEADMAN is Professor of Dramatic Art at the University of the Witwatersrand, South Africa, and an award-winning director in the theatre. He is founding co-editor of the *South African Theatre Journal*, and is author of numerous essays on South African theatre.

SOLOMON TSEHAYE is the Director of the Eritrean Bureau of Cultural Affairs. He was both a fighter and a playwright over a twenty-year period during the Eritrean liberation struggle of 1961–91, and was the first winner of the Eritrean National Literary Award in 1995.

CAROLE-ANNE UPTON is Lecturer in Drama at the University of Hull, UK. Her interests include African and Caribbean theatre in French and English, and Modern Irish drama. She is also a translator and director.

JATINDER VERMA is a founding member of Tara Arts, the first and foremost professional theatre company to be established and run by Asian immigrants in Britain. His work has sought a fusion of Indian and western techniques, and has been performed in the UK (at the National Theatre and in local communities), as well as overseas.

GEORGE WOODYARD is Professor of Spanish and Portuguese at the University of Kansas, Lawrence, USA, and has long had an interest in Latin American theatre. He is also a member of the Advisory Editorial Board of the *Cambridge Guide to Theatre*.

# Foreword: A letter from Kingston

WOLE SOYINKA

*Dear Martin*

This comes to you from Kingston, Jamaica, which has been aptly described as a clone of Lagos, Nigeria, a city that you may remember! It would not surprise you therefore to learn that *The Beatification of Area Boy* is being reincarnated in these parts, but the ramifications will surely stretch your imagination. Since you were very much involved in bringing that play to Leeds, I thought you might like some news of its latest adventures, which are the result of an exchange programme between Emory University and the University of West Indies. Wedged in between the two, as initiator and facilitator for the specific undertaking, is a production company known simply as The Company Ltd. It is not a theatre company but a group of 'enthusiastic volunteers' who periodically organise theatre practitioners – mostly amateur and semi-professional – into a production. Yes, I think that is an accurate way of describing the process: just as in Nigeria, there is no full-time theatre professionalism in Jamaica.

It is a long haul from Leeds where you helped so generously to facilitate the production of *Beatification* by the West Yorkshire Playhouse, not forgetting the further assistance you rendered to one of the actors who could not return to Nigeria after the performances on account of his prominent role in the production. Kingston is much closer to the birthplace of *Beatification* than Leeds, and I had looked forward to making up for the disappointment of not having its premiere take place in Lagos, its true milieu.

Well, the wonder of it all! This is probably one of those rare instances when a play has succeeded beyond the wildest dreams of an author even before rehearsals have begun. Does that sound like wishful thinking? Not when the sociology of an environment virtually begs for such a script, and there are committed artiste-citizens on the spot who see the possibilities, and resolve to exploit the coincidence in truly imaginative ways.

Kingston is a violent city. The nature of the violence in Kingston differs, however, from that of Lagos. Here, the area boys are the products of *garrisons* – as they are known locally – created and often maintained by politicians. The youths grow up in an atmosphere of mutual, predatory neighbourhood hostility. You do not stray from your own turf on to another – the result can be fatal. The politicians have apparently made it their life mission to maintain these bunker relations in their constituencies – for political control and sense of power even when out of power.

Each garrison – they go by such names as Barbican, Tel Aviv, Georgetown, Tivoli Gardens, Trenchtown, etc. – has its own schools, some have their own police, clinics and internal judicial system – or more accurately, means of dispensing justice, etc. The children grow up, attend school (or drop out), marry etc. within these garrisons, rarely into another. The zones are just suburban quarters, the same as you'll find in Lagos or any other city. They are defined by nothing more than the usual innocent-looking street, playground or neighbourhood shop – but you cross that demarcation strip at your own peril. Taking public transportation through other zones – as is unavoidable – means one thing only: don't descend at the wrong bus stop!

I should mention something also about the theatre where *Beatification* is scheduled to perform. We had a choice of a number of theatres, but the Ward Theatre, which is in the same contentious 'inner-city' category, happens to constitute a war-zone of its own. Remember the new – well, the seventies replacement for the old – Glover Hall in one of those Lagos side-streets that link Broad Street and Marina? It was a favourite stage for Orisun Theatre and the 1960 Masks whenever we performed in Lagos. And you will recall of course that parking your motor car to attend a show meant first 'seeing to' the area boys. If not, you might find your side-mirror missing on return, or your car sitting on wooden or cement blocks with one or two or all four wheels missing – or the entire car vanished into thin air! Of course we maintained an easy rapport with the area boys – it was mutual respect – and I don't recall any of our supporters undergoing such instructive experiences. Mind you, the 1960s were an immeasurably different climate from the Lagos of the 1980s till now – nowadays the thug is armed, waits for you to leave the theatre and then calmly demands your keys. He might also just shoot you for the fun of it – even after you have surrendered your keys!

It was a case of no contest – I settled for the Ward Theatre immediately we drove up to the building. It was as if I had been transported to Broad Street or Yaba, Lagos! Groundnut sellers, cigarette hawkers, rickety stalls with the usual knick-knacks were all on display, lay-abouts lolled on broken walls, tree stumps and pavements, in various stages of boredom and alert opportunism. Present and vacantly ambu-latory was the mandatory quota of an indulged street lunatic or two . . . summatively, in short, an exterior of dust and noise and vitality but – an efficient sound-insulated interior. (I prefer productions without unscripted 'noises off'.) The environment of Ward Theatre is unbe-lievably the environment of Glover Hall of the 1960 Masks/Orisun Theatre days – maybe just a touch more risk-laden. Here, if you want the uptown crowd at your production – and hardly any productions can make their way without that clientele – you first let your prospective audiences know that they can park their vehicles in a designated park-ing lot at a shopping mall, well-lit and policed, and that shuttle buses will be available to bring them to the Ward. Well, my production hosts – The Company Ltd – decided that they would break this tradition with *Beatification*! Involving the City Council and some business compan-ies, they set out to clean up the Ward Theatre environment, engaged the locals in the exercise, and plans have been laid out for landscaping and general reclamation.

You will have surmised already that this will be a very different kind of animal from the West Yorkshire Playhouse production – for one thing, it is a community-theatre-project-within-a-community-project. The Company's motivations for the production, plus the context, tal-lied neatly with what I had envisaged for Lagos, except of course that their goals went much further. It was an opportunity to break the 'garrison mentality' among youths, and this constituted the group's primary goal. There was a formal launching of the 'Area Boy Project' in February – it was a most eloquent affair! Every aspect of Kingston civic life was present – the media, business firms, local councils, university, hotel management, politicians, tourism, social workers, the Minister of Culture and of course – representatives of the troubled inner city population – the area boys themselves. It was a new experience for me to listen to all these sectors articulate a *problem* in a situation where they had been brought together by an artistic project, one which, they felt, could provide the beginnings of a *solution*! Monetary and material pledges were made and, as I write, they are being fulfilled, and new ones made by others who have been following the project in the news. They call up the television station, the newspapers or The Company.

The first step of The Project was a talent-scout throughout the inner city. This was a bold device that took the project leaders into those fortified ghettoes. There, they auditioned youths and then brought the successful ones together – seventy altogether! It was the first undertaking of their lives across zones, the first time they were able to see that their age-mates across the street did not hide devil's horns beneath their rastafarian locks, that there was not a gun lurking behind every lamp-post. Encouraged to narrate and reproduce their experiences for the stage, they – as is proved again and again in every corner of the world – revealed unsuspected creative talents in all directions. For eight weeks they rehearsed their own scripts under the guidance of the project leaders and had their first outing just two weeks ago, in the same Ward Theatre, in a show that was appropriately titled *Border Connections*. The enthusiastic response of the audience was amply deserved. They have since performed at various venues, mostly open air, including the Independence/Emancipation celebrations, weekend of 1 August 1997. Ah, the days of your Unibadan Travelling Theatre (and memories of Geoffrey Axworthy!), of Ogunmola, Duro Ladipo or Orisun Theatre at Mbari, in sports fields, marketplaces and expropriated courtyards!

Such was the initiative of these kids that they started their own newspaper – *The Area Boy News*! – an eight-page mimeographed edition with cartoons, Agony Column (quite witty), poetry, etc. which they sell to raise funds. At the early stages when funds were somewhat slow coming in, they undertook a walkathon on their own, raising 13,000 Jamaican dollars (about US $450) for the project. Their enthusiasm obviously swept ordinary folk off their feet, the same energy and vitality that electrified the air when all seventy of them poured into the Ward Theatre stage from all sides of the auditorium to plunge into their opening number!

Eleven of the seventy had been selected for minor roles for the second stage of the project – the play itself; others are apprenticed to the technical department – design, set and costume building and lighting. You may recall that Orisun Theatre had its beginnings with just such a component of area boys, so you can imagine the weird sensation that their presence triggers off in me – back to the 1960s in my sixties! Their lives have been more violent, of course. One actor lost a brother in a shoot-out, and then his father was wounded, and is still invalided, in yet another. A girl (15) has been looking after both herself and her junior sister since they were abandoned by their parents when she was 11. The father gives her a small stipend which she ekes out with after-school jobs. Another girl lost an eye in circumstances that have probably traumatised her, since she tells a strange, improbable story of how it was supposed to have happened. She has refused medical aid, even examination, insisting that she is not really blind in the eye but that she has acquired a kind of special sight that enables her to see into the supernatural world! After rehearsals, some may find that they have to stay the night with friends because the passage home has become too hot! I had a drink in a bar in Barbican one late afternoon and learnt that a woman was shot later that evening – caught in a cross-fire – in front of that very bar.

Some of the company turn up late or do not turn up at all for rehearsals because the shifting war-zone made it unsafe at the time – indeed a strapping sixteen-year-old was locked up at home by his mother for three days: she was scared that his physical over-development would make him a target of enemy violence . . . and so on, and on. (Of course some of the company simply do not turn up, and then wonder why there should be any fuss!) For all of them, however, this is a break that they never envisaged in their wildest dreams. They are paid only their transport fare, though fed when attending rehearsals – courtesy of Kentucky Fried Chicken, one of the project sponsors. Some have already obtained short-spell scholarships to receive further training with dance company groups like Ashe. For their *Border Connections* they learnt how to design and make masks – each of the seventy made his or her own mask for one of the more sobering skits in the show – an indictment of the forces that use them as cannon fodder, blighting their childhood and lives. The greatest experience for all of them, however, has been to be able to do the impossible – go into the enemy camp, and perform to an enthusiastic audience.

Now, perhaps you will appreciate the extravagant claims I made at the beginning. *Beatification* itself has run into difficulties – professional theatre does not exist in Jamaica, alas!, and a professional *attitude* is a strange concept for many. Add to that the usual problem of funds and, well, after two weeks of rehearsals, we are not totally confident of the fate of this production. The strange feeling for me, however, is that this seems so secondary, almost trivial, given the transformation the project has wrought in the lives of these garrison kids, and the possible – just possible – re-thinking it may begin to provoke in the minds of the politicians. How they will undo the evil they have done to these young lives, I do not know, and certainly *Beatification* is not the magic wand whose wave will achieve the miracle – those power-blinded men are a long, long way from beatification. The *potential* social implications are, however, far-reaching, and the level of identification and commitment of these young reformers is often startling. Can you imagine what it means to listen to a thirteen-year-old girl from the garrison declare, with a laugh that had just a hint of menace: '*Anyone who wants to remove me from this project had better start looking for a tractor*'? She was referring to her father who had come once or twice to express misgivings about her participation.

Several of them have narrated their lives on video, assessing the impact that the Area Boy project has already made on them in its brief existence, quite apart from unlocking their creative assets. For both sociologists (and psychologists) as well as theatre practitioners they provide some remarkable insights into the actual operations of theatre on the human personality. A few titles of the sketches and songs will give you an idea of the main thrust of their performance, and explain why one of the younger project supervisors voiced a fear that the movement would not last, because 'the politicians will kill it': *Youth Oppressed; How we come to Dis; Mi Son Dead; Mi Hungry, Mi Angry; Skeletal Dance; Isn't There another Way? Put Down de Gun: Look ina Yu'self* etc. That last item is indicative of their refreshing impulse to self-criticism, in addition to the robust indictment of the negative forces in their lives – social marginalisation, political manipulation and violence as sung, danced and mimed in other items such as *Youth Oppressed; Mi Hungry, Mi Angry* etc. Let me emphasise again that all the sketches, songs and thematic outlines are provided by these youths themselves. All their advisers do is provide the aesthetic structure and rehearse them, as well as minister to their logistical needs.

That young supervisor's fears will prove unfounded, I am convinced, the politics of Jamaica being very different from the politics of Nigeria, even in the less malevolent (in hindsight) sixties. And the message of the youths can by no stretch of the imagination be interpreted as partisan. So I do not see the Area Boys Crew training backstage in the use of fire extinguishers, etc. for self-defence, as became the norm for Orisun Theatre at the height of the sixties' political madness!

Well, that is the state of play for now. I cannot think of a more appropriate experience to share with you on this occasion of your *festschrift*, given its overall theme. Repression takes many forms, some quite subtle, and the tools of resistance must adapt to its every manifestation, which is nearly always unique. Hopefully, the foregoing will provoke pleasant memories of the work you were involved in during your stint in Nigeria with the university equivalents of the area boys – 'same difference' really, most of the time, I am sure you'll agree.

A footnote – I cannot resist it – provoked by one of these same politician types who try to prove that they are not illiterate, but are indeed up-to-date on contemporary trendiness. Having had my fill of it in the United States, I was confident that, in Lagosian Kingston, I had escaped, for a while at least, the rampaging beast of Political Correctness. I was due for a shock. After the Emancipation Day performance by the Area Boys Crew – as they style themselves – a lady something from the Town Council's cultural division got up to make a speech that was supposed to be a vote of thanks for the various performing groups. She spent most of her time on *Border Connections* – but not on the performance. No, her recriminations were reserved for the hapless organisers and their choice of name for the project. Why 'Area Boy'? she demanded. Why was the opposite sex ignored? She launched into a public tirade against what she regarded as its overt sexism, totally forgetting even to commend the kids – boys or girls – for their performance.

The pall of Political Correctness was cast over what, until then, had been very simply a festive and thought-provoking outing at a national occasion.

Of course this political functionnaire was fully aware of the origination of the project, had had more than ample opportunities to speak to the project leaders whom she knew personally, and with whom she frequently interacted. That course was far too rational. Where would Political Correctness be without grandstanding? What she would have learnt, had she opted for that course, was that most of the running of the group was done by democratic decisions. The project leaders had in fact made the suggestion to the group that they might want to consider a different title for themselves – 'Area Kids', 'Area Youths' or whatever. The boys had no objection, it was the girls who vociferously rejected any change in the name. They wanted to be known by the title of W.S.'s play and nothing else. T-Shirts, stickers, brooches (bearing their individual names), all donated by supporting firms – everything must be 'Area Boy', including even the name of the club which, again on their own, they have formed, and to which they have elected their own officers.

Who did that politician/civil servant instantly remind me of? That schoolteacher in your part of the world (somewhere near London, I recall) who denied her pupils the opportunity to attend a ballet based on *Romeo and Juliet* because she considered Shakespeare's treatment of heterosexual love stereotyped and politically incorrect! In the implacable war against the imbecilities of Political Correctness, do let the forces of creative rationality – theatre regiment – know that we have a volunteer army in Kingston, Jamaica, ready to take on demented schoolteachers and other p.c. philistines at a moment's notice!

*Wole Soyinka*

# Preface

The origins of this book lie in the determination of its editors and their colleagues to mark the retirement in 1998 of Martin Banham as Professor of Drama and Theatre Studies and Director of The Workshop Theatre at the University of Leeds.

A *festschrift* was an obvious way of allowing some, at least, of Martin's many friends and colleagues the opportunity of honouring his achievement as teacher, scholar and academic. What was less immediately clear was the precise form such a book might take. It is a testament to the breadth of Martin's interests and expertise that this collection of essays could quite easily have concerned itself with the history of British theatre, or with Shakespeare, or Victorian melodrama (especially or even only Tom Taylor!); with designing for the stage, or with part or the whole of that great range of educational and developmental uses to which drama and the theatre have been put. All would have been both appropriate and legitimate. In reality, however, our choice of subject was a simple one. Since he began his academic career in the 1950s at the University of Ibadan (a time fondly recollected by Wole Soyinka in his Foreword), a large part of Martin's heart has belonged to the theatre of Nigeria. Indeed, the importance of his influence on the creation of the modern theatre of that troubled country has long been recognised. (Only recently, Martin was greatly embarrassed, on meeting a young theatre director who had just returned from a visit to West Africa, to be greeted by 'Martin Banham? You're a legend!'.) Prompted, no doubt, by the extraordinarily rich and diverse theatrical culture of West Africa, Martin's interests grew quickly to embrace the theatres of Africa generally, and these interests have remained very much at the centre of his teaching and research ever since. The contributions made to this volume by Wole Soyinka, Femi Osofisan, Ian Steadman, and Jane Plastow and Solomon Tsehaye go some way, we hope, to recognising and reflecting what has been a genuine and life-long passion. The other essays found here, dealing with theatres and theatrical activity in the Caribbean, in North and South America, in India and in Britain, similarly seek to acknowledge not only Martin's belief in the social power of theatre, but his continuing fascination with performance of all kinds in a variety of cultural contexts. It is the persistent strength of that fascination which lies behind and accounts for two of his greatest achievements.

On his return to Britain in the late 1960s, Martin established The Workshop Theatre at the University of Leeds, and went on, in 1969, to create with Trevor Faulkner what was the first (and remains the longest-established) MA in Theatre Studies in the country; although the title would doubtless cause him some embarrassment, it remains true that he is one of the 'founding fathers' of theatre studies as an academic discipline in British universities. From the beginning (and long before it became financially expedient to do so), the MA was committed to recruiting students from around the world, and to exposing them to and challenging them with a rich diversity of multicultural theatrical practice. African students were always a theme, especially students from West Africa, from Nigeria, Ghana, Cameroon and Sierra Leone; but Kenyans, Tanzanians and Ugandans also featured, as did Americans, Syrians, Iranians, Chinese, Japanese, Australians, Koreans, Canadians, Turks, Lebanese, Brazilians, Indians . . . as well as most varieties of European, including, of course, Britons. Many have gone on to achieve distinction as academics or practitioners (Martin has always resisted conventional distinctions between the two), their numbers swelled by the many research students whom he has supervised. One of the latter, Father Jacob Srampickal, makes his own contribution to this book. Whether student or supervisee, all, we may say without hesitation, would acknowledge the magnitude of the debt owed to Martin, as would students of the BA programme in English Literature and Theatre Studies inaugurated under his leadership in 1989.

In his editorship of the *Cambridge Guide to Theatre*, Martin was able to draw on his expertise as an Africanist, his experience as a teacher of students from many cultures, his own professional travels (often under the auspices of the British Council) and an international network of colleagues and friends in the academy and 'the profession' to create a unique, fascinating and endlessly informative scholarly reference work. Whilst he would be the first to acknowledge the collaborative nature of the enterprise, and the huge contributions made by Sarah Stanton and others at Cambridge University Press, by the Editorial Advisory Board (two of whom, Christopher Innes and George Woodyard, appear here), and by a host of contributors, it is hard to imagine anyone else who would have possessed the breadth of knowledge and experience, the wisdom and the patience, necessary to give birth to so monumental an undertaking. Moreover, although he appears himself as contributor only sparingly, his *imprimatur* is felt everywhere within the book. In the space of twenty pages are to be found entries not only on Stanislavsky, Stein and stage lighting, but on Sri Lanka, stage food and 'Stainless Stephen' (a music-hall comedian and childhood hero). In its ambition, the richness and range of its variety, the rigour of its scholarship, its occasional flashes of wit and general lightness of touch (the last two qualities fast disappearing from the contemporary academic scene), the book stands as clear testament to the character of its editor.

These were qualities which we wished to celebrate in our *festschrift*. Our initial approach to the Press was greeted with warm support, but it was also made clear, quite properly, that any book could not 'only' be a *festschrift*, but must also stand on its own as a serious contribution to theatre scholarship. We hope and believe that we have achieved that, not least because anything else would be a grave disservice to Martin's achievement. Our punning title, with its implications of the positive, the optimistic and the up-beat, attempts to mirror in our own (perhaps rather unfashionable) argument – that theatre can and does 'make a difference' to the societies and cultures of which it is part – something of the character and career of the man we seek to honour, for whom theatre has always 'mattered'.

*Richard Boon and Jane Plastow*

# Acknowledgements

We are grateful to Sarah Stanton and Victoria Cooper at Cambridge University Press for their invaluable advice and support, and to our contributors for their generosity and professionalism in contending with tight deadlines and requests for further information and clarification; and for the trust they placed in us as their editors. We are also grateful to Mark Batty, Chris Jowett and Nicola Wildman for technical help of various kinds. Appreciative mention must also be made of friends and colleagues who freely gave advice and support or who, in the planning stages of this project, offered suggestions, ideas and even contributions which, sadly, finally fell outside the scope of the book: Christopher Banfield, Ruby Cohn, Tony Green, Peter Holland, Eldred Jones, Dragan Klaic, Tice Miller, Yasunari Takahashi, Peter Thomson and Don Wilmeth.

Finally we are particularly grateful to Ms Nora Lenderby, who very generously provided us with free accommodation during a research visit to London.

# 1 Introduction

JANE PLASTOW

*Theatre Matters* is an assertive title, but it embodies an idea that the editors and contributors to this book all, in very different ways, see as central to our engagement with the theatrical form. If I were writing this in parts of the South[1] I might not feel the need to make the assertion so emphatically because it would be more self-evident. In countries such as Nigeria and South Africa, and in some parts of India, theatre productions, companies and playwrights have engaged, often head-on, with the ruling classes in debates about government and social and political reform. The impact of such interventions can be seen most clearly in the level of state response. Banning orders, censorship, imprisonment and, in the most extreme cases, murder, as in the 1996 state killing of the Nigerian writer Ken Saro Wiwa, have often been the lot of those who have used theatre to take on the state, and it should be noted that several of those featured in this book have lived with the knowledge that their work may at any moment cost them their freedom, or possibly their lives. If theatre did not matter, as in such immediate ways it palpably does not matter in most of the western world, state responses would not be so extreme.

In other instances the theatres we are debating here are not dealing with political embattlement but, as in the Caribbean pieces, the essay by Jatinder Verma and the plays of the native American playwright Tomson Highway, as discussed by Christopher Innes, with the creation of identities and a sense of self-worth. Here the notion that is being interrogated is that a people without some sense of communal identity become fundamentally disempowered and negated at a profound level of their personal sense of being. In all the cases examined that negation has arisen because of the process of colonisation which

I

has uprooted or disenfranchised communities. The theatre not only examines the resultant sense of loss of self-worth but also attempts to take part in the healing process of asserting culture and identity, so that the people involved can begin to re-value or even to re-invent themselves in the context of their contemporary post- or neo-colonial situation. What both approaches to making theatre have in common is a belief in function. This does not in any sense crudely privilege message over aesthetic sensibility, but rather posits a theatre where function and aesthetic importantly cohabit in the same performance arena.

The impact of cultural interventions can never be neatly measured and this, I think, is one reason why politicians, economists and various types of development agencies, who usually have control of the purse-strings, are so often reluctant, world-wide, to fund cultural expression. Paradoxically, those same agencies may at times fear the uncontrollable nature of creative expression and so, again, be reluctant to support the arts. This book examines a diverse range of theatrical engagements with the state and society in order not to prescribe, but to examine how committed theatres of various kinds work and the kinds of impact they make on the people exposed to that work. The style and content of each practitioner involved is unique, responding to particular realities in specific times and places. What this book seeks to do is to further debate both on how and why theatre might 'matter', and about the range of ways in which theatre which might loosely be described as 'committed' has sought to express itself.

The people who have contributed to this book come to their subject from a range of different perspectives which quite obviously colour their approach to the subject. Those who are primarily playwrights, like Soyinka and Osofisan, are able to give us a very personal, immediate argument for why they work as they do and what impact they seek to make. Others – Srampickal, Verma, Heritage, Tsehaye and myself – all have a degree of academic interest, but are also practically engaged in making theatre in the societies we examine, and we bring to our arguments, I think, an interpreter's eye as well as in some cases a creator's vision. The third category of writers are the 'straight' academics; here there is, I think, a different flavour to the writing, with a greater sense of objective overview than is present in the essays by the practitioners.

I think this variety of overlapping perspectives in itself sets up various arguments about how judgements might be made about theatres which seek to 'matter'. It seems quite obvious in the writings of Soyinka, Heritage and Srampickal that some of those most profoundly affected by the theatres they discuss are the people who are actually drawn into the creative process. For participants this theatre quite incontrovertibly matters and has had a revolutionary effect often on both their lives and their thinking. It is much more difficult for more distanced writers to make those kinds of first-hand judgement. It is also easier for the practitioners to make statements about the kinds of audience they wish to reach and the impact they are at least trying to make than it is for outside observers. What the academy is perhaps best placed to do is to give the overview, to compare and contrast away from the hurly-burly of actual practice, so that writers such as Innes can give us examples from two very different places which yet have powerful linkages of situation and intent, Steadman surveys the South African scene in a crucial period of flux while Upton and Woodyard examine how the work of individual playwrights, over the course of an entire career, shifts, adapts and re-positions itself in response to changing national contexts.

However, it is surely significant that it is often quite difficult to find the material which demonstrates the impact of theatre in a particular time and place. The artefact, the play itself, is usually not difficult to unearth, but – with the exception of South Africa where so much theatre until recently was declaring itself as primarily aimed at effecting political change that the issue of impact could not be ignored – how much a production actually affects participants, audiences or society more widely has not usually been seen as being of primary interest to those who study theatre. Academic study of theatre has too often perhaps been dominated by a literary approach which views the text in isolation from the conditions of its creation and performance. For the academics who have contributed to this book it has sometimes proved very difficult to find evidence of the impact of particular theatrical events on those involved in, or witnessing, a production. However subjective such material may be it is surely significant to know how an audience might react to a play by Osofisan in Nigeria or Halac in

Argentina. Theatre's best chance of having an impact is not, I would argue, in the literary text, but in the live performance which is, after all, what makes theatre different and not simply a form of literary aberration. If my argument has any strength it then follows that those of us who wish to understand the contemporary significance of theatre need not only to read texts and interview authors, but also to see plays, ask questions of audiences and take notice of reactions appearing in local media. Theatre that 'matters' must be theatre in interaction with society, and the text-based study to which the academy has so often limited itself is surely as partial a basis for making judgements as a deaf man watching an orchestra.

Contributors not only see the theatre they are involved in from different perspectives of engagement, they also work from very different imperatives and in radically varying modes. None of these are inherently contradictory. To quote from Soyinka's foreword to this book: 'Repression takes many forms, some quite subtle, and the tools of resistance must adapt to its every manifestation, which is nearly always unique.' A playwright will always bring not only his or her own sensibility to their work but is also bound to be affected by the conditions and kinds of repression and oppression against which they work. I have already mentioned the two obvious divisions of psychological and overtly political theatre which are very clear in this book. But even within such broad areas each writer brings a very different perspective to bear.

At one extreme the work of the Eritrean and South African playwrights during their countries' liberation struggles had obvious propaganda objectives, both political and social. Halac, Boukman, Osofisan and Soyinka might all be called political propagandists in various of their plays. Even the work Srampickal records in India could be seen to fall under the umbrella of social propaganda. Propaganda has become something of a dirty word in the west, where it is too often equated with coercion and the excesses of either fascism or eastern European state communism. From discussions with many southern practitioners and playwrights I do not think the word propaganda has the same pejorative connotations in relation to much of their work. Neither Femi Osofisan nor Alemseged Tesfai has any problem with seeing himself as a propagandist – they see political and social evils and wish to use theatre to help rectify these – therefore they make propaganda. They do not see this as brainwashing but rather as bringing 'obvious' truths into the clear light of day in opposition to states which wish to obscure the truth about oppression in order to continue their domination of the people. The idea that propaganda may be a tool of empowerment is one which several writers featured here might see as relevant.

Where Osofisan differs from Alemseged and from many other playwrights considered here is that he believes that the way to make propaganda effective and to effect change is to target the middle and upper – and especially the student – classes in his plays. Osofisan argues – of course from a primarily Nigerian perspective – that peasant and workers' revolts are inevitably crushed by the ruling classes, and that therefore it is that latter class which must be brought to see the injustice of its behaviour and effect reform. This argument can be seen clearly in plays such as Osofisan's *Morountodun*[2] where hope lies in the conversion of a rich bourgeois woman to the cause of the oppressed peasantry, although ironically in a play which draws on actual Nigerian history, even with such a conversion, peasant revolt is still crushed. Still Osofisan seeks to hold up a mirror to his bourgeois audiences so that *à la* Brecht they will see their world from a startling new perspective. Soyinka too is most famous for his complex stage productions which reach predominantly bourgeois audiences, and he has often been criticised for being elitist. Yet Soyinka has another side. He was instrumental in setting up guerrilla theatre groups in Nigeria in the 1970s, and his work in Jamaica interestingly combines the populist and bourgeois strands of his theatre practice, both of which he sees as being equally important in working towards democratic revolution.

Paul Heritage's contribution continues the debate when he discusses a Brazilian theatre group which puts on populist and classical theatre, both in the open air and in a laboriously constructed theatre, dug out of the underworld of the *favela*. Heritage makes a powerful argument for the rejection of an either/or position in relation to the conventional/classical or developmental/populist debate about how to make theatre that 'matters'. For the Brazilian group both are instruments – in different but related ways – of liberation and the creation of a culture of self-valuing for the disempowered people of the margins.

This more embracing consciousness of how theatre can matter relates to the psychological theatres of the Caribbean, of Jatinder Verma and of Tomson Highway. Here it is the very act of making theatre which is perhaps more important. For here we are dealing with people who have been so displaced or denigrated that the world, and to some extent they themselves, may have come to see them as invisible, culture-less and without identity. To explore identities – and not in any kind of eulogistic manner – is central to this theatre. For one of the greatest evils of colonialism was to strip people of their belief in themselves and their very being. As the Kenyan novelist and playwright, Ngugi wa Thiong'o, argues:

> The biggest weapon yielded and daily unleashed by
> imperialism against . . . collective defiance is the cultural bomb.
> The effect of a cultural bomb is to annihilate a people's belief
> in their names, in their languages, in their environment, in
> their heritage of struggle, in their unity and ultimately in
> themselves.[3]

The theatres of Walcott, and even more strikingly perhaps of High-way, speak to a people struggling to re-identify themselves against a history of loss, defeat and denigration which at its most extreme, as among some of the Canadian Native Americans, threatens to drive a people into acts of self-annihilation; surely the ultimate triumph for a colonial power.

Interestingly here the Francophone Caribbean experience is different again. Boukman proves a playwright very difficult to pigeon-hole with an œuvre ranging from plays advocating international revolution to the more recent Délivrans!, which seems to come from a place nearer to the work of such as Walcott in its more internalised debate over identity. Influenced by French assimilationist philosophies, by Césaire's negritudism – which arguably is a by-product of and reaction to assimilationism – and most strikingly by Frantz Fanon (it is surely extraordinary that the tiny island of Martinique has produced these two hugely influential figures, and almost inevitable that Boukman writes to some extent in response to them), Boukman's theatre is possibly the most obviously internationalist of any of those examined here. Identity is asserted in relation to other struggles which are seen as parallel to, and in some ways even the same as, those of the Martiniquans. The French imperialists thought they could create an international body of essentially similar French people throughout their empire, as opposed to the British who often sought to emphasise difference in order to perpetuate a policy of divide-and-rule. Possibly this has a bearing on Anglophone writers' often more culturally specific work, whereas Boukman continually seeks to put the Martiniquan situation into a series of international perspectives covering not only the Antilles but also Africa and the Middle East.

The status of Africa in this text which deals with so many peoples who come from, relate to, or have had experience of that continent, is fascinating. For the undisplaced Africans of Nigeria and Eritrea, Africa is the site of struggles for freedom from colonial and post-colonial oppression, but it is a reality in a way that Steadman seems to argue it is not even for South Africans. Steadman refers to the *myth* of Africa, and of course most South Africans – largely due to embargoes on travel resulting from apartheid – effectively know less of other Africas than they do of pervasive American culture which is continually beamed into the country via various forms of media and economic linkage.

In South Africa there is also the debate as to who can claim to be African in that country whose people result from a history of centuries of invasion and migration. And then Verma brings another perspective to bear when he talks of Kenyan Asians who have chosen largely a kind of collective amnesia in relation to their African roots, and who, in England, generally choose to fillet a sixty-year sojourn in Kenya from the group memory and instead look back to another kind of myth of Asia as the source of community identity.

Finally, the Caribbean people have yet another perception of history and identity, torn between awareness and myth of Africa and America seen through the prism of either British or French colonialism. For many playwrights in this book, whether their work is overtly political or more concerned with the forging of communal identities, myth, memory and history are continually invoked in an endeavour to find who a people might be and how they can identify themselves in relation to contemporary realities after the trauma of the period of colonial adventurism. What strikes the reader is that in this endeavour myth is often as important as, if not more important than, more conventional history in articulating states of consciousness, possibly because myth, as in the work of Osofisan and Highway, can often be invoked dynamically, re-imagined and re-worked to create a bridge between past and future.

Issues of identity in the neo- and post-colonial eras relate closely to the issue of nation, which is another theme that recurs in many different guises in this book. At its most extreme in Alemseged Tesfai's *The Other War*, and more obliquely in the work of Highway, theatre is used to protest against forms of actual genocide. But in almost every other practitioner's work, with the possible exception of Srampickal, the interrogation and assertion of identity either implicitly or explicitly involves an examination of the notion of nation. The questions of to whom the nation does or should belong are continually raised in both ethnic and class terms. Verma examines not only Kenyan-Asian identity but also that identity in relation to the place of Kenyan-Asians as British citizens who relate in different ways to their Asian, African and European experiences and memories. Walcott looks at the heterodox identity of the people of Trinidad and at how that affects their sense of community, and implicitly, by extension, their sense of nation. In South Africa and Nigeria the discussion is more about who owns and therefore essentially constitutes the nation. Race is crucially part of this debate in South Africa, but in Nigeria ethnicity also plays a part, along with class and (an often-present issue in the political South) the relative place of urban and rural peoples. In some cases theatre is invoked literally to write the nation into being, but in others it is used to question what is the nation, who is the nation and to whom will it belong?

Ultimately it seems necessary to explain why some areas of the world and some kinds of theatre are not represented in this book. The editors are not unaware that there is minimal representation in this work of white or 'First World' playwrights or practitioners. This is largely because of the post/neo-colonial positioning of the text. We have chosen to focus on work which 'matters' predominantly in relation to the very difficult construct of nationhood, conceived either geographically or ethnically, and work which aims in some way to speak to and/

or for that whole 'nation'. A sense of urgency in writing or playing the nation into being or into a sense of where it should be going seems to lie at the present time mainly with the post- and neo-colonial peoples. In contrast most contemporary western political theatre is not only already exhaustively analysed by academics, but actually makes, I would argue, precious little impact on either audiences or the state. (I would exclude here various Eastern European theatres which have been omitted mainly because they had a different kind of history in relation to colonialism rather than because they have not made an impact.) The theatre that might claim to 'matter' by this book's criteria in the west is possibly more issue- or locality-based theatre focusing on single issues, minority rights, local community identity, etc. We in no way seek to devalue this work: it is simply beyond the remit of this book.

A coda to this introduction – which possibly resonates interestingly with Wole Soyinka's final paragraphs. There are no women playwrights or theatre impresarios included here, and only two (western) women contributors. This does not mean women are invisible in creating theatre that matters. It does mean that it is still often hard for women, particularly in the South, to command the resources needed to bring theatre into being. In many of the cultures under consideration, to be a woman performer is still likely to bring accusations of immorality, and even those women who do perform are usually forced to give up the profession when they marry, or as the price of marrying in order to carry out a 'proper' role as wife, mother and home-maker. Moreover, in many places women commonly have less access to education than men, and it is noticeable that often only highly educated women, who thereby command a measure of economic independence, are enabled to transgress societal mores sufficiently radically to become writers and makers of theatre. Many women playwrights like the Nigerian Tess Oumwene and the Ghanaians Ama Ata Aidoo and Efua Sutherland have been able to write largely because they were protected by the respectability of an academic career. In other cases women can often only continue to work in theatre if they marry someone else in the profession. It is to be earnestly hoped that any future book dealing with this area of theatre will be able to include women speaking to the nation just as vociferously as their men.

NOTES

1 In the body of the text we have usually used the term 'Third World'. Such terms are notoriously difficult because they can often be seen as patronising or pejorative. In this book 'Third World' is broadly used to describe the poorer countries which came into being during the colonial period. 'South', as used in this Introduction, refers in a more political sense to those nations which have suffered under-development at the hands of the rich, capitalist, political 'North'. These categories are broadly, though not exclusively, geographically based.

2 Femi Osofisan, *Morountodun and Other Plays* (Ibadan: Longman, 1982).

3 Ngugi wa Thiong'o, *Decolonising the Mind* (London: James Currey, 1986), p. 3.

## 2 'The Revolution as Muse'
## drama as surreptitious insurrection in
## a post-colonial, military state

FEMI OSOFISAN

. . . the only safe place I've ever known is at the centre of a story, as its teller. (Athol Fugard)

We might say then . . . that Osofisan's play is, ultimately, a celebration of the Revolution as Muse. (Abiola Irele)[1]

### I

Except by surreptitious tactics, the voice of protest in a one-party state cannot be pressed to the public ear. When the state in question is, in addition, under the iron grip of military dictatorship, and one too that is stridently intolerant of criticism and opposition, protest in whatever form becomes a gamble with danger, unless formulated with especial cunning. In particular, in the field of drama, a recourse to ruse becomes *de rigueur*, if only because, in theatrical performance, the fate of several persons is involved; hence the artist must accept it as a primary obligation to proceed through such strategies of enlightened guile that will ensure that his or her collaborators do not become the careless victims of official thugs. Happily, however, against the inert silence which autocrats seek to impose upon their subjects, the dissenting artist can triumph through the gift of metaphor and magic, parody and parable, masking and mimicry. With this gift, properly deployed, the terror of the state can be confronted, demystified. But it has to be a conscious tactic of deployment, one that has also to be constantly re-tuned and re-honed to the particular moment, a covert and metamorphic system of manoeuvring which, for want of a better term, I have summarised as 'surreptitious insurrection'.[2]

## II

How does this system operate? To answer this question, we must first take a rapid tour through the history of my own country, Nigeria, in order to understand the turmoil which constructs my plays, and against which my plays are constructed. Nigeria became 'independent' from a century of British colonialism in 1960. But in reality, like everywhere else from where the British departed, ours was no more than a 'flag independence', a situation where economic control remained in London, while the local leaders left behind were stooges carefully selected from among members of the elite sympathetic to British interests. These were people who had accepted to serve as agents for the British policy of 'indirect rule', and so enjoyed a privileged status under colonialism.

Thus in Nigeria political leaders from our conservative, Muslim north, who had resisted western education and missionary influence, and had even initially opposed the granting of independence, came to power. And the southerners, who had embraced western education, who had even travelled to Britain or to America to acquire knowledge of western systems, and so were to a large extent deeply westernised in their outlook, were not loved at all nor trusted by the duplicitous Britons, and ended up in the opposition parties.

Thus the stage was set, in our 'independent' country, for conflict, if not chaos.[3] Since our new rulers had scant understanding or sympathy for parliamentary systems, the government was soon mired in ineptitude and corruption, and became embroiled in a bitter war with its more voluble and more aggressive opponents. Then came the rigging of federal elections in 1964, which proved to be the final straw for the fragile democracy. All hell broke loose. The western section of the federation in particular – that part controlled by the opposition party – reacted in an orgy of looting and arson, and political homicide.

This state of anarchy provided the excuse for a section of the army, under some effervescent young idealists, to seize power, killing the prime minister and several of his ministers, who happened to be mostly from the north. (The army rebels were mostly southern Christians and Igbo.) The victory of the progressive forces – if 'victory' indeed it was – lasted only a couple of months. A savage reprisal followed from northern officers, accompanied by the massacre in the north of Igbo people. The latter were thus forced to flee to their homeland in the east, where they finally declared a secession from the Nigerian federation. But the incipient 'republic of Biafra' which they announced was doomed from the first to failure – a federal onslaught under the government of General Gowon brought the rebellion to an end in 1970.

### III

It was thus a nation which had undergone a terrible bloodbath, and was now subsumed under military might, that provided the backdrop for the work of my generation when we came to young adulthood and began to write seriously in the early 1970s.

It was a nation of myriad paradoxes, in a time of paradoxical riches. Peace had been won on the battlefield but, on the home front, a different kind of war was just beginning. The nation yearned for freedom, for the impulse to liberate its enormous potential for creativity, and put its muscles behind the wheel of modernisation. But the soldiers were everywhere with their guns and bayonets, haughtily feathering their own nests alone, stifling initiative with their decrees. Power for them was merely an excuse to line their own pockets, and all the noisy programmes of 'development' announced with tedious frequency and fanfare became convenient drainage pipes through which national wealth was greedily siphoned into private bank accounts. Incredible wealth was flowing into the nation's coffers from the discovery of oil and the prodigious revenue it brought. Yet for the majority of the people misery and squalor formed the dough of their daily life. The more money the nation earned, the more the official corruption pullulated, and the worse grew the impoverishment of the common folk. Amazingly, against all the euphoria of Independence, the gap widened even more distressingly between the haves and the have-nots, and our nation, even in the midst of its oil, sank further down the list of the world's poorest. Now and then public anger over these accumulated grievances, ferried by a sympathetic press, exploded into violence, but these protests were always scattered and random – pockets of striking workers here, a farmers' uprising there – and never anything at all like 'the great revolution' expected. Indeed, each outburst only helped the soldiers, for in its wake would come another *coup d'état*; a more brazen sector of the military would replace the previous one, and business would be resumed again as usual.

This has been the repeated scenario of political life in Nigeria, this game of musical chairs of military regimes and abortive civilian revolts which has led us to our present entrapment in the snare of the IMF–World Bank Structural Adjustment Program (SAP).

Clearly, if we are to escape from this wasteful and tragic cycle, there must be a revolution: the soldiers must be made to climb down from the saddle of power; the lower classes empowered; and an enlightened leadership, composed from all sectors of the population, must be created to replace the present usurpers. And, in the light of market developments in the post-communist era, an honest, patriotic and committed middle class must be assembled, gifted enough to lead the urgent work of repair and raise the investment necessary for industrialisation and the building of infrastructures.

Obviously it is quite easy to make these prescriptions; what is hard is to say how to bring them to fruition. It is clear however that not all revolutions have to be violent or bloody. And, in my opinion, one vital prerequisite for the task of salvaging our country is a committed educated class. As I see it, of all of the various 'communities' which make up Nigerian society it is the educated community, armed with a proper ideological consciousness, that can successfully undertake the building of a dynamic modern economy, towards which we yearn to stir our country.[4] Hence the really vital battle, I believe, is to be waged by the educated class – which in our country does not necessarily constitute a privileged elite, at least not since the advent of SAP.

Now I know that the received wisdom in radical circles is that any properly progressive work is one carried out with/among the masses, or at least in the circle of the dispossessed. And in our environment this would mean the peasants, who form the majority of the population, or the urban wage-earners, who are clearly the subaltern class in our cities. I know of course that among the peasants some valuable work has been going on under the rubric of the Theatre for Development. Nevertheless, while I recognise the potential usefulness of this kind of work, and have on some occasions participated in it, my feelings remain that in the age of marauding multinationals, and in our peculiar circumstances as a fledgling, neo-colonial state trapped at the periphery of world capitalism, these approaches are not enough by themselves. They are not only riddled with self-contradiction,[5] but are fundamentally insufficient to provoke the desired change to the macro-society without some additional kind of intervention.

In any case, because of the dissonant heterogeneity of our country it is impossible at the moment to find a common language to address the 300-plus ethnic groups of peasants, a fact that opens them to exploitation by tribal tin gods and wily politicians. To reach them at all, and unite them behind a common ideal, we would still have to pass through the members of the educated class. In a similar manner, the workers' population is relatively thin and confined to only a few cities: at important moments, it is to those educated among them that leadership is normally entrusted. Thus the educated class spreads into every group and every community: properly mobilised, they can form a decisive revolutionary army that will arrest the present drift of our society and, in the manner of the Asian Tigers, transform it into a flourishing modern and industrial economy. While Theatre for Development projects continue at various micro-sites, a simultaneous battle must also be waged at the larger, but intangible, level of consciousness.

## IV

So what is the role of the playwright in all this? My argument so far has been that the educated class is at the core of development in any modern economy, and that the failure of our society in Nigeria, and in other African countries, is to be traced to the lamentable decadence of that class.

As a playwright, therefore, it is this question that obsesses me. Almost all of my plays, since I became a self-conscious dramatist, have been passionately devoted to it, and dominated by it.[6] In some works I am trying to expose this class failure and probe its causes. In others I am denouncing its corrosive agents, while in others I am ridiculing its antics. And in still others I am trying to stir the class out of its customary apathy into combat, provoking it into anger and active resistance. Sometimes I am trying to do all these things in the same play. I am constantly, ceaselessly pounding at the educated class, trying to lance, and heal from within, that abscess which Fanon so presciently identified long ago as our distorted consciousness, and which shows itself in collective amnesia and inertia, in cowardice, and an inordinate horror of insurrection. Deliberately, I put pepper on the open sore of the educated class's consumer mentality, its limp mimicry of foreign cultures.[7] I insist again and again that this class, to which I myself belong, has a historical responsibility to lead society from misery into prosperity, from the darkness of under-development to the dawn of technological modernity. I attack its criminal complicity in the betrayal of our people, showing how it is because of the willingness of certain of its members to form an alliance with the military that the democratic movement remains unborn. Likewise, I reveal how it is that because some elements of the military have learnt how to insinuate themselves into the class, and manipulate it with cynical opportunism, the rest of society has been successfully co-opted or cowed, as a result of which corruption has grown to become the national ethos. In the quest for an alternative to all this parasitism, I turn official historiography and mythopoesy on their heads, insisting on their hidden partisan agenda, and offer a dialectical counter-narrative, in which history is seen from the lower side, from the perspective of those who are society's victims. This is why female heroes are so prominent in my plays, since the empowerment of women is crucial to this prospective programme of liberation and modernisation.

All the same I divide this class into two – between those whose ideas are already formed, whose positions are therefore already secure on the social ladder, and those whose minds are still in formation, but who will be potential recruits into the class. And it is to the latter, mainly, that I direct my work. Unlike the situation in the developed countries perhaps, students in our higher institutions occupy a unique place on the train of social formation, which no doubt explains the phenomenon of student power in Third World politics. Students are young and dynamic, alert to injustice and wrong, capable of compassion, quick to learn or unlearn. They are just old enough to be excited by the competitiveness of opinions and the selectivity of choice, but not old enough to be saddled yet with the burden of family or other responsibilities. This means that they can readily be summoned for 'instant action', advantageous for those causes requiring protest marches or agit-prop activity (though disadvantageous for those needing more reflective response). Assembled from disparate backgrounds and cultures, they comprise the various ethnic, gender and social types and, along with the army, are the ones who most truthfully constitute a 'nation' in more than just the geographical sense. Furthermore, and perhaps most important of all, students are also ideologically pliant and hence neutral, not yet frozen within the theology of any particular camp or cult. For me, therefore, this is the ideal moment to reach them as growing citizens. One year afterwards is already too late. By then the student has graduated, and turned into someone else – a banker, a journalist, an accountant, a lawyer, an army officer – an established member of the professional middle class, in whose hands directly or indirectly the destiny of our nation has been trapped since Independence. Henceforth, it is these ideas the student has imbibed from the campus that will largely guide his future life and decide the manner of his intervention in public life. The committed dramatist who is able to reach that undergraduate student before s/he fully matures therefore, while his or her allegiance is still fluid, is obviously taking a more than decisive step in the work of communal rehabilitation.

## V

Still it must not be imagined that this work, even when clearly elucidated, is easy to accomplish. The state obviously has a stake in the formation of its citizens. A corrupt state, in particular, has an interest in seeing that its subjects do not become enlightened for, as it knows, knowledge is the first weapon of freedom. To the slave-master, any initiative that aims to break the chains of the slave is subversive, and must be suppressed. So with the dictator, for whom the progressive artist is always a target. Hence the playwright who pursues the kind of agenda I have outlined above must be ready for official reprisal in the form of censorship or even direct elimination. Especially under a military regime, whose laws are capricious and vindictive, and where even death sentences against opponents can be backdated, the dramatist who wants to survive and still keep doing his work is obliged to operate with the tactics of a cultural guerrilla. And it is in such a context that playwriting becomes an act of surreptitious insurrection.

Furthermore, the committed playwright must remember that it is not only the antagonism of the state that he needs to anticipate; there is also the potential hostility of the audience. Most of those who come to the theatre come in search of entertainment, for 'relaxation' from the agonising realities of their life through a momentary escape into the fabulous world of illusion. Nothing would horrify them more therefore than to be called upon to 'think' at such outings. Hence a play that seeks to win attention cannot afford to present itself like a political tract or a religious sermon. Besides, if the ideas on stage push against prevailing popular positions or currently accepted norms and practices, as they must, response from the spectators cannot be expected to be spontaneously warm or sympathetic, unless the playwright takes care to package his play, cleverly, through the furtive masks that art itself can furnish. These strategies will differ of course from play to play, and from occasion to occasion, depending on the particular crisis the playwright has chosen to confront, as well as the circumstances of performance, and so on. In the remaining part of this chapter I will try to illustrate my own procedures with one concrete example.

For me, then, as I said earlier, so absorbing has been the post-colonial experience of anomie that I have been unable to divorce my work from it, or from the urgent need to change it. Each week, at least since the coming of the soldiers and the discovery of oil, our life in Nigeria has been marked by unending crisis, a situation which, from a certain grey perspective, is paradoxically propitious to the creative imagination. Thus, virtually all my plays have taken their inspiration from one immediate crisis or other, to the extent where it is rare that I choose a theme to write on. Rather, it is the theme that chooses me. When, for instance, at the end of the civil war the government of General Gowon grew monumentally corrupt, the need to confront it publicly prompted me to *The Chattering and the Song*, in which I found metaphors to explain why the regime had to go and in what way social justice could be established in its aftermath. Corruption among local government officials during the Obasanjo–Murtala military regime inspired the fierce satirical portraits of *Who's Afraid of Solarin?* as, later on, the same anger against the betrayal of public aspirations by politicians during the civilian regime of Shehu Shagari led to *Midnight Hotel*. However, I confess that these dramatic works (now numbering more than forty plays) are not always the product of conscious decision or clear illumination. Not long ago, for instance, worried about the gradual collapse of all traditional and modern civil institutions in a gleeful collusion with General Babangida's military regime, I wrote *Aringindin and the Nightwatchmen*, for which comrades from the left angrily berated me at the time, but which, in the present dispensation of things, has proved to be a horribly prophetic piece. How I wish we had all taken the omens seriously! Perhaps we would have pre-empted the course of history, and saved ourselves the present anguish.

However, the example I wish to focus on here relates to the problem of armed robbery, which has grown to alarming proportions in Nigeria since the end of the civil war. So serious was the phenomenon that at one time the nation was virtually under siege from robbers who struck at random, at any hour of day or night, and killed and maimed at will. In the end, following a massive public outcry, the military government under Gowon was forced to react with a drastic solution. A decree was passed which made armed robbery punishable by public execution, and special tribunals were sworn in to enforce the law. The public cheered with relief.

Thus, week after week, to public acclamation, condemned robbers were routinely lined up in different state capitals, and executed by firing squads. This 'Bar Beach show' – so-called because the Lagos Bar Beach was the most notorious location for these executions – soon turned into a regular carnival, with large crowds and television cameras, complete with drummers and ringside gamblers, and sometimes presided over by state governors and their glittering coterie of officials.

But it became apparent, after a while, that this brutal, simplistic approach was not the solution. Clearly the executions assuaged nothing beyond the public's vulgar desire for vengeance. The crowds gathered mostly for primitive titillation, drawn by bloodlust, and not for any lesson in deterrence. In any case the robberies did not abate, but grew even more violent and more daring. Instead of sanitising society, the executions staged before cameras were only further brutalising us, killing our sensitivity, numbing us to the horror of death, degrading our sense of the worth of human life. Because men were being so freely and so openly slaughtered like goats, we too began to behave and treat one another like goats.

In the end, therefore, the problem called to me to respond, to try and open our eyes to this collective barbarity, this terrifying hysteria – all obviously stage-managed by the property-owners of our ruling class. It was necessary to counter the widespread fallacy that robbery, particularly on the scale at which we were witnessing it, was merely the result of personal evil, of greed or envy or sloth, of the penchant in some recalcitrant individuals to become wayward and harm others without compunction. I was concerned to demonstrate how the robbers, with all their repellent acts, were themselves victims of our unjust socio-economic set-up; and how the rest of us were already directly implicated in some form or other of public looting, undetected because more covert.

All the same, the reason for this collective stain did not derive from any endemic, national flaw. It was not because we as a people were more disposed than other societies towards criminality, but simply because in the kind of society we had fabricated for ourselves, crime had become an obligatory practice in the rites of survival. And so robbers were not an aberration, but were a creation of the society itself, which such unconscionable measures as public execution would not eliminate but instead aggravate. It was we ourselves who manufactured our own robbers, and the solution therefore lay in a more sobering prescription – altering our social and political set-up, creating a more equal society, and democratising our polity, starting with the removal of soldiers from power.[8]

Fine enough – but how should these ideas express themselves *on stage*? Given the controversial nature of the topic, and the sensitivity towards it of both the rulers and ruled, conventional drama in the western sense of it – as for instance in the Shavian tradition – was obviously inappropriate. By experience I had learnt already the inadequacy, for our audience, of the form of conventional western drama, based as it is on the primacy of words.[9] The drama which our people savour is still one in the mould of 'total theatre', that is, a multi-media production, in which dialogue is no more important than other paralinguistic signs. There must·be music and song, dance, colour and spectacle. The only problem here, however, is that unless the playwright exercises control, the message can be subsumed by the theatrical game itself.[10]

Hence, in search of an appropriate form, the wise thing was to turn back to our traditions. How, I pondered, did our predecessors proceed to deal with sensitive issues without incurring the wrath of the rulers, or the antagonism of their audience? In Africa, we are no strangers to art forms that are designed to entertain, as well as instruct or condemn. And one tradition that immediately came to mind was the folk tale in performance. For not only do these tales combine entertainment and instruction, but they also have the kind of techniques to shelter the outspoken artist from official harm. As many observers have noted, oral performers are able to voice trenchant criticism, even while keeping their audience amused, and even when the target of their barbs sits on the throne. The theatrical elements of the genre make it the most popular art form in the community, but are these adaptable to a modern stage with paying spectators? One can isolate its elements: a protean one-man cast, with or without the accompaniment of musicians, who narrates *and performs*; a story located in *fabu*-land, whose protagonists are frequently non-human figures with, in particular, the trickster figure of the Tortoise as hero; the involvement of the audience through the use of music and antiphonal chants; and, finally, a moral that summarises the play's didactic purpose. It seemed exciting as a vessel for the ambitions of my own play.

In scanning through the extant repertory of folk-tales, I found that there was no dearth of stories dealing with the topic of robbery. One of these, *The Tale of the Tortoise and the Market Women*, fascinated me. According to this story, our restless hero discovers the trick of mesmerising the market people through the use of song. Repeatedly, he uses this trick to lure the traders to sleep, making away with their goods each time. All attempts to catch him fail, as all the guards the traders employ also prove vulnerable to this strange hypnosis. Then the elders in turn are sent to keep guard and, finally, the king himself; but all to no avail. In desperation, the people decide to build a Glue-Man, a figure well-known to all story-tellers of the black world. In the end, Tortoise is caught, disgraced, and punished.

Was there a means by which, on the modern stage, this simple but splendid tale could be successfully adapted?

## VI

*Once Upon Four Robbers*[11]
'*The lights in the auditorium are still up. But suddenly, from somewhere in the theatre, and while some are still finding their seats, a voice rings out: "Aaalo-o!", it calls.*' This is the traditional opening formula for the raconteur, known at least to the older members of the audience. Startled, they sit up. Then at once, all around them, several

voices give the familiar response: 'Aaalo!' The astonishment increases. This is how a story normally begins, at home, when a story-teller, or an elder, entertains the household, and particularly the children. No one in the audience has expected anything like this, in this place. When they bought a ticket earlier on, and came into the theatre, they had believed that it would be business as usual – lights would dim in the auditorium, then the stage would light up, ushering them straight into a mirror, into some scene which would be the replica of their daily life. And from that moment onwards all they would be required to do was to stay attentive in their seats, like spectators at a tribunal, and peep, through a missing fourth wall, into the privacy of men and women like themselves going through some conflict such as they themselves customarily experience. Then, after a while, the lights would dim again on the stage, they would applaud, politely or enthusiastically, and as the auditorium lights went up again, they would find the exit and return to their homes.

But now, something different is happening. The narrator, now clearly discernible, utters his formula again. And those who responded the first time are now nudging others around them, encouraging them to do as they themselves are doing. And again, for the third time, the narrator calls. Now the game is understood, the response is carried enthusiastically by most members of the audience. It is their world after all, from infancy, one in which they used to be at ease, which they are glad to discover again. When the narrator proceeds to the next stage of the game, they are prepared. They know he[12] is going to start a song which will be familiar to them, and that they will be required to join in singing the chorus. So when the narrator begins the song, 'Itan mi dori o dori', the whole audience answers appropriately with 'Alugbinringbinrin!'. He sings, delighting them with his voice and his music, summarising the story he is about to narrate, infecting his listeners with his mirth and vivaciousness. And as he moves among them, and goes gradually towards the stage, he captures them completely in his spell, just as the traditional raconteur does.

But something new to the tradition is happening now. As the narrator weaves his way through the singing spectators, so some of them are seen to rise from their seats and move along with him. Many more join them. Lights also begin to dim in the auditorium, and to come up on the platform[13] towards which the narrator and his crowd are moving. Now they are gathered on stage, the narrator surrounded by those who have followed him. From among the latter he asks for volunteers to play roles in the story he is about to enact, and sends someone for costumes and props. Several hands go up; the narrator selects those he wants, assigns parts to them, gives them their costumes and props. He thanks the rest of the crowd, and sends them back to their seats. There is great laughter in the house, as some realise at last what has happened: they have been pleasantly conned, and the so-called 'volunteers' are in fact real actors planted among them. Others, who have not yet caught on to the trick, sit in wonder about this unusual beginning, and about what is to follow. But no one in the audience is merely apathetic now: the players have revived for them the traditional practice of theatre as collective fun, as a game of fantasy in which they themselves are active participants. Now they are ready not only to follow the story, but also to intervene at any moment in it.

Still there is more cause for astonishment. When the play starts, the characters on stage are – armed robbers! The revulsion, the terror, which this evokes in the audience can only be properly imagined by someone who has lived in Nigeria since the end of the Biafran war in 1970. Certainly the last thing the audience expects to see, in the brief interval it has come to spend in the theatre, is this unpleasant reality. It wants to be wooed away to an escapist dreamland where everything is rosy and cheerful and safe, where the world is nothing but fabulous spectacle. But – robbers? Horror! The fearsome soldiers on the street at least have a face and a name, they can be identified, appealed to, bribed or bought, cajoled, or countermanded with appeals to a superior officer. But the robber is a god without a face, arbitrary and volatile, hardened to carnage, and operating clandestinely, beyond compassion, with unbridled cruelty and carnality. A beast of primordial times, beyond all human control, why on earth must this dreadful figure pursue them even to their place of escape? Deliberately, taking a tremendous risk, the playwright has brought these terrifying figures on to the stage, right at the outset of the drama, to stir the audience into a violent unease, into a tension pulsing with dramatic irony. Will it work?

23

The play proceeds; the tension gradually thaws. The robbers are mourning the loss of their leader, executed that morning, and one of them is deciding to quit. This evidence of humane feelings, of common vulnerability, soothes the audience: empathy begins:

MAJOR. Hold it, Alhaja. Listen to me, if only for the last time. The party's over and it's going to be every man for himself from now on.
ANGOLA. You hear!
MAJOR. Face the truth man! Ever since this new decree on armed robbery, we've been finished! You can only walk that far on the edge of a blade. Sooner or later, the blade cuts in.
ANGOLA. And so you'll run, isn't it? Like a cheap half-*kobo* pick-pocket in the market pursued by women. You think –

. . .

MAJOR. Listen, Angola, Hasan, Alhaja! Listen to me, this is the end. The guns will get us in our turn, unless we quit.
HASAN. But for what? Where do we go?
ALHAJA. Nowhere. They've trapped us with their guns and decrees.
HASAN. All we have left is the Bar Beach. And the six feet in the ground.   (*Once Upon Four Robbers*, 8–9; 15)

These are not just evil men after all? Shaken by the unfolding argument, the audience begins to recognise and acknowledge the robbers as *human beings* like themselves, not just as negative *types*. More: the robbers may even begin to win sympathy, as they play on their identity as members of the underprivileged class, forced to take to crime because of the prevailing injustice of the economic system. With touching bravado, they accept the fatality of their choice to live as pariahs:

ANGOLA. Right, Aafa, so the journey ends. At the Bar Beach, in some market place, at the outskirts of town. What does it matter? For those not in the privileged position to steal government files, award contracts –
HASAN. Alter accounts –
ANGOLA. Grant sick leaves –
HASAN. Sell contraband –

MAJOR. Collude with aliens –

ANGOLA. And buy chieftaincy titles as life insurance! No, let our
obituaries litter the public places . . .   (*Robbers*: 24)

Then, at this juncture, on to the stage walks Aafa, who in the culture is
recognised not only as a Moslem priest but also, because of that position, as a man in possession of supernatural powers. His song on entry is
also familiar, commanding response: for it is axiomatic that when a
priest chants 'Ataiyatu' in a gathering, the adherents of Islam present
there will almost spontaneously respond with a chorus of 'Lilahi', and
join in the rest of the song:

> Ataiyatu: lilahi
> Azakiyatu: lilahi
> Ike Oluwa: lilahi
> Ige Oluwa: lilahi
> Ko lo ba Mohamadu: lilahi
> Ataiyatu Salamatu: lilahi!
> > (*Robbers*: 16)

Thus the audience's involvement is further enhanced, and its initial
anxiety mollified.

The universe of the play shifts, happily at this point, from that of
banal reality, to that of folklore. On our traditional stage, magic and
incantation have always held a great fascination for the audience. (No
Yoruba play, for instance, is ever complete without it.) In the modern
theatre, the effect is no less entrancing. The Aafa, in response to the
pleas of the robbers, gives them a magic boon, which will allow them to
rob henceforth without violence, but only with song. As we watch, the
robbers try the boon out on a crowded market. It works! The traders
hear the song, and are immediately sent to sleep, and the robbers carry
away their goods. Our sympathies are now split between the robbers
and their victims. And it is a long way already from our initial position
of pure revulsion for the robbers.

When the next scene opens, the market is in a state of efferves-
cence. The traders, surrounded by soldiers, are in great spirits, packing
up after a day of extraordinary sales at the market. They boast of the

profits they have made under the protection of the soldiers, and reward them generously with drinks:

BINTU. Sergeant, today's my lucky day, you can have the wine free. You and your men have been wonderful.
MAMA ALICE. Yes, Bintu, call the other soldiers to share the wine. I don't think Sergeant will mind. They all deserve our gratitude.
SERGEANT. Yes, they can leave their posts now. The sun's falling anyway.
*(Bintu goes to call the soldiers)*
MAMA ALICE. You're right. We're already packing up. Our problem is going to be how to carry our profits home. Some of us will need porters!
SERGEANT. I'm glad. I need a promotion.
MAMA ALICE. If they ask for a recommendation, come to me. All the market women will sign for you. Ah, the goddess of the market woke up with us today. Right from dawn the customers have been pouring in.   (*Robbers*: 37–8)

In honour of the soldiers, the market women call out a song, and a dance begins. It is at this moment of general rejoicing, filled with laughter and bantering, that disaster strikes. The robbers return with their song, and sweep away the profits.

A complication now enters the drama. One of the robbers, Major, who had earlier on threatened to quit, seizes the whole loot at gunpoint, and tries to abandon the others. Their efforts to dissuade him are in vain – but notice how the confrontation unmasks the social and economic contradictions in society, and reveals how ordinary people must fend for themselves whichever way they can to survive. It is a grim struggle, and there is no honour anywhere, even among thieves:

HASAN. You're filthy, Major. Your mind has grown rotten.
MAJOR. You can't understand? This is the end. The beginning. I am leaving the filth. I am leaving you.
HASAN. How long? How long will it last?
MAJOR. For ever.
HASAN. It will follow you, the filth.

MAJOR. This is money! Money! A new life. No more scurrying in the smell of back streets . . .

. . .

ANGOLA *edging towards him*. You cannot escape. No act of betrayal will alter your kinship.
MAJOR. Stand back or I shoot! There is no kinship, I have crossed to the other side of the street.   (*Robbers*: 52–3)

Major is determined to leave, to build a better life for himself 'out of the gutters', as he says. However, just as he turns away the soldiers, who seem to have recovered from their hypnosis, return. Major is wounded and arrested, while the others make their escape. And to our shock, the soldiers themselves quickly pounce on the loot, and agree to share it among themselves.

The next scene shows the soldiers preparing the execution ground. Their conversation, as they erect the stake, is structured deliberately to show how they themselves are simply pawns in the hands of the ruling class. Alhaja, widow of the executed robber baron and the only female member of the gang, who has all along pleaded for group solidarity and compassion, comes in now, in a final desperate bid to save Major. She seduces the soldiers with her natural charms and sympathetic arguments, and sends them off with a resolve to free Major from jail before the execution.

The other robbers rush in to congratulate her, thrilled, with the exception of the sceptical, unappeased Angola:

ANGOLA. We shall be here, when they bring him trussed up. They'll walk him up that platform and shoot him like a dog. He'll get the death all traitors deserve. In a common market, among the smell of stale meat and rotten vegetables. He won't even make the Bar Beach.
ALHAJA. Tell me, what do you gain from such hatred?
ANGOLA. He foamed at the mouth! You saw it, he was going to shoot us.

. . .

A companion! He was no longer with us, he had crossed to the other side of the street.

ALHAJA. Yes, Angola. And that's why he's dearer to me.

ANGOLA. The lost sheep, eh? Don't tell me, I know the parable. And I know he'll be the first to scoff at it.

ALHAJA. What does that matter? He's still one of us.

. . .

ANGOLA. Major will be shot, like a dog.

HASAN. And afterwards?

ANGOLA. After what?

HASAN. After his death. Yours. Mine. After our death? After the next betrayal, the hammering of boards together for the state-approved slaughter? What will be left?

ANGOLA. I don't understand . . .

HASAN. You trade in death and danger – by government decree your life's the cheapest commodity in the market, and you don't understand! Listen to Alhaja, man! There'll be nothing after us, you hear, nothing but the empty stalls and their solidarity of suffering, the blood stains . . .

ALHAJA. The market waiting for new corpses, for my sons . . .

HASAN. We're doomed, my brother, and only our solidarity saves us. From the cutting of the cord, earth to earth. You know the myths! What else do they recount but the unending tales of the powerless against the strong. And it's a history of repeated defeat, oppression, of nothing changing . . .   (Robbers: 78–80)

But their joy is short-lived. Even as they dance they see, coming towards them, the dreaded execution squad, with Major and the seduced soldiers in tow. Alhaja's ploy has failed. The robbers have to dash for cover, and watch proceedings in helpless rage. However, when the soldiers take up positions, to fire, Alhaja is unable to stay silent. She runs forward with a last plea, prompting the others too to break cover and, their identity broken, they fall into the irate hands of their former victims in the crowd. A big scene of mutual recrimination and denunciation follows. The whole notion of 'guilt' is complicated: all are driven by the pressures of life under an unjust economic structure:

HASAN. . . . Every one has his dream. Everyone has a point at which the dream cracks up. I have sworn never to be a slave in my own father's

28

land. All I wanted was the right to work, but everywhere they only wanted slaves.

SERGEANT. You could have come to me.

HASAN. The family circuit, eh? Like a huge female breast eternally swollen with milk. But it's a mere fantasy, isn't it? The family breast can be sucked dry, however succulent, it can shrivel up in a season of want . . . The world's a market, we come to slaughter one another and sell the parts . . .

SERGEANT. It's not true! It can't –

HASAN. No? Ask these women. They'll chop each other to bits at the jingle of coins.

MAMA ALICE (*Angry*). It's all right for you to talk. You stalk the street drunken, and idle, and strike at night. But we have got to feed our families, haven't we?

BINTU. We've got to pay the rent, pay the tax.

MAMA UYI. For the tax man has no friends.

YEDUNNI. And the headmaster wants his fees, threatens to send the children into the street.

MAMA ALICE. Brothers die and must be buried.

BINTU. Sisters have their wedding day.

MAMA ALICE. Children fall ill, needing medicine.

MAMA TOUN. Needing food . . .

SERGEANT. You hear that? You've been robbing from victims!

MAMA ALICE. The market is our sanctuary.

HASAN. A slaughterhouse. Each hacking off the other's limbs. Kill quick, or be eaten.    (*Robbers*: 90–3)

The crowd is all for immediate lynching. But in the end, when the Sergeant orders the execution to begin, magic again intervenes.

The whole scene, under Aafa's spell, freezes. He comes in, again as the story-teller, and asks the audience to decide. Should the robbers be shot or freed? What of the soldiers? Lights return abruptly to the auditorium. Through Aafa's insistence, a lively debate ensues among the audience, with opinion swaying now in favour of the robbers, now against them. Finally a vote is taken, and the narrator announces the majority decision. Lights return to the actors on stage, and the audience watches as they carry out that decision. The robbers are either executed, or, as happens on most nights of production, liberated. And if the latter, the instructions are that they should descend on the audience and begin to rob them as they go away!

## VII

Each night, as the audience disperses, it is in tumult. I mix into the crowd, unobtrusively, and I listen. The arguments are fierce. The government is vilified, then defended. There is a plurality of passionate voices. Positions are taken and then renounced, and then affirmed again. Those who voted 'for' now wish to vote 'against', and vice versa. No one is at ease.

The playwright is hardly remembered: the arguments run as if the audience has just left a real event, not an invented tale. And I smile. *Once Upon Four Robbers* has achieved its immediate purpose, which is to end the apathetic response to the issue of armed robbery and public executions. Hitherto, because of the brutality they cause and the distress they bring to so many homes, robbers have been seen as callous villains to be brutalised in their turn, done away with, with equal vengeance. But without denying or hiding their callousness, the play has been able to present a different perspective, and show these outcasts as possible victims themselves of the social order. In such a case then, the play reveals, the robbers are closer to us than we thought, because we in the audience share the same oppressors.

And not only this: the play reveals to us a frightening identity of ourselves, as latent candidates for the stake. For all of us are stealing in one way or the other – the rulers and their cronies; the poorly paid civil servants who thrive on 'kick-backs'; the higher ones who prepare the execution papers; the police personnel, who can make ends meet only by graft; the 'business-men', whose wealth is built on inflated contracts and fraud, but who are rewarded by society with lavish titles and honours; all of these people, referred to euphemistically as 'pen robbers', do even more damage to the economy, and enjoy much larger loot than the armed robber on any outing. Hence the frustration and the anger of the lower classes; of the many roaming the streets without employment; of the ordinary clerks and typists and teachers who work with only a minimal, miserable wage, and eke out their lives in sub-standard shacks. These are the people who eventually crack one day, and take to crime.

In executing them, we bring no solution to the problem at all, we only compound it.

In any case, public executions, organised like state carnivals, complete with brass, fanfare and drums, constitute a potent danger to us and to our sense of worth. How will we value human life when, every week, we see men slaughtered like beasts before cheering crowds?

## VIII

*Once Upon Four Robbers* was written and performed in March 1978 with my students at the University of Ibadan Arts Theatre. This was in the last year of the Murtala–Obasanjo military regime, which had itself displaced the discredited Gowon military regime.

At the time, I worked entirely within my own extremely limited resources. So hostile was the Establishment then that I never had direct access to the theatre until opening night, and so invariably began all my rehearsals somewhat clandestinely, in my little office or in the apartment of one of my colleagues. All auditions and rehearsals had to be done in these crammed places; the script typed out on stencil by ourselves, using office hardware after closing hours (none of us had a typewriter at the time), the actors trained *in camera*, initiated to secrecy. These were the years when my reputation was still in the making; when, in spite of at least three successes in the theatre, many in the profession still considered me an impudent upstart, especially because I was challenging their staid traditions and the established names in the field. It is a delight to triumph against such obstacles!

Of course the disadvantages in this method of working could be overwhelming. But given our motivation and enthusiasm, the constraints turned out to be unexpectedly fruitful. First, the quasi-conspiratorial atmosphere allowed the cast to develop, and rapidly too, a genuine team spirit, and to accept one another's failings pleasantly like a family at siege. There was always a sense of adventure and excitement, which no doubt compensated for the lack of financial remuneration and the ostracism by the 'elders' of the profession. The actors gave freely of themselves, and wonderfully too, with cheerful dedication. Rehearsals were like a treat, and proudly we named ourselves the Kakaun Sela Kompany, after that ancient creeper whose sap served to staunch wounds on the farm.

Second, the difficulties of our circumstances compelled us into a system of close collaboration, so that our rehearsals were truly creative workshops. At each meeting the script was analysed (again), interrogated, re-worked. Everyone contributed without inhibition, and was accepted, or rejected, without acrimony. The text we started with in rehearsals underwent enough reconstructions that, by the time we came to production, it had become a completely different, living thing. This was particularly useful to me, still in that initial process of learning my craft, developing what nowadays has become a defining practice: namely, the incorporation of directing and performance into the motors of my writing process (which explains why I most often direct the premiere of my plays).

Third, working without resources brought us back to reality, and taught me – even before Grotowski – to develop a dramaturgy that is more apt to our circumstances in Nigeria. For not only do the available theatre houses in our country number hardly more than a dozen, but professional companies are few, and financial and other resources for the arts are difficult to find. Thus, impelled by a propitious beginning, I have made a conscious choice over the years to develop scripts which can be performed by amateur actors, using their bodies and voice mainly; working in an open space without sets or technological gadgetry; without elaborate costumes or make-up; with room for improvisation and audience participation. This has facilitated the mobility of the plays, and explains why they are so frequently performed.

Fourth, our way of working helped the actors to develop without strain a high degree of versatility. And I learnt that the actor, once allowed to be a collaborator in the play's process of becoming, turns into a splendid ally: he is able to free himself from the tyranny of the text, because the text is a process which he himself embodies. This is perhaps not easy to explain to outsiders. But perhaps the best way to express it is that after a while, the actors become implicated in the work's parturition to such a degree that without prompting they can identify weak spots in the plot and either correct it (while retaining the flow of action) or alter the mode of presentation without frustrating in any way the play's intention.

*Robbers* was therefore created in collaboration, first with my students, and later, as we incorporated aspects of their response, with our audience. My role as playwright was to instigate the script; have it thoroughly interrogated in production; and afterwards shape its final form. Now the play could take on a life of its own, get on the road . . .

### IX

The impact on the audience of *Robbers* was, as I said, profoundly stirring. A great debate ensued, and the play became notorious. (When we tried to perform it for a film a year later, at the Sango market in town, outside the campus, the film crew ran into such enormous problems from state agents that we had to abort the project. And similarly, a production some years later in Ilorin was banned on orders from Lagos.) Night after night audiences debated the issues, and came out of the hall still arguing. On occasions I was confronted with sometimes angry, sometimes bewildered, spectators, but no one came out indifferent. Not long afterwards, the issue developed into a nation-wide debate, and everywhere people argued whether it was right or wrong that robbers should continue to be executed in public. Until, in the end, the Carnival thankfully ceased . . .

But did this result come from the play and the debate it stirred up? Only an egregious ego would make me answer in the positive. Social phenomena are hardly ever the result of any one single event. But I would like to believe that the play had had its own part, however small, in the final result.

What I can say with more confidence, however, is that the play did not succeed in altering the socio-economic make-up of our society. All that happened, in the face of complaints and agitations by various progressive organisations and movements, was that a new military regime replaced the former one.

This has been the pattern in our country. Each time that agitation mounts, and the call for change becomes impossible to ignore, negative forces quickly come into a new re-alignment. Progressive forces are out-manoeuvred, and a new wing of the retrogressive flank bullies its way into power.

I have continued to write plays and, like others on other fronts, tried through theatre to empower my audience and help them to transcend our tragic cycle. I continue to believe that victory will come when the educated class is fully mobilised, and from that faith I continue to write and perform plays for this community. But the menace remains just as palpable; comrades abandon camp; and life is short. Sometimes, inevitably, the spirit flags. But as the old saying goes: *ars longa, vita brevis.*

NOTES

1 Fugard, cited in S. Gray, *File on Fugard* (London: Methuen Drama, 1991), p.82; Abiola Irele, introduction to Femi Osofisan, *The Oriki of a Grasshopper and Other Plays* (Washington: Howard University Press, 1996), p. xxx.

2 See Femi Osofisan, 'The Terror of Relevance: Reflections on Theatre Practice in Contemporary Nigeria', paper given to the 'Mediums of Change' Conference of the Africa-95 Project, University of London, 1995; unpub. ms. in the possession of the author under the original title of 'Mediums of Change/Change of Medium'.

3 For useful further reading, see Chinua Achebe, *Morning Yet on Creation Day: Essays* (London: Heinemann, 1975) and Wole Soyinka, *The Open Sore of a Continent* (Oxford University Press, 1996).

4 See Abiola Irele, 'The African Scholar', *Transition* 51 (1990), 56–69.

5 See Michael Etherton, *The Development of African Drama* (London: Hutchinson, 1982).

6 Useful critical accounts of my work include three volumes by Muyiwa Awodiya, ed., *Excursions in Drama and Literature: Interviews with Femi Osofisan* and *The Drama of Femi Osofisan: A Critical Perspective* (Ibadan: Kraft Books, 1993 and 1995) and *Femi Osofisan: Interpretive Essays (I)* (Lagos: Centre for Black and African Arts and Civilisation, 1996). See also Chris Dunton, *Make Man Talk True: Nigerian Drama in English since 1970* (Oxford: Hans Zell, 1992) and Sandra Richards, *Ancient Songs Set Ablaze: The Theatre of Femi Osofisan* (Washington: Howard University Press, 1996).

7 For further explication of these ideas, see Frantz Fanon, *Black Skin, White Masks*, trans. C. L. Markman (New York: Grove Press, 1968), and Amilcar Cabral, *Return to the Source: Selected Speeches* (New York: Monthly Review Press, 1973).

8 See Niyi Osundare, 'Social Message of a Nigerian Dramatist', *West Africa* 3262 (1980), 147–50.

9 See Biodun Jeyifo, 'The Reinvention of Theatrical Tradition: Critical Discourses of Interculturalism in the African Theatre', in Erika Fischer-Lichte, J. Riley and M. Gissenwehrer, eds., *The Dramatic Touch of Difference* (Tübingen: Gunter Narr Verlag, 1990), pp. 239–51.

10 For a fuller discussion of this issue, see Olu Obafemi, 'Revolutionary Aesthetics in Recent Nigerian Theatre', *African Literature Today* 12

(1982), 118–36, and Femi Osofisan, 'Drama and the New Exotic: The Paradox of Form in Modern African Theatre', *African Theatre Review* 1 (1983), 76–85.

11 Femi Osofisan, *Once Upon Four Robbers*, third edition (Ibadan: Heinemann, 1994).

12 I use the male pronoun, rather than the cumbersome 's/he', merely for convenience. It should be understood, however, that the narrator may just as well be female as male: there is no sexist bias whatsoever in the trade.

13 I use terms such as 'platform' or 'proscenium' only loosely. The performance area may in fact be no more than an open space with no technical resources at all. My plays have performed successfully on beaches, in market-places, in the centre of a wedding party, in a sitting-room, and on a bandstand in a small village bar.

## 3 Making theatre for a change: two plays of the Eritrean liberation struggle

JANE PLASTOW AND SOLOMON TSEHAYE

The Eritrean struggle for freedom from Ethiopian colonial rule lasted for thirty years, from 1961 to 1991. It was a war that led to exile for more than half a million of the country's three-and-a-half million population and internal displacement for many more. More than 65,000 Eritrean fighters as well as an unknown number of civilians died in a conflict which pitted guerrilla forces against black Africa's largest army, made up of 300, 000 troops. Eritrea received almost no external help, whilst Ethiopia was supported initially by the United States and later, from the mid-1970s, hugely by the USSR. In this genocidal war no Eritrean was safe. For, as well as conducting a formal military campaign, Ethiopia sought to cut off the guerrillas' supply and information lines by napalming villages and terrorising and torturing urban-dwellers; most horrifically of all, Ethiopia even tried to breed out Eritrean identity through encouraging the impregnation of Eritrean women by Ethiopians, either through marriage or rape.

The David-and-Goliath nature of the struggle makes the story of this liberation war extraordinary, but what makes it unique is that the Eritrean People's Liberation Front (EPLF) was simultaneously conducting wars against colonialism *and* against the feudal ideologies which had dominated Eritrea for thousands of years. This is the story of two plays which were produced by EPLF Cultural Troupes in support of those dual aims, and the story of how theatre was used as part of the armoury of resistance by the liberation forces.

Many liberation struggles have recognised the importance of the cultural tool in fighting colonial oppression, and generally it would appear that the longer and more bitter the struggle for liberation the more the cultural weapon is likely to be brought to bear.[1] The Eritrean

Liberation Front (ELF) established itself in 1961, initially with only isolated groups of hit-and-run guerrillas, and slowly grew into a major force in response to Ethiopian oppression. This organisation was hier-archical, factionalised and largely undemocratic in its workings. Con-sequently a group of more socialist-minded fighters split off in 1970 to form the EPLF. From the mid-1970s to the early 1980s the two Fronts fought a bitter civil war against each other, a war which eventually resulted in EPLF victory.[2] Throughout this period cultural activity had been given a low priority, although a number of eminent national musi-cians had performed in support of the ELF in the early 1970s.

In 1975 the EPLF started to promote cultural events, events which quickly acquired a format that was to remain broadly the same throughout the war. These were essentially variety performances. They ran for three to four hours, and were dominated by music, song and dance, designed both to entertain and to inspire support for the milit-ary and social struggles. Eritrea has nine ethnic groups and – since the EPLF saw it as essential to give equal value to all these cultures, in order to promote national unity and to oppose Ethiopian policies of promot-ing the Ethiopian Amhara culture[3] as supreme throughout the empire – the cultural forms of all nine ethnic groups were represented in every cultural programme.

All performances were given at night. Indeed, because of the ever-present fear of the Ethiopian air force nearly all activities, from farming to transporting supplies, had to be carried out during the hours of darkness. An announcer, or master of ceremonies, controlled the performances, which were conducted by cultural troupes number-ing about thirty people, many of whom had multiple roles as singers, dancers, musicians and actors. To bring the audience together and arouse a spirit of resistance the shows usually began with some eight or ten songs and dances. These both represented the various ethnic groups and celebrated the cause of the liberation struggle.

In all these cultural performances music was the most important factor. Music and dance were the cultural forms with which the people, whether fighters, refugees or villagers, in liberated or semi-liberated areas, identified most closely. Drama had been introduced to Eritrea during the period of Italian colonisation from 1890 to 1941, and had been largely a neo-naturalistic, elitist form, which had been seen only in urban areas prior to the liberation struggle. Plays, therefore, could only take place once the audience had been 'warmed up'. These performances varied from crude agit-prop sketches lasting some 30 minutes to, especially in the later years of the war, much subtler naturalistic pieces, which might last an hour or more. After the drama, music and dance again took over, interspersed with poetry readings and, perhaps, further short skits. A show would generally run from around 8.00 pm until midnight, when the audience would disperse, either back to their villages or, in front line areas, on sometimes long walks back to their units.

No research was ever conducted into the effectiveness of the cultural weapon in the Ethiopia–Eritrea war, although both sides expended considerable effort in producing artistic propaganda.[4] Formal discussion was rarely a follow-up activity to these presentations. But the Eritreans certainly saw cultural activities with multiple functions as an integral part of the struggle. First, life during the war was very hard, with minimal opportunities for relief. A cultural performance might take place in any particular area at most once in a month and the entertainment value of these events must have been considerable, offering a chance for relaxation and escape from the tensions of a fighter's life. Second, they were also, of course, agitational. When a new offensive was being planned cultural programmes were aimed particularly at strengthening morale and reminding people of just what they were fighting for. Finally, these events were seen as education. Fighters were ordered to attend as part of the EPLF's on-going commitment to educating a fighting force which was for the most part composed of illiterate peasants who had had minimal exposure to either new ideas or to cultures other than those of their own home area.

### If It Had Been Like This

The first play we are considering, *Kemsie Ntezechrewn Nehru* [*If It Had Been Like This*], is an early work in terms of liberation theatre. It was written in 1980 by Afewerki Abraha, specifically for the occasion of the 8 March International Women's Day.

Afewerki Abraha was at the time the leader of Brigade 23's Cultural Group, although like many other Eritrean cadres he had a variety of positions within the EPLF. Afewerki had lived in the capital,

Asmara, before training at the Ethiopian Polytechnic Institute in the northern Ethiopian town of Bahr Dar. After a year working for the Ethiopian petrol-refining industry he had been sent to the USSR to take an MA in chemistry. It was from Russia, via Germany and Italy, that he made his way to the EPLF in 1975. The exceptional quality of Afewerki's written reports for Brigade 23 was noted and he was assigned to develop the Brigade's cultural work. He consequently led the Brigade Cultural Group, producing agit-prop plays and poetry as well as serving as the group's announcer. Afewerki Abraha is now the Eritrean consul to the UK and in 1995 he published a novel, *The Chains*, which explores the colonial background to the Eritrean liberation struggle.

In 1980 the brigade was the highest level of organisational grouping in the EPLF.[5] Brigade 23 was stationed in north-east Sahel, in the foothills of Eritrea's northern mountains (to which the EPLF had been forced to withdraw after the strategic retreat of 1979, when the Ethiopian army, with massive Soviet arms support, mounted a series of offensives aimed at eradicating the Eritrean forces). At this time the EPLF was organising Cultural Troupes in all the Brigades. These people were still fighters who, like everyone else, could be and were called upon to fight in times of crisis. But for most of the time the members of the troupes, selected from those who appeared to have an aptitude for the arts, were full-time artists, who would rehearse a new show for around a month, and then tour it to the various fronts as well as to liberated and more dangerous semi-liberated areas for civilian consumption.

*If It Had Been Like This* was a ground-breaking farce in support of equality between the sexes. Here it is necessary to understand the degree of oppression women have traditionally suffered in Eritrea. The division between male and female roles has been extreme. Men were the breadwinners and domestic rulers. They chose what the money was spent on, they chose when to come and go and they expected to be served in all their desires by wives whom they could beat freely for any supposed transgression of their wishes. Women were despised domestic chattels, often married off at extremely young ages, who had to defer to their husbands in all matters. In the EPLF a third of all fighters were women, and they served as equals with the men. The issue of women's rights therefore was, and still is, of central importance to the social programme of reform in Eritrea, and many cultural works were produced in subsequent years in an attempt to re-educate society into considering issues of equality between the sexes.

Afewerki Abraha explained in an interview for this chapter[6] that he had become concerned with women's issues as the result of personal experience. He had noted on the one hand how conservative traditional women could be, defending the status quo in male–female relations even when this militated against their best interests, while on the other he had seen how tough women were when they joined the Liberation Front. Afewerki claims that, compared with men, very few women ever deserted the EPLF, and he noted with initial surprise that they could be cruel fighters; the Eritrean stereotype of women saw them as timid and gentle. Bearing in mind these contradictory experiences, and motivated by the EPLF's commitment towards the promotion of women's rights, Afewerki decided to write a play which would expose the absurdity and injustice of 'normal' male and female roles in Eritrea.

The central premise behind *If It Had Been Like This* was simple. The audience was shown a society where gender roles had been reversed. No explanation was given for where, how or why this might be. It simply was so, and the impact of the play lay in the audiences' amazement at witnessing such a society and being forced to conceive that such a thing was even possible. The plot was minimal, for in this play it was not the story that mattered so much as the witnessing of daily life through the glasses of role-reversal.

The play opened with the announcer asking the question 'If it was like this . . . ?' The audience then saw a man doing the housework. Amongst rural audiences this image alone was sufficient to throw the watchers into confusion. As is usual with African audiences, spectators are seldom silent during a show, and this opening tableau on occasion provoked enormous debate. Some thought they were being shown an image of a primeval past, some believed it must represent an incredibly distant place 'such as Japan', while others decided it was merely the product of a wildly ridiculous imagination. When the announcer concluded the play by asking the question implied in the title – 'What if it *were* like this?' – the result was often a flat and very vocal denial from an audience outraged by the mere possibility of such a state of affairs.

Much of the play relied on slapstick comedy to deliver its message. The central characters were an urban man and his wife. But in this play it was the woman who went out to work, who stayed out late drinking, bore children from another man, and then came home to beat her husband. The man meanwhile stayed at home and brought up the children.

The secondary characters were the neighbours. While the women were out working the husbands gathered, as Eritrean women commonly do, to drink coffee and talk. These men discussed their wives as women would 'normally' discuss their husbands. Some described how they were beaten if everything was not to their wives' liking, while others said their wives were sweet, came home early, bought them clothes and stayed faithful.

When the wife finally came home she beat her husband because there was no food immediately ready. This involved the woman jumping up to reach her much taller spouse, to predictable laughter. The husband cried and neighbouring wives appeared to adjudicate and say he had been beaten enough. Meanwhile the men shyly peeped around doorways, only to be sent home by their wives who said this was none of their business. Further cultural taboos were breached when children were named by women, and moreover named after grandmothers who were clearly identified as leaders in the community.

Essentially, Afewerki challenged every commonly accepted aspect of male domination, and exposed its absurdity and injustice by positing a society where injustice was not eradicated but inverted. Audience reaction was often a mixture of hilarity and anger. Fighter audiences were not totally unprepared for the message of the play and among them laughter predominated, but in civilian audiences anger often took the upper hand, with men railing at the husband for being so weak and women berating the wife for transgressing Eritrean cultural mores. In some more remote villages the play was simply incomprehensible, with men assuming it was intended as an attack on their promiscuity. Afewerki Abraha argues that when *If It Had Been Like This* was being performed there were in fact *two* plays going on: one on the stage, and a second among the audience, as spectators tried to digest the uncompromising material before them. The range of responses reflected the different levels of awareness among those who witnessed the play. To a western observer, perhaps what seems most noteworthy was that villagers tended to criticise their own sex on stage; this was especially true of the women, who were furious with the wife for rejecting traditional womanly values. In the west, we have become so accustomed to seeing men as the oppressors of women that we frequently do not like to acknowledge the fact that women have often internalised their oppression so deeply that they can, in fact, control their sisters' attempts to liberate themselves more viciously than any man.

*If It Had Been Like This* ends without reconciliation. Roles are not re-reversed and equality is not achieved. Audiences were simply left with the taste of this outrageous comedy in their mouths, and the debate that it provoked was enormous. The play became so renowned that it was retained in the Brigade's repertoire throughout a two-year period of touring, and was requested wherever they went. Even in 1995, when we were carrying out research into Eritrean theatre,[7] *If It Had Been Like This*, along with *The Other War*, were the plays interviewees most commonly recalled from the days of the struggle.

### The Other War

*Eti Kal'a Quinat* [*The Other War*] was a slightly later piece than *If It Had Been Like This*. It was written in 1984 by Alemseged Tesfai, who was in charge of literary and drama development work for the EPLF for much of the last decade of the liberation war. In 1979 the EPLF decided it was time to re-organise cultural activities and to give them higher priority amongst the ever-growing liberation forces. A Division of Culture had been first established in 1975, but this was now re-structured, based at Arag in Sahel, and full-time cultural development officers were appointed. A Central Cultural Troupe, drawn from the best performers in all the Brigades, was also established.

The business of actual performance was held up for some time; first because the Troupe had to dig out a base. For five months Division of Culture personnel dug out of the hillsides offices, homes and even a 12 × 6 m rehearsal hall. Everything had to be underground for fear of aircraft attack, although in calmer periods people usually slept outside where it was cooler than in the underground warren. Life for all personnel was hard. Besides preparing cultural shows and materials, a considerable part of each day had to be spent on tasks such as collecting firewood and water, and preparing fighters' food (which centred on a diet of lentils and sorghum).

The one luxury for figures such as Alemseged was that writing was *part* of their work, and they could therefore devote uninterrupted time to developing their creative abilities. As in the case of Afewerki Abraha, Alemseged Tesfai had no training in the arts. He had been a lawyer by profession and had worked for a short time for the Ethiopian government. Like Afewerki, Alemseged was sent abroad for further training, although in his case it was to the USA, where he took an MA in Comparative Law and began work on a PhD. In 1974, however, after four years in America, he quit his studies and made his way back to Eritrea to join the EPLF. Alemseged had developed a love of literature, cinema and music from an early age, and now he developed an interest in journalism and research and helped to create educational curricula for EPLF-controlled schools. During his time at the Division of Culture he wrote the first two text-books in Tigrinya (the most commonly used language in Eritrea), on literature and drama, as well as an historical novel. He also wrote three plays, the last of which was *The Other War*.

In order to equip himself as a playwright, Alemseged studied the few texts available to him in the Front's libraries – mostly naturalistic play-texts, such as Chekhov and Ibsen – before setting about producing works for performance by the Central Cultural Troupe.[8] *Luul* and *Anqtzi* [*Meningitis*] were the first two plays. The eponymous heroine of *Luul* is a factory-worker, and the story tells of her work as an underground EPLF militant. *Meningitis* was written as a direct response to an outbreak of a disease which periodically sweeps in epidemic proportions across the Horn of Africa. The play described the work of EPLF bare-foot doctors in combating infection. As with all Eritrean plays at this time, Alemseged's writing was essentially naturalistic in form, following a tradition which had been introduced to the country under first Italian and then British colonial rule.[9] Such a form had nothing in common with indigenous cultural traditions, which was why it took considerable effort to educate people to accept and appreciate drama. Alemseged himself has acknowledged that this was a problem, but points out that because Eritrea was cut off for so long from exposure to other nations and to new ideas, the development of syncretic forms of theatre which have brought together indigenous and imported cultural forms so successfully in other parts of Africa was completely unknown to the EPLF.

*The Other War* was developed from an experience in Alemseged's own life. Many years before, as a junior official in the Ethiopian Ministry of Finance, he had been taken by a minister on a tour of southern Ethiopia. In the Ogaden desert – which is inhabited by ethnic Somalis who have long fought an irridentist struggle to join with Somalia – he was introduced to local Ethiopian military leaders. Here he was told that the leadership had decided their war was unwinnable in military terms, so instead they were encouraging Ethiopians from the dominant Amhara ethnic group to have children with the local population in order to breed out Somali identity. The story horrified the future playwright, and many years later in his homeland he realised that the same tactic was being employed by the Ethiopians in Eritrea. This Ethiopian contribution to strategies for genocide became the starting-point for *The Other War.*

The play concentrates on a single family. The mother, Letiyesus, has two children. One, her son Mikael, is a liberation fighter whom we never meet. The other is a daughter, Astier. At the beginning of the play Astier, her two children, Solomie and Kitaw, and her Ethiopian-army husband Assefa have just arrived unexpectedly from Ethiopia to live with Letiyesus in the Eritrean capital of Asmara.

Letiyesus is appalled that her daughter has married an Ethiopian. She views Astier as a traitor and her baby son as less than human because he is the product of an Ethiopian 'donkey'. So far this is the kind of portrayal one would expect from a piece of nationalist propaganda. However, as the action unfolds, we learn more of Astier's life story, and a rather different gloss is put on matters. Assefa is Astier's second husband. When she was very young she had been married off to an Eritrean, Zecharias. From this marriage she had her first child, Solomie. Astier bitterly explains how she came to feel alienated from her family: 'Remember when you married me off to Zecharias? That's when you lost me. Yes mother, you and father gave me to a drunkard, just because his parents had money and some fancy titles. You didn't even notice that I was only half his age.'[10]

Zecharias had physically and sexually abused his wife. But after his death in Ethiopia, Astier had met Assefa, who loved her and treated

44

her well. Consequently, she feels her loyalty is to Ethiopia, and she is happy to work in Eritrea as a local official amongst women, even when this means imprisoning and fining those who do not attend obligatory political meetings. The Assefa we meet at first is also presented as a very reasonable figure. He flatters Letiyesus, wishes to be seen as part of her family, and urges his wife to be tolerant and sympathetic towards her mother.

Domestically, then, it might appear to be Letiyesus who is in the wrong. But in this play we can never forget the background of the liberation struggle. In the very first scene we hear how Ethiopian soldiers abuse Eritreans at the numerous checkpoints which were manned on every road out of Asmara, and we are constantly reminded of Mikael, the fighter son whose fate is unknown. By the third act our sympathy for Astier, and even more for Assefa, begins to evaporate. The act begins with Letiyesus clearing up after a wild party which Assefa has held the night before, where he and his friends celebrated what they believed to be the imminent crushing of the EPLF. We then hear that Astier, as a neighbourhood or *kebele* officer, has been rigorously fining and punishing many people for minor transgressions. Finally Assefa tries to persuade Letiyesus to tell him where Mikael is, claiming that he can protect her son from the annihilation which he says is about to be visited on all the guerrilla fighters. He even claims he has a helicopter at his disposal. But when Letiyesus refuses to tell him anything, Assefa loses his temper and for the first time shouts at his mother-in-law: 'Don't you feel sorry for your own son? *Em-mama*, your son will be eaten by vultures!' Letiyesus replies: 'So he will be eaten by vultures! What of it? Is he any better than all his comrades?' And for the first time the absolute opposition in the political positions taken by these two is made overt.

By Act 4 Letiyesus and Assefa have abandoned any polite fiction that they might live as a 'normal' family. Their mutual hatred is clear to see, and Assefa ultimately explains that to him Kitaw represents a future where Eritrea will be fully Ethiopian:

I, Assefa, planted my seed in your own daughter's womb. Kitaw was born. Kitaw walks the earth, just like your Mikael. My roots are firmly planted in Eritrea and no power can ever pull them up.

> So, get this straight. Eritrea no longer belongs to the Mikaels, it
> belongs to us, to the Kitaws.

Letiyesus is horrified. She had thought Assefa at least loved his son,
but now the child appears to be just another weapon in the battle for
Ethiopian control of Eritrea. Letiyesus decides to flee to her village in a
liberated area, taking Solomie and her neighbour, Hiwot, with her.
Solomie is delighted to join the struggle but she begs to take her baby
half-brother with her. The grandmother initially wants nothing to do
with the infant who, as Assefa's offspring, to her symbolises Ethiopian
oppression, but her friend finally persuades her to steal the baby, not
out of love, but because this loss is what will most hurt Astier and
Assefa.

> Think Letiyesus. He told you he is going to rule this land
> through his son, didn't he? He dared to say to you that this land
> belongs to Kitaw, and not to Mikael. Well then, brace up! Take
> the child away from them. Snatch him, Letiyesus. He is your
> flesh and blood too. Burn them inside, just as they burned you.
> Don't let them use our own wombs to rule us!

They even re-name the child, from Kitaw, which means 'punish them'
in Amharic, to Awet, the Tigrinya word for 'victory'. This child will be
denied to the Ethiopians as a tool for undermining Eritrean identity
and instead will be remade into an instrument for vengeance and the
achievement of Eritrean independence.

The last scene of the play shows Astier and Assefa at home, desperately waiting for news of whether their son has been found. Finally
we hear that the fugitives have passed safely through to the Eritrean liberated area. Astier is devastated and Assefa turns on her, denouncing
her untruthfully as a secret sympathiser of the struggle before leaving
his wife a prisoner in her own home, her life in shreds.

*The Other War* is a play emanating from hard struggle. Soft sen-
timent is banished in favour of close analysis of how the personal and
the political remorselessly interact in this world of total war. We can
understand and sympathise with each character's position individu-
ally, but the overarching brutality of the Ethiopian army of occupation
finally compels the audience, like Letiyesus, to abandon Astier to her

fate as one who has betrayed her people. The play is, however, relieved by moments of delightful comedy. The scenes between Letiyesus and her beloved grand-daughter are full of touching, affectionate banter, and there is the unforgettable moment when Solomie, cross with her step-father, is ordered to bring him the traditional water to wash his feet. On this occasion she omits, however, to dilute the boiling water with cold. Assefa is duly scalded and the child gets her revenge on the hated Ethiopian. (Alemseged Tesfai told us that this incident was based on his own memories of his little sister similarly scalding an older brother who had annoyed her.) It is also notable that the play is peopled with strong women. Many African playwrights have been criticised for writing women who are little more than ciphers; Alemseged makes his own contribution to the EPLF desire to promote women's rights by pre-senting a group of powerful and complex female characters.

The title of *The Other War* refers to the fight which went on away from the front line of the military struggle. When Eritrea under-took a UN-monitored referendum in 1993, 99.8 per cent of the people voted in favour of independence. This was symptomatic of how the population felt about the freedom struggle, and in the towns and cities a covert war was conducted every bit as bitterly as the open war tak-ing place in Sahel. Alemseged's play opened a window on that struggle within ordinary domestic life, and brought the covert war home to his audiences amongst the fighters and in the liberated areas of Eritrea.

### Making and touring an EPLF play

Until fairly late on in the struggle authorship of material produced for the EPLF was not publicly acknowledged. The war was seen as a collective effort, and therefore all useful activity was to the collective credit. This also meant that work was open to criticism and altera-tion if such was seen as beneficial to the working of the Front. *The Other War* was circulated amongst various cadres for their comments before it went into rehearsal. At this stage the play provoked consider-able controversy. The main target of criticism was Letiyesus. It was considered that she showed too much weakness in weeping over her misfortunes, and that a revolutionary mother should be portrayed as always strong and resolute. Further, it was argued that Astier's strength overwhelmed that of her mother and that it was not good to show any sympathy for her. These essentially were propagandist arguments, and Alemseged rebutted them, saying that characters had to be shown to be fully human. Later, most critics agreed that Alemseged had been right to stand by his judgement, since in performance they felt Letiyesus' strength came through more clearly than on first reading. In later years, when the play had been made into a video, Alemseged said that criticism abroad was very different. Here Letiyesus was criticised again, but this time for being too cold, especially towards the small boy whom she effectively stole from her daughter, and some felt that Alemseged was criticising inter-ethnic marriage. Alemseged passionately rejects this last criticism, arguing that it is not love he wishes to condemn in any guise, but the *manipulation* of love to serve the interests of oppression of any one group by another.

Finally the play went into rehearsal by the Central Cultural Troupe, to be incorporated in a major tour. In some groups rehearsing a playscript could be problematic. Many of those joining the EPLF were illiterate, and the Front undertook a major commitment to give all its recruits a primary education. This took time, and in the early years not everyone could read well. Most of those in the Central Cultural Troupe were, however, fully literate in Tigrinya, the language in which all plays were written.[11] There was a particular benefit for Alemseged in working with the stable Central Cultural Troupe. He knew all its members and wrote the parts in his plays to fit the particular personalities of his actors.

*The Other War* is a short play lasting just under an hour, and has a cast of only six. It was rehearsed over a period of a month, and rehearsals took place in the afternoons between 2.30 and 5.30. As we have noted, the cast had other duties to perform at the same time: collecting firewood and making food were jobs that had to be shared daily, and in the mornings everyone had to work on what remained the most important part of the Cultural Troupes' programme, the songs, and music. (This was a particular limitation on rehearsal time for the actress who played Astier, since she was also one of the group's leading singers.)

It was common practice at this time for the writer of a play also to direct his work. It is essential to understand that no one in the EPLF, or indeed in Eritrea generally at this time, had any professional training in theatre. Learning was for everyone a matter of trial and error. Alemseged therefore directed his play, although actors were free to debate points they found contentious, and to suggest changes. In practice, actors were not likely often to challenge such a man as Alemseged over major points: he was far more educated than any of his cast, and had considerable status within the Division of Culture. Directing had to be carefully managed, since actors often found it difficult to be flexible in experimenting with role portrayal. This was a particular problem for less literate actors when it came to learning their parts. Words were frequently learnt by rote, and so any subsequent modifications to the script were hard for actors to assimilate. In the case of *The Other War*, because Alemseged had access to the best actors and wrote roles with particular actors in mind, many of these problems were minimised. The final production was a tight piece of naturalistic acting which was, given Alemseged's available theatre reading, unsurprisingly reminiscent in style of the early pioneers of naturalism, such as Ibsen and Shaw.

*The Other War* became part of a major Cultural Troupe tour which lasted for about a year in 1985–6. The group went to all the war fronts around the Sahel region, where the major part of the EPLF forces was still contained by the Ethiopians. They also went to safer areas to the rear, and then on to semi-liberated areas in the west of the country, around Barka, Barentu and Gash-Setit. As their name implies, the semi-liberated areas were those regions of the country where neither side exercised full control, and in these places members of the EPLF had to be constantly on the alert for Ethiopian incursions. During the tour the Ethiopians made a major attack on the western town of Barentu, and Eritrean forces had to retreat. Since the Cultural Troupe had been performing in the area they also had to flee and crossed the border into Sudan. Here the tour continued among the nearly one million Eritrean refugees in eastern Sudan. This was not the first time cultural troupes had visited the diaspora. Strengthening support for, and understanding of, the struggle among the enormous refugee population was seen as important. In later years the Central Cultural Troupe would go as far as Italy and America to perform to exiled Eritrean communities.

Touring was an arduous business. The Troupe had two vehicles to ferry their thirty-strong company. But they also took with them all their equipment, and even a portable theatre. Before going anywhere the leaders of the target community were informed of the intention to perform and it was up to them to publicise the event among the people. These communities also had to arrange accommodation and food for the Troupe.

At about 5.00 pm on the day of performance the company would begin putting up the stage. This was a wood-and-metal affair, raised only some 70cm off the ground, but very wide. There was also a set of curtains which boxed in the sides and covered the top of the stage area. The Central Cultural Troupe was better resourced than Brigade Companies or the other cultural troupes formed amongst children, women, disabled fighters and even Ethiopian prisoners of war, but all aimed towards the same kind of proscenium staging. In this practice we can still see the dominant influence of western naturalist theatre which has been so pervasive over many years in many parts of colonial and even post-colonial Africa. Carrying and erecting such a stage was an enormous task, yet it was not part of any indigenous tradition, and can have done little to assist in the performance level of a show.

Once the stage was up the electricians took over. Very few areas outside the major towns in Eritrea have access to mains electricity so the Troupes took their own generators. When on occasion these failed, lighting was provided by bonfires built close to the stage; this became less of a problem in later years when the Troupe acquired better generating equipment. Normally a performance was ready to begin by around 8.00 pm and would be finished by midnight, although on those occasions when fighters were being entertained in front-line areas performances might start later and go on until dawn, since audiences could not make their way back to the lines during the hours of darkness.

Audiences were not provided with the facilities of western naturalist theatre. In most places performances had to be in the open air, and in order to facilitate the huge numbers of people (often several thousand) who attended each show, the Cultural Troupes utilised Eritrea's ubiquitous hills and mountains. Normally the stage would be set up at the bottom of a hillside, so that the audience could seat itself on the slopes of these natural amphitheatres. The exact content of the show would vary from place to place. A scripted play might remain unchanged, but in areas where a particular ethnic group predominated more songs and dances from that culture and in that language might be included. Current events could also affect the content: in particular, poems were often included which were written to comment on battles, victories, defeats and other events which might have taken place within the last few days.

The tour of *The Other War* was hugely popular with all kinds of audiences. As in the case of *If It Had Been Like This*, there is no systematic research available on the play's impact, but in performance it was clear that Letiyesus was no weakling, and the domestic agony of a family torn apart in various ways by the years of struggle must have struck a chord with many of those watching. In this case the playwright did not accompany his work on tour. Indeed for some two months of the time *The Other War* was on tour, Alemseged was engaged in front-line fighting during a period of military crisis, when all available personnel were called upon to carry arms. Unusually for plays which came out of the EPLF Cultural Troupes there is a video record of *The Other War*, which makes an accurate understanding of how it was produced much easier than for other productions.

The video recording happened by chance. Videos were quite often made in the 1980s of the dance and song elements of Cultural Troupe shows, both as a record and in order to reach wider audiences. On this occasion, however, the video crew happened to see a rehearsal of *The Other War* and, liking the play, they chose to record it. On the video Alemseged was publicly credited as playwright for the first time. The recording became widely known and popular amongst Eritrean communities in exile, and later amongst richer Eritreans (those with their own video recorders) in the urban areas, providing a unique glimpse into the creativity of the EPLF and the lives of those engaged in that 'other war' of civilian resistance to Ethiopia.

Propaganda theatre has been utilised by any number of liberation and political movements, and it has often been a popular and effective means of winning hearts and minds. Many plays produced by the EPLF were simple propaganda, intended to raise morale in the resistance forces. But *If It Had Been Like This* and *The Other War* demonstrate that liberation theatre can be much more than crude agit-prop. These plays resist the common temptation of propaganda to be prescriptive and doctrinaire. *If It Had Been Like This* is much closer in its method to developmental or educational theatre than to agit-prop. It is a truly open-ended play in that it resists any temptation to tell its audience what to think. Much more cleverly, and demonstrating considerable trust in the abilities of audiences to think for themselves, *If It Had Been Like This* presents a situation which is bound to shock its audience, rather after the fashion of Brecht, into reconsidering a state of affairs which it had previously considered perfectly 'normal', right and proper.

*The Other War* is rather more of a hybrid. The element of propaganda is clearly present in the untrustworthy Assefa and the constant reminders of Ethiopian atrocities. However, Assefa is only gradually exposed. In the first half of the play it is Letiycsus' sins towards her daughter which are revealed, and which are shown to have a direct bearing on the evils of the present. Insofar as Letiyesus is a representative of pre-revolutionary Eritrea, Alemseged seems to be using this character to raise at least the possibility that inequalities in traditional Eritrean society may be partially responsible for some of Eritrea's contemporary problems. And if the Ethiopians seem by the end of *The Other War* to represent a virtually unmitigated force for evil, then the Eritreans are by no means purely virtuous. *The Other War* combines its propaganda with considerable social analysis.

What seems ultimately most striking about these two very different plays is the unusual trust they demonstrate in their audiences. We have already explained that very few Eritreans were accustomed to drama, and playwrights might have been expected to give in to the temptation to simplify their messages, or simply to preach in order to ensure that uneducated audiences would understand their meaning. In both plays, however, this route is rejected. Afewerki Abraha refused to give his play a neat resolution. He simply presented the facts as he saw them and left audiences to think for themselves, even when the evidence shows that that thinking process did cause considerable difficulty for some people. Alemseged Tesfai rejected peer pressure to lionise Letiyesus in favour of an approach which deliberately problematises certain aspects of Eritrean traditional society.

It seems enormously heartening that such relatively complex plays are the ones which lived on in people's memories, even fifteen years after they were first performed. Here were two playwrights, divorced to some degree from the majority of Eritreans by their vastly superior education, and with no formal training in theatre, who yet managed to produce plays to which people could relate while at the same time finding them immensely provocative. What more could any playwright desire? Perhaps the message for those of us who work in the related, albeit less severe and demanding, areas of community, developmental or educational theatre is that we too should display more trust in the interpretative abilities of our audiences than has sometimes been the case in the past, and that truly challenging performances, either intellectually or conceptually, are indeed the way all who are involved in developing theatres might dare to go forward.

NOTES

1 If we look at the recent examples of struggles to end white rule in South Africa and Zimbabwe we see that the cultural weapon became increasingly important as a means of politicising the people and drawing attention to their struggle. It may be that this stems from an increasing understanding that identity is closely related to culture, and that the reclamation of indigenous cultures is an important part of asserting self-value in the face of what has often been a long colonial campaign to denigrate culturally subject peoples.

2 For further information on the Eritrean liberation struggle see Lionel Cliffe and Basil Davidson, eds., *The Long Struggle of Eritrea for Independence and Constructive Peace* (Nottingham: Russel Press 1988); Dan Conell, *Against All Odds: A Chronicle of the Eritrean Revolution* (Trenton: Red Sea Press, 1993); and Ruth Iyob, *The Eritrean Struggle for Independence: Domination, Resistance, Nationalism* (Cambridge University Press, 1995).

3 The Amhara were the dominant ethnic group in Ethiopia from 1270 until the overthrow of Mengistu's regime in 1991. They were only one of some seventy ethnic groups within Ethiopia and made up some 20 to 25 per cent of the population, but Amharic language and culture were promoted in all parts of the country at the expense of the cultures of all other indigenous peoples.

4 After the overthrow of Haile Selassie in 1974 the military junta which took control of Ethiopia quickly recognised the potential of agit-prop theatre. From around 1976 the government promoted agit-prop plays in the theatre houses of Addis Ababa and gradually spread the form through the use of cultural groups run by compulsory mass organisations such as the national Youth, Women's and Farmers' Associations. Later on,

Eritreans were forced to produce cultural programmes in support of the Ethiopian regime, although few people attended these performances.

5 From 1984 the increased size of the EPLF encouraged a new structure. Divisions were established as the largest unit, which each brought several brigades under a controlling umbrella.

6 Interview with Afewerki Abraha, July 1997.

7 The impetus for this chapter came from the work of the Eritrea Community-Based Theatre Project. This is an on-going project which is working with the Eritrean Bureau of Cultural Affairs to develop practical training in community and educational theatre skills, and to research Eritrean performance forms. Part of the remit of the first research project in 1995 was to investigate theatre produced by the EPLF.

8 Alemseged Tesfai kindly agreed to several interviews regarding his involvement with EPLF cultural work. Interviews took place in September 1995 and October 1996.

9 Drama in the western mode had first been introduced to Eritrea following colonisation by the Italians in 1890. The opera house built in Asmara was exclusively for the use of Italians, but Eritrean staff working there began the process of introducing drama to their countrymen. After the British took over in 1942 schools began to put on short educational plays and excerpts of Shakespeare in English, and this promoted the expansion of amateur drama groups in urban areas, mostly run by teachers. All these groups saw drama as completely separate from indigenous forms of performance. There was no attempt to bring disparate performance modes together, and most actors and playwrights aspired to a form of naturalism in their plays.

10 All quotations from *The Other War* are taken from a ms. translation into English by Paul Warwick, Samson Gebregzhier and Alemseged Tesfai. A text is due to be published by Methuen as part of an anthology of African plays in 1998.

11 We know of no play written in any other Eritrean language than Tigrinya. This is probably because the very limited educational opportunities open to Eritreans prior to independence tended to be concentrated near the capital, which is a Tigrinya area, and because the Ethiopians discouraged the development of Eritrean cultures in favour of promoting Amharic.

# 4 Race matters in South African theatre

IAN STEADMAN

I am Black / Black like my mother / Black like the sufferers /
Black like the continent. (Mthuli ka Shezi, *Shanti*, 1972)[1]

We all know that we are fragments / of a common segment /
Cemented by the blood of a common struggle / We are a people
with a common destination / We are the children of Shaka.
(Matsemela Manaka, *Pula*, 1982)[2]

. . . the 'black man good, white man bad' syndrome is as dated
in our theatre as last month's fish and chip wrappings.
(Raeford Daniel, 1992)[3]

My strength is with black people . . . if you have the numbers
you have the power. (Mbongeni Ngema, 1996)[4]

## Race and nation in the theatre

Since 1976 a great deal of published opinion about South African theatre has drawn attention to the themes of racial discrimination and
African nationalism. In debating these themes, theatre scholars and
critics have neglected other themes as well as important developments
in the forms and styles of performance which have emerged in the last
quarter of the century.[5] But there is an area of that debate which, it
seems to me, can be enriched by yet further discussion, especially at a
time when the euphoric response to South Africa's political miracle has
begun to be replaced by more pragmatic debate about sustaining political transformation.

The history of the struggle for liberation from apartheid reflects
an historical tension between at least two broad fronts: between on the

one hand a majority non-racial tradition, and on the other a range of racially focused separatist traditions which, for convenience, can be described here as Africanist. The victory of democratic non-racialism against apartheid has not seen the demise of the Africanist position. On the contrary, as the new democracy struggles to transform constitutional blueprints into political and economic realities the Africanist voice has become more and more prominent. Extreme versions of the Africanist position, articulating a racism as virulent as that which underpinned the system of apartheid, have also appeared in cultural debates within South Africa. Just at the historical conjuncture which has seen the demise of apartheid, new forms of race-thinking are becoming prominent in South Africa. Valentin Mudimbe[6] reminds us that assertions of the rights of racially defined groups are frequently based on new racist theories which simply relativise the presumed relations of difference between the groups but do not actually challenge the binary oppositions which are used to construct the notion of the 'other' group. Since the election of a democratic non-racial government in South Africa there has been a renaissance in racially exclusivist thinking. It is important now, as it was under the apartheid system, that this be resisted and opposed. Yet in the face of this challenge there is silence in some quarters of the South African academy.[7] Why this silence? Has nervousness taken root so deeply that any voice critical of race-thinking will be deemed to be a racist voice? Are South Africans so nervous of speaking about race that they undervalue the extent to which race still matters in a post-apartheid society? In this chapter I look at some race matters in South African theatre, and specifically at how the notion of 'Africa' is invoked in South African theatre, all in the service of a theatre which was intended to play an active role in the struggle against apartheid.

In the last quarter of the twentieth century the special role played by South African theatre has been well documented. In the struggle against apartheid theatre practitioners demonstrated that theatre can play an important role both in mediating social consciousness and, indeed, in constituting it. I am particularly interested in the persistence of arguments about how Africa figures as both race and nation in cultural debate, and in the implications of this for further scholarly and creative work in South African theatre. The figuring of Africa is not restricted to South African debate. Chinua Achebe asks: '. . . what does Africa mean to the world? When you see an African what does it mean to a white man?'[8] There are two suppositions here: that an African identity is constructed by the gaze of the European,[9] and that there is a necessary distinction to be drawn between 'Africans' on the one hand and 'whites' on the other. These suppositions express the habit of thought and speech that is one subject of this chapter. The habit of thinking and speaking on behalf of a continent and on behalf of an assumed homogeneous race – one in which the expression 'African' has come to mean 'black' and in which 'black' has come to mean 'African' – has haunted commentary on African literature and theatre for decades. In the invocation of 'Africa' there frequently occurs a discursive conflation in which race, culture, nationality and ethnicity are harnessed to a conception of 'blackness', and in which differences of religion, language, gender, social status and many other multiple subjectivities of African peoples are erased in the interests of an organic 'national' identity. In this process, notions of pure or 'authentic' cultural expression are assumed to be somehow reflective of that national identity, and there is an assumption that culture is congruent with nation.

In South Africa these ideas provided important sources for a great deal of anti-apartheid theatre which, with few exceptions since the 1970s, was greeted with enthusiasm by audiences and critics who shared the moral viewpoint of black artists in their stance against apartheid. But as attention moved in the 1990s away from the clear target of apartheid to the less clear and moving target of a rapidly transforming post-apartheid South Africa, the simple, often didactic, formulae of anti-apartheid theatre became unsustainable. Some of the attempts to analyse why this should be so have focused on the limited possibilities of 'protest' and 'resistance' in South African theatre, but there have been few attempts to look at theatre's figuring of Africa in the context of a fast-changing society and how that figuring helped theatre make a contribution to social and political change.

Since the 1980s a considerable body of South African theatre scholarship has dealt with the race theme. On the one hand there has been a focus on the essentialism of black theatre.[10] On the other there have been anti-essentialist critical voices which have tended to downplay race against other subjectivities, such as class and gender.[11] Now, at a time when race-thinking is enjoying a renaissance in South Africa, it is useful to look again at some of the issues involved, to see how Africa has figured in black theatre, and to look again at the pros and cons of racial figuring in the theatre.

South Africa has moved rapidly from a repressive totalitarian social structure based on race, traversing a political terrain characterised by a resurgence of different competing nationalisms to a new constitutional dispensation, still to be tested, promising a 'new' South Africa. It would be utopianist to imagine that this rapid change will mean the end of thinking about race and nation in the country's theatre. But the *ways* in which race and nationalism are theorised as influences in cultural expression give some cause for concern. The problem demands investigation primarily because some of the most prominent of South Africa's theatre practitioners, and some of the scholars who have explicated their work and described the significance of it, are seduced by race-thinking even when conscious efforts are made to challenge it.[12]

Recent debates elsewhere about race-thinking offer some lessons to South African theatre practitioners and critics at this historical moment. Some of these issues have been thoroughly rehearsed in the American academy, perhaps most passionately in exchanges between Henry Louis Gates and Joyce Ann Joyce.[13] Gates prefers to see race as a trope[14] in American literature, but Joyce demands 'a characteristically Black art . . . to mold healthy African-American minds' against the 'serpent's bite' of what she calls 'Euro-American criteria of art' and 'artistic criteria established by the European and American white hegemony'.[15] Her words echo the militancy of an earlier generation, in which voices like Amiri Baraka, Ed Bullins, Ben Caldwell, Jimmie Garrett, William Mackey, Ron Milner, Sonia Sanchez and Larry Neal gave prominence to the black arts movement of the 1960s. Joyce, in repudiating what she considers to be Gates' betrayal of the notion of a 'black aesthetic', seeks a return to the energy of the 1960s movement in black arts.

The features of this debate are well enough known in the American academy. What is less well known is the influence of American conceptions of a 'black aesthetic' on theatre in South Africa since the 1970s.

### The black aesthetic in South African theatre

The Black Consciousness Movement (BCM) in South Africa claims many philosophical and cultural sources. The black arts movement in the United States was one influence, especially in the theatre. Black consciousness in South Africa made theatre practitioners aware of just how functional their art could become in the struggle against apartheid. The process started in 1968.

The significance of the year 1968 as the 'cultural moment' of a whole generation has been extensively documented, but it is of interest that South Africa barely features in the published record which traces events from Prague to Paris and from Tokyo to Chicago. Authoritative accounts like David Caute's *Sixty-Eight*[16] do no more than make passing reference to South Africa as a *cause célèbre* for American and European students in their rejection of the policies of their university administrations. Yet the revolutionary actions of students throughout Europe and North America, as well as elsewhere, were matched in South Africa, and the process commenced in 1968. That was the year in which black students rejected their traditional alliance with the predominantly white National Union of South African Students, and decided to form their own black South African Students' Organisation (SASO). From 1968 SASO played a prominent role in the development of black consciousness.

During the years preceding the apocalyptic events of 16 June 1976, when black schoolchildren confronted the apartheid state, the BCM made a radical impact not only upon political developments, but also upon practices of cultural expression in South Africa. The movement, owing much to the intellectual leadership of Steve Biko, was barely eight years old in 1976. The philosophical fountainhead for many of the pronouncements by Biko and his comrades included Third World theories of cultural and political liberation, like those of Frantz Fanon.[17] An additional influence was the impact of the black arts movement in the United States on the cultural activities of the BCM.

The year 1968 was significant for the black arts movement in the United States. In that year Larry Neal articulated the relationship between black arts and the black power movement:

Black Art is the aesthetic and spiritual sister of the Black Power concept . . . The Black Arts and the Black Power concept both relate broadly to the Afro-American's desire for self-determination and nationhood. Both concepts are nationalistic. One is concerned with the relationship between art and politics; the other with the art of politics . . . the motive behind the Black aesthetic is the destruction of the white thing, the destruction of white ideas, and white ways of looking at the world.[18]

Neal's words were reinforced in many quarters in the USA, particularly by compilers of anthologies of black plays. Clayton Riley, for example, in introducing his anthology of plays by Ben Caldwell, Ronald Milner, Ed Bullins and Leroi Jones, uses similar terms to describe black theatre which he sees as: 'Creating a mythology out of a consciousness durably shaped by a continuum of Black experience.'[19]

These sentiments were by no means simply imported into South Africa by supporters of the BCM, but they supplemented similar notions by black-consciousness leaders in South Africa. Plays by representatives of the American black arts movement were produced in South Africa by black consciousness groups[20] which were cognisant of the parallels between the black theatre movements of both countries. In words which echo the sentiments expressed by Neal, Biko and his comrades formulated, after 1968, the programme of black consciousness in South Africa. Artists and intellectuals, following Biko, asserted the need for a militant 'cultural struggle' in the programme of political consciousness-raising among black people seeking political and psychological liberation. Emulating the journals and magazines of the time in the United States (publications like *Black Dialogue, Journal of Black Poetry, Liberator*, and *Black World*), the BCM established its own *Black Review*,[21] dedicated to reporting progress in the growth and development of the BCM. The BCM adopted principles for a two-pronged struggle against apartheid. On the one hand, following Fanon, it appropriated Third World philosophies of cultural struggle against colonialism and imperialism. On the other, it appropriated an Afrocentric search for a black identity with 'Africa' as its centre. These two influences – a 'Third-Worldist' notion of structural blackness and an African dream of essential blackness – have functioned in tandem in the black consciousness movement. In black consciousness theatre, however, some slippage has on occasion occurred. Fanon's concern with theories of liberation and independence conceived more broadly as a diasporic struggle has sometimes been reduced in black consciousness theatre to a concern with an African myth of essence and authenticity. Mafika Pascal Gwala, in a 1973 essay,[22] attempted to articulate the role of theatre in relation to black consciousness more broadly conceived as a black rather than an African struggle. He argued that a 'new approach in theatre' was emerging, and suggested that an 'authentic national culture' could come only through black involvement. This 'authentic national culture', having first been given an 'identity basis' through the BCM, would develop and take hold via a 'black sub-culture' which would 'act as a counter-culture'. These sentiments illustrate many of the claims made on behalf of the BCM in the 1970s. In appropriating ideas from the black arts movement in the United States, a national-istic conception of *African* identity sometimes became prominent, at the expense of Riley's more broadly defined 'continuum of Black expe-rience' and at the expense of Fanon's search for a more broadly defined Third World struggle. One play which reflects how important is the difference between these two concepts is *Shanti* by Mthuli ka Shezi.

Mthuli ka Shezi was an active politician as well as a playwright. After having served as Students' Representative Council President at the University of Zululand, he was elected as the first vice-president of the Black Peoples' Convention (BPC) at its inaugural conference in July 1972. In December of that year he was 'killed while defending the dig-nity of Black people'[23] by allegedly being pushed in front of a train at a railway station.[24] The circumstances surrounding his death caused a sensation[25] and made him, like Biko, one of the many black-conscious-ness leaders to become symbols of the struggle against white oppres-sion, especially among practitioners of black-consciousness theatre. Before his death Shezi wrote the play *Shanti*,[26] which was produced by the Peoples' Experimental Theatre (PET) before being banned in South Africa.

In 1983 a spokesman for a leading black-consciousness organisa-tion in South Africa described the major thrust of black conscious-ness as being to establish an 'alternative' society.[27] This focus upon the need to conscientise black people and to lead them to an alternative political, social and economic dispensation was underpinned at all times by the search for an alternative cultural aesthetic such as that urged by Larry Neal in 1968. To achieve political liberation it was necessary to assert cultural liberation. Indeed, the collected writings of Biko[28] demonstrate this, for Biko's writing presents a continuing dialectic between the political and cultural counterparts of black liberation: 'Black culture above all implies freedom on our part to innovate without recourse to white values. This innovation is part of the natural development of any culture . . . The adoption of black theatre and drama is one such important innovation which we need to encourage and to develop.'[29] The theatre, providing occasions for lived experience to be played out on stage, would fulfil an important role in the processes of consciousness-raising. Perhaps the clearest indication of the role played by theatre in the dissemination of black consciousness ideology during the first half of the 1970s lies in the wording of the state's charge sheet in the 'Treason Trial' of 1974–5:

> In that during the period 1st December 1968 to 31st October 1974, and in the Republic, the accused, at all relevant times members and/or active supporters of the South African Students' Organisation (hereinafter referred to as SASO) and/or the Black Peoples' Convention (hereinafter referred to as BPC) and/or the Peoples' Experimental Theatre (hereinafter referred to as PET) and/or the Theatre Council of Natal (hereinafter referred to as TECON) and/or the Students' Representative Council of the University of the North (hereinafter referred to as Turfloop SRC), did wrongfully, unlawfully, and with intent to endanger the maintenance of law and order in the Republic or any portion thereof, conspire with one another and/or with one or more or all of the aforesaid organisations and/or their members or active supporters and/or others, to commit one or more or all of the following acts . . .[30]

It is significant that of the five organisations which were brought to trial, two were theatre groups. PET and TECON, in presenting plays and performances of militant poetry and sketches aimed at dramatising the ideals of black consciousness as expressed by leaders like Biko, were clearly considered to be subversive. The role of theatre groups such as these in the development of black consciousness has received scant attention, and it is only when the more obvious political manifestations of black consciousness are illuminated by a study of literary and artistic manifestations that a clear picture can be obtained of black consciousness in a broader cultural context.[31] A culturally expressive form like theatre was seen by the state as a danger to security, for among the various acts specified under the main charge were references to those of the accused who conspired 'to make, produce, publish or distribute subversive and anti-White utterances, writings, poems, plays and/or dramas'.[32] The state's description of such theatre as 'inflammatory, provocative, anti-White, racialistic, subversive and/or revolutionary'[33] reflects the official attitude to theatre at the time: theatre, for the state, certainly made a difference, and needed to be policed.

PET's prominence in the trial of 1975 is some measure of the significance of black theatre in the mobilisation of black consciousness on the Witwatersrand.[34] *Shanti* encapsulates in its theme many issues which defined the ideals of black consciousness. The play is superficially a story about an African man's love for an Indian woman, their friendship with a Coloured man, and the struggle of all three against an oppressive political system. Thematically, then, it is a call to 'blackness', and it defines three population groups in words reminiscent of the BPC constitution[35] as black according to a common resistance against discrimination. In *Shanti*, black consciousness is asserted as the only means to the necessary union of all blacks, a union which must precede liberation.

The action is set in the 1970s and the plot is episodic, with thirteen very short scenes covering many different locales.[36] The play begins with Shanti, an Indian woman, kneeling on the floor weeping over a letter she has just read. From offstage there is a song, and a voice is heard, intoning and insistent, asking how long pain and suffering must continue to be endured. The play then depicts the relationship between Shanti and her lover, Thabo, an African law student, and their relationship with Koos, who is classified as 'Other Coloured' because his mother is Sotho-speaking and his father was a white farmer. The play speaks directly to the audience, arguing that all sufferers under the political system, whether African, Indian or Coloured, are united as blacks, and should join together to fight the apartheid state. Its action is essentially presentational, with the audience addressed directly on matters ranging from resistance to black unity. Thabo is destroyed by the apartheid state and the play concludes with a repeat of the first scene as Shanti learns of his death.

*Shanti* is designed to present events and ideas as a platform discussion or lecture-demonstration. Shezi's language is built up out of short slogans and sentences in the service of a message about the organic identity of all black people. Throughout the action of the play the reader is aware of the text as merely a scenario for theatrical performance. The scenes are presented in too staccato a fashion to allow for any dramaturgical sophistication. Far more important than complex or subtle verbal dialogue are physical tableaux, of which there are a number in the play. The first, of the weeping Shanti, initiates the action, and the image recurs as the closing tableau. As such it represents an iconic rendering of the title character's predicament: a black woman broken by the oppressive system under which she lives, as the offstage voice calls out 'How long shall it be Lord / how long must we carry this burden / how long must we yield?' In townships like Soweto, where audiences could include members from many language groups and social classes, playwrights in the 1970s appreciated the importance of such theatrical representation over more literary sophistication, conceiving their theatre as a deliberate medium for proselytism and conscientisation. The simple proposition which the play makes is that black unity must occur before oppression can be overcome. In Scene Three, Koos says :

> Yes, I am Black and inferior
> To no man. Why must I care what I am being called then:
> Coloured, Cape Coloured, Malay, 'The Other Coloured'.
> I am Black.
> Black like my mother
> Black like the sufferers.
> Black like the continent

and the stage directions have him '*boldly*' standing centre stage as Shanti and Thabo kneel on either side of him and repeat the last three lines.

Shanti, Thabo and Koos, intellectuals like Shezi and the members of PET, were operating in a world of consciousness which was structurally different from that which would make the play 'related to the lives of all Black people'.[37] This aspect of the work of black consciousness theatre practitioners has arguably beset the BCM as a whole and has provided the substance for some criticism not only of the notion of a black aesthetic but of the aspirations of the BCM in the political sphere.[38] It has been argued that the notion of a black aesthetic in literature and drama reflects a major contradiction in the BCM; that the movement neglected class and overstated race as the basis for a critique of South African society. In the case of *Shanti* this has been seen as attributable to a *petit-bourgeois* vision at the heart of the play.[39] These criticisms and others which extend the criticism of black-consciousness essentialism in general[40] have been partially based on a misreading of the sentiments of people like Biko, and even beyond Biko to Fanon. False oppositions between race and class have been set up by scholars commenting on the thought and pronouncements of Biko and Fanon. While the charge of essentialism can certainly be laid before practitioners of the theatre such as the PET producers of *Shanti*, simply to apply these criticisms to Biko and Fanon is to misread them both, and to underestimate the political efficacy of black consciousness.

The relative status of race and class in Fanon's thought is important for our consideration of the 'anti-essentialist' argument. He argues:

> When you examine at close quarters the colonial context,
> it is evident that what parcels out the world is to begin with
> the fact of belonging to or not belonging to a given race, a given
> species. In the colonies the economic substructure is also a
> superstructure. The cause is the consequence; you are rich
> because you are white, you are white because you are rich. This
> is why Marxist analysis should always be slightly stretched
> every time we have to do with the colonial problem.[41]

Fanon does not deny the ultimate importance of class and economic factors: he merely asserts the active role of racism in the ideological structuring of social relations. Biko follows Fanon in this, and frequently demonstrates the importance of looking at race in context.

As early as June 1970 Biko acknowledged this by stressing the need to forge links with the broad mass of black society,[42] and by August of the same year he was discussing the way race was ideologically used to mystify power and privilege.[43] Furthermore, the BCM did something concrete in this regard, for example, by setting up a Black Workers Project. The BPC Newsletter 'Inkululeko Yesizwe' of August 1974 makes extensive reference to black trade unionism, western economic relations with apartheid, and the capitalist base of apartheid; indeed, the reports of the many commissions set up by the black consciousness organisations testify to a wide-ranging effort in the field.[44]

A simple condemnation of black consciousness for not displaying a class and economic awareness is therefore a distortion. The 'anti-essentialists' position has been as reductive in this regard as the essentialism they have attacked.[45] Arguments in South African theatre studies about a dichotomy between race and class similarly reflect a tendency in the 1980s to marginalise race, or at best to subsume race in class analyses.[46] Biko warned against those who rejected race as a factor in political and cultural analysis: 'They do so by dragging all sorts of red herrings across our paths. They tell us that the situation is a class struggle rather than a racial one. Let them go to van Tonder in the Free State and tell him this. We believe we know what the problem is, and we will stick by our own findings.'[47]

### Beyond African nationalism: the 'black' aesthetic in South African theatre

Black consciousness exerted a profound influence on South African cultural life. In the political sphere, the organic notion of strength and unity in blackness was a crucial weapon against white racism, and contributed in no small measure to the collapse of the apartheid state. Against notions of liberation conceived as a product of the unity of all people oppressed by apartheid, however, the theatre also frequently invoked an essentialist *Africa* as its dream of liberation. The notion of a diasporic rather than an African identity has shaped the thinking of a generation of black scholars in the 1990s, especially in Europe and the United States, who have recently shifted the debate away from romantic notions of a united Africa toward more pragmatic arguments about race and diasporic identity. This shift in perspective away from Africa toward the concerns of a black diaspora – a shift from essential black-ness to structural blackness – has not been fully achieved in South African black theatre despite the efforts of some of the black conscious-ness theatre practitioners, primarily because of the seductive influence of the Afrocentric myth. Fanon's concern with the black diaspora's struggle against imperialism became reduced in much South African black theatre to a concern with an invented organic African identity. Critical response to the development of black theatre has not demon-strated 'epistemological vigilance'[48] against the myths of Africanism, and at the heart of some Africanist thinking in the theatre is a stereo-typical view of race which involves what Kwame Anthony Appia describes as being 'seduced by the rhetoric of ancestral purity'.[49] Not-withstanding the empowering impact of black-consciousness thinking in South Africa, many of the arguments of black artists and theorists were attributable to a misguided appropriation of ideas which were themselves misguided appropriations of a rhetoric of ancestral African purity.

Throughout the 1980s and into the 1990s there was a noticeable resurgence in this kind of Africanist thinking in South African theatre. There is, of course, an important restorative and celebratory function in art which rejoices in an image of Africa as unified and harmoni-ous, but that same image renders political arguments sentimental. And Africa looms large in political argument both in South African theatre and in political debate outside the theatre. In plays such as *Pula* by Matsemela Manaka (see, for example, the quotation given as epigraph to this chapter above), and in many others, the call to Africa and to a notion of blackness conceived as African, enjoyed a renaissance.[50] Bey-ond the confines of the theatre, in sometimes quite romantic versions of 1960s Africanist thinking,[51] the same sentiments were expressed. The Afrocentric assumptions of journalists, editors, artists and scholars became a feature of post-apartheid South Africa. The irony in this is that Fanon's rejection of western imperialism was replaced by another kind of imperialism in the thinking of Africanists, for whom the model of black struggle was to be found not in the black diaspora's struggle against western imperialism but in the assumed nation of Africa as defined primarily by African-Americans.[52] Another way of looking at this is to suggest that a new imperialism placed black America at the centre of the dream of black unity, with Africa relegated to the periphery as some distantly remembered model.

In the critique of anti-essentialism beyond the South African context, a feature of the debate about black aesthetics has been the place of Africa in the black struggle. Mudimbe and Appia, in attacking the romanticism of the Afrocentric idea, are not without their detractors. Tsenay Serequeberhan[53] argues that although there is a 'legitimate critique of essentialism' it can be overstated:

> beyond our ethnic identities, the heritage of the differing
> African liberation movements makes possible for us a historical
> and political world in which we all share as Africans. This
> 'sharing' does not presuppose any kind of metaphysical or
> mystical African one-ness. It only calls for the recognition that,
> beyond color and race, our being African is grounded in a shared
> history of subjugation, struggle, and liberation: a history we
> affirm and choose to perpetuate . . .When Aimé Césaire affirms
> that Négritude is a 'concrete rather than an abstract coming to
> consciousness' and an affirmation of our blackness, or when
> Patrice Lumumba writes that '[we] are Africans and wish to
> remain so', what is being upheld is not a 'metaphysical or
> mythic unity' but an identity in the context of concrete social,
> political, and historical struggles.[54]

Katya Gibel Azoulay[55] agrees with Mudimbe and Appia in arguing against essentialist notions of race, but argues further that a 'strategic essentialism' is important. She suggests that race will always matter in a race-conscious society and that notions of race-neutrality are myopic. Furthermore, she argues that although the African-American experience has been romanticised and mystified as a distinctively black experience, there is nevertheless a 'shared experience of racism which in turn conditions the manner in which we situate ourselves in the public sphere of a society historically and politically governed by the discourse of race . . . race may indeed be theorised in the academy as a social construct, but it is *also* an *experienced* thing'.[56]

This polarisation between essentialist and anti-essentialist notions of black identity is unhelpful, as Paul Gilroy has shown.[57] He supports the notion of diasporic black identity, which acts against essentialist and nationalistic conceptions of black culture, and does so because it avoids totalising black experience in a nationalistic way, while acknowledging the importance of black struggles against colonialism and imperialism.

These ideas provide a possible direction for black theatre in South Africa. What is needed is an epistemological reappraisal of the way Africa is thought about as an organic image of black unity and nationhood. For black theatre practitioners and for scholars interested in their work, there is a need to distinguish between two dreams about black unity. Maishe Maponya offers two different perspectives on black struggle in South Africa. On the one hand, he has invoked the African dream of essential blackness: 'Wake up Mother Afrika / Wake up / Time has run out . . .'[58] and on the other hand he has invoked structural blackness: 'as long as blacks do not have equal rights there'll always be black theatre . . .'.[59] In the latter assertion he links his work, and the potential of black theatre, to the concerns of black theatre in the diaspora. That is to say, when he changes focus from a romance with Africa in plays such as *The Hungry Earth* (with its refrain of a lost harmony in Africa since the arrival of white settlers), to grappling with contemporary South Africa and its problems in plays such as *Umongikazi* [*The Nurse*] (which deals with oppression and exploitation of healthworkers in contemporary South Africa) and *Gangsters*[60] (which depicts the methods of security police in dealing with political activists under apartheid), his work reflects the concerns of the larger black struggle against discrimination. When Matsemela Manaka changes focus from the realities of black survival in the mining compound in his play *Egoli*,[61] to the dream of a once-unified Africa in *Pula*, the theme of unity which is central to each play becomes more mystified. In the earlier work, a central image in which two black men break the chains which bind them becomes a striking metaphor for the struggle for liberation and the need for unity in order to achieve freedom. In *Egoli*, Manaka analyses the exploitative system which underpins apartheid, and asserts in a powerfully theatrical way the need for black unity in the struggle against all forms of discrimination. In the latter play, as indicated in the epigraph to this essay, Manaka's search for liberation and unity is not forward-looking, into the possibilities of the future, but turns backwards, into the mists of time and the dream of a distantly remembered pastoral Africa which was organically at ease before the arrival of white settlers.

Notwithstanding the restorative and celebratory functions of much African music, poetry and fine art, in black theatre the Afrocentric dream of a master narrative with its roots in the dawn of civilisation is little more than a romantic narrative of origins and imagined unity, offering a utopian dream of an organic nation congruent with an organic culture. The alternative dream, of a black aesthetic with its roots in the diaspora, offers a vision which is both politically and culturally strategic. On the one hand it recognises the importance of black struggles against all forms of oppression, while on the other it recognises and celebrates difference, hybridity, and cultural exchange and continuity. South African theatre beyond apartheid needs this difference. Black theatre beyond apartheid stands to achieve more in the ongoing struggle against racial discrimination than it will ever gain from its romance with Africa.

NOTES

The financial assistance of the Centre for Science Development (HSRC, South Africa) towards the research upon which this paper is based is hereby acknowledged. Opinions expressed and conclusions arrived at are those of the author and are not necessarily to be attributed to the Centre for Science Development.

1 Mthuli Shezi, *Shanti*, in *South African People's Plays*, ed. Robert Kavanagh (London: Heinemann, 1981), p. 72.

2 Matsemela Manaka, *Pula*, in *Market Plays*, ed. Stephen Gray (Johannesburg: Ad Donker, 1986), p. 73. The play was first performed in 1982.

3 Raeford Daniel, 'Arresting Ma Rainey', *Cue*, Grahamstown Festival, Monday 6 July 1992: 1.

4 Mbongeni Ngema, interviewed by Newton Kanhema, *The Sunday Independent* (Johannesburg, 9 June 1996): 9.

5 Loren Kruger, in a prefatory note to 'The Drama of Modernity: Plays, Pageants and Public Spheres in 20th Century South Africa', a seminar presented at Northwestern University on 12 April 1995, observes that critical writing on the subject 'has tended to take for granted the authority of what might be called the protest drama paradigm'. I am grateful to Dr Kruger for comments made on earlier drafts of this chapter.

6 Valentin Mudimbe, *The Invention of Africa: Gnosis, Philosophy, and the Order of Knowledge* (Bloomington: Indiana University Press, 1988), p. 129.

7  In the pages of *The Sunday Independent* (Johannesburg), for example, the education supplement throughout 1996 carried arguments in favour of a quaint 1960s Africanist vision of social transformation. The significant challenges to this vision, in the same supplement, were pseudonymous. See also note 51, below.

8  Chinua Achebe, interview, in Kwame Anthony Appia, *In My Father's House: Africa in the Philosophy of Culture* (New York: Oxford University Press, 1992), p. 73.

9  Appia, *In My Father's House*, p. 71.

10  See, for example, Robert Kavanagh, *Theatre and Cultural Struggle in South Africa* (London: Zed Press, 1985); and Martin Orkin, *Drama and the South African State* (Manchester University Press, 1991).

11  See, for example, Keyan Tomaselli, 'The Semiotics of Alternative Theatre in South Africa', *Critical Arts* 2.1 (1981), 14–33; and Kelwyn Sole, 'Black Literature and Performance: Some Notes on Class and Populism', *South African Labour Bulletin* 9.8 (1984), 54–76.

12  For examples see Bhekizizwe Peterson, ' "A rain a fall but the dirt it tough": Scholarship on African Theatre in South Africa', *Journal of Southern African Studies* 21.4 (1995), 573–84. I don't exempt myself from the charge of overstating, during the 1980s, the importance of race as a determinant in South African theatre. My interests at that time were primarily descriptive, bringing to the attention of a disinterested academy some of the important theatre being created behind the scenes. Because the academic establishment at that time had constructed black theatre as an absence, I was attempting to reconstruct black theatre as a presence.

13  See Henry Louis Gates, Jr., and Cornel West, *The Future of the Race* (New York: Alfred A. Knopf, 1996); Henry Louis Gates, Jr., ' "What's Love Got To Do With It?": Critical Theory, Integrity, and the Black Idiom', *New Literary History* 18.2 (1987), 345–62; 'The Trope of a New Negro and the Reconstruction of the Image of the Black', *Representations* 24 (1988), 129–55; *Loose Canons: Notes on the Culture Wars* (Oxford University Press, 1992); Joyce Ann Joyce, 'The Black Canon: Reconstructing Black American Literary Criticism', *New Literary History* 18.2 (1987), 335–44; ' "Who the Cap Fit": Unconsciousness and Unconscionableness in the Criticism of Houston A. Baker, Jr. and Henry Louis Gates, Jr.', *New Literary History* 18.2 (1987), 371–84; *Warriors, Conjurers and Priests: Defining African-Centered Literary Criticism* (Chicago: Third World Press, 1994). See also Kenneth Warren, 'Delimiting America: The Legacy of Du Bois', *American Literary History* 1.1 (1989), 172–89; and Michael Awkward, 'Race, Gender, and the Politics of Reading', *Black American Literature Forum* 22 (1988), 5–27.

14  Gates, *Loose Canons*, p. 56.

15  Joyce, *Warriors, Conjurers and Priests*, p. 3.

16 David Caute, *Sixty-Eight: The Year of the Barricades* (London: Hamish Hamilton, 1988).

17 Frantz Fanon, *The Wretched of the Earth* (Harmondsworth: Penguin, 1967).

18 Larry Neal, 'The Black Arts Movement', *The Drama Review* 12.4 (1968), 29–30.

19 Clayton Riley, ed., *A Black Quartet* (New York: The New American Library, Signet Classic, 1970), p. vii.

20 For example, in July 1972 TECON produced William Mackey's *Requiem for Brother X*. See *Black Review* (1972), 201–3.

21 *Black Review* (Durban: Black Community Programme, 1972, 1973 and 1974).

22 Mafika Pascal Gwala, 'Towards a National Theatre', *South African Outlook* CIII, 1227 (August 1973), 131–3.

23 *People's Experimental Theatre Newsletter*, vol. 1 no. 1 (September–October 1973), an unpublished document attached to the *Attorney-General's Report, 1975: Annexures and Typescript Documents from the 'Treason Trial' of 1974–5*, National English Literary Museum, Grahamstown.

24 BPC Newsletter: *Inkululeko Yesizwe*, August 1974, annexure to the *Attorney General's Report*, 1975.

25 *Black Review* 1972 carries a report which describes Shezi in hospital before his death and relating the events leading to the incident:

> According to this account, he had originally quarrelled with some white employees of the Railways following their unacceptable treatment of some black women at the station some days before the fatal accident. On a subsequent occasion on 12 December, while passing through the Germiston station, he was apparently spotted by one of the white men he had quarrelled with. This man gave chase and caught up with him and following a short scuffle, pushed him onto the rails in front of an oncoming train . . . Five days after he had been taken to hospital, Mr Shezi died following excessive bleeding.

26 Apart from the text in Robert Kavanagh, ed., *South African People's Plays* (London: Heinemann, 1981), pp. 63–84, reference is also made to the typed manuscript originally used by the People's Experimental Theatre and attached to the *Attorney General's Report* as Annexure 8 in the notorious 'Treason Trial' of 1974–5. Copies of the documentary exhibits from that trial reside in the National English Literary Museum in Grahamstown.

27 Ishmael Mkhabela, 'Black Consciousness Lives', *Sowetan* (9 September 1983), 7. Mkhabela was speaking as publicity secretary of the Azanian Peoples' Organisation (AZAPO).

28 Steve Biko, *I Write What I Like*, ed. A. Stubbs (London: Heinemann, 1978).

29 *Ibid.*, p. 96.

30 Main Count, unpublished ms., *Attorney-General's Report, 1975*.

31 Tom Lodge, *Black Politics in South Africa Since 1945* (Johannesburg: Ravan Press, 1983), p. ix, says with reference to his comprehensive study of black politics since 1945:

> I have concentrated on explicit types of resistance which have directly confronted the authorities or the employers of labour. The story of the more introverted kinds of resistance . . . deserve . . . separate and extended treatment of their own.

Kavanagh, *Cultural Struggle*, provides a useful critique of *Shanti* in relation to the political struggle against apartheid, and Orkin, *Drama and the South African State*, pp. 152–8, provides a brief commentary on the political function of the play.

32 Charge Sheet, *Attorney-General's Report 1975*, p. 4.

33 *Ibid.*, p. 6.

34 For information on the development of PET, see *PET Newsletter*, 1973, p. 1.

35 The BPC constitution (*Attorney General's Report 1975*) says:

> Black shall be interpreted as those who are by law or tradition, politically, economically, and socially discriminated against as a group in the South African society . . .

36 The scenes are divided, in the typed ms., into acts – but not consistently so. I follow here the Heinemann edition of the play in this regard, and number them consecutively as thirteen scenes.

37 *PET Newsletter*, 1973, pp. 15–16.

38 See, for example, Kavanagh, *Cultural Struggle*, p. 171.

39 Orkin, *Drama and the South African State*, p. 156.

40 See, for example, various issues of the *South African Labour Bulletin* (Johannesburg, 1984 and 1985) which addressed the question of essentialism and 'organicism' in the literature of black consciousness.

41 Fanon, *The Wretched of the Earth*, pp. 30–1.

42 Biko, *I Write What I Like*, p. 18.

43 *Ibid.*, p. 19.

44 For example, the 'Report of the Urban and Rural Politics Commission' (Exhibit, *Attorney-General's Report 1975*). These attitudes were shared by theatre practitioners, many of whom exemplified in their work the ambiguous role of black intellectuals. Although in part the beneficiaries of privilege, they were nevertheless also in part organic leaders of rebellion. Saths Cooper of TECON, as Public Relations Officer for BPC,

was the author of a pamphlet in support of a bus strike in Chatsworth, which described the economic and power privileges enjoyed by whites behind the structures of apartheid (see Annexure 6, *Attorney-General's Report 1975*). Sadecque Variava, the organiser of PET, reveals his clear understanding of the same issues in his poem 'Rape of the Land' and in an article on black consciousness (see *PET Newsletter*, p. 1).

45 As Lodge, *Black Politics*, p. 324, has argued:

> merely because its exponents and identifiable followers were relatively socially privileged and hence unrepresentative of the black community as a whole did not mean they were not popularly influential . . .

46 Cf. Paul Gilroy, *There Ain't no Black in the Union Jack: The Cultural Politics of Race and Nation* (University of Chicago Press, 1987), p. 12.

47 Biko, *I Write What I Like*, pp. 89–90.

48 Mudimbe, *Invention*, p. 36.

49 Appia, *In My Father's House*, p. 61.

50 See, for example, Duma Ndlovu, ed., *Woza Afrika!: An Anthology of South African Plays* (New York: George Braziller, 1986). Ndlovu's introduction talks freely about 'the African way of life' and 'basic African elements' in the very different plays collected in the volume.

51 See, for example, Malegapuru William Makgoba's series of articles on African identity and culture written for local newspapers in 1995 and 1996. In one of them, under the heading 'Wits needs to capture the essence of Africa' (*The Star*, 5 June 1995), he argues that the University of the Witwatersrand in Johannesburg:

> should be an African university that draws its inspiration from its African heritage and environment; not a transplanted tree, but one growing from a seed that is planted and nurtured in the African soil . . .

which, though unacknowledged by Makgoba, appears to be influenced by T.M. Yesufu, *Creating the African University: Emerging Issues in the Nineteen-Seventies* (Oxford University Press, 1973), p. 40:

> The truly African university must be one that draws its inspiration from its environment, not a transplanted tree, but growing from a seed that is planted and nurtured in the African soil.

52 Among the many authorities invoked by South African Africanists is Molefi Asante, *Afrocentricity* (Trenton: African World Press, Inc., 1986), but the list is endless. The debates surrounding Makgoba's Africanist arguments (see above, note 51) have emulated the debates in the African-American academy over the work of scholars like Martin Bernal and many others too numerous to mention here.

53 Tsenay Serequeberhan, 'Reflections on *In My Father's House*', *Research in African Literatures* 27.1 (1996), 110–18.

54 *Ibid.*, 114–15.

55 Katya Gibel Azoulay, 'Outside Our Parents' House: Race, Culture, and Identity', *Research in African Literatures* 27.1 (1996), 129–42.

56 *Ibid.*

57 Paul Gilroy, *The Black Atlantic: Modernity and Double Consciousness* (London: Verso, 1993), pp. 86–7.

58 Maishe Maponya, *The Hungry Earth*, in *Doing Plays for a Change* (Johannesburg: University of the Witwatersrand Press, 1995), p. 3.

59 Maishe Maponya, *Sunday Post* (Johannesburg, 4 July 1980), 4.

60 All three plays are published in Maponya, *Doing Plays*.

61 Matsemela Manaka, *Egoli* (Johannesburg: Ravan Press, 1980).

# 5 Dreams of violence: moving beyond colonialism in Canadian and Caribbean drama

CHRISTOPHER INNES

Canada and the West Indies are very different societies: geographically, economically, racially and culturally. Yet in two important aspects they share comparable problems. Each has a colonial history, as well as a highly diverse and ethnically mixed population; and in each almost all the present population comes from elsewhere. Over the last three decades both have been preoccupied with creating a distinctive 'national' culture, rejecting previous dependency on the literary tradition of the imperial power, but without any obvious alternative to draw on – and in formulating this new identity, the stage has played a significant role.

Even here, the contrasts would seem far more crucial than the parallels. To state merely the obvious, the Caribbean is primarily a 'black' area, largely rural and still impoverished, only very recently independent, and with practically no pre-established indigenous theatrical infrastructure (experienced actors, professional directors or designers, even stages). In a sense this might be seen as a conceptual advantage, since starting from an artistic ground-zero encouraged experimentation with other native forms of presentation, particularly dance and carnival, from which a distinctive style of physical acting emerged. At the same time, the severe practical limitations meant that only a writer as dedicated as Derek Walcott could develop the conditions for the performance of his plays or an audience for them. And indeed, at least until the 1980s, Walcott was the sole Caribbean dramatist of any stature, while his Trinidad Theatre Workshop (TTW) remained the only company with extensive expertise. By contrast, Canada is predominantly 'white' – indeed still dominated by the earlier colonisers, French as well as British – with more than a century of effective self-government, and an urban industrial base that had built a network of theatres going back to the nineteenth century, even though it was only in the late 1960s (coincidentally at almost exactly the same time as in the Caribbean) that Canadian playwrights began to emerge.[1] As a result, the assertion of national identity in Canadian drama was almost entirely thematic, while the style of presentation carried over from standard European acting or directing; and there was no single focus to theatrical activity.

However, one element of the Canadian cultural mosaic had been given no voice in this new cultural assertiveness – indeed, continued to exist in (and still today, retains) a colonised relationship to the dominant post-colonial society. This, of course, was the North American Indians, who not only subsisted on isolated reservations, but had absolutely no exposure to a theatrical tradition. It was barely ten years ago when the first play by a Canadian Indian hit the stage. The Indians had been one of the earliest subjects of the new Canadian drama, with *Indian* (first produced for television in 1963) and *The Ecstasy of Rita Joe* (1967). But their plight had been depicted by an Anglophone of Ukrainian origin – both these plays being the work of George Ryga, a radical socialist who had already an established reputation as a novelist. Indians had acted in the second play (even though the Indian title-role of Rita Joe herself was taken by a white actress, while one of the other leads had to be brought in from the United States) and indeed these Indian performers identified completely with the roles.[2] Yet, however attuned to the psychology of racial exploitation, or documentary in their sources, these plays used the Indian as the most extreme example of general social injustice; and they can hardly be counted an authentic expression of the Indian experience.

This only came with the first plays by Tomson Highway in the 1980s – and it is no accident that Highway's most significant play to date, *Dry Lips Oughta Move to Kapuskasing*, is strikingly similar to Walcott's most widely produced drama, *Dream on Monkey Mountain*.

Indeed, the parallels are remarkable, even though there is no question of influence. There is no evidence that Highway had read or had the opportunity of seeing any of Walcott's work before 1989, when *Dry Lips* was first performed in Toronto; and Highway insists that all the elements of his play are drawn from traditional native thought,

Cree tribal symbolism and his experience on the Manitoba reservation where he grew up. There is a gap of more than twenty years between the two works; each expresses a widely different cultural context, and was written for very different audiences – even if Walcott's *Dream on Monkey Mountain* was first publicly performed in Canada, as part of the 1967 Caribana Festival (also in Toronto). Yet despite the distances between them, the themes are directly comparable, and the form is the same. Both are dream-plays – indeed both contain a double dream: a nightmare of murder and revenge inside a dream of liberating re-birth, which becomes a hopeful new reality with the rejection of false images. Both centre on the distorting deception of a white 'Goddess'; and both present a 'Trickster' as one of the central figures. In both violence is linked with comedy. Both also require a highly physical form of acting, developed through their own performing groups, and rely heavily on symbolism.

Beyond such stylistic similarities, Walcott and Highway each depict the self-alienating psychology of the colonised, and propose a healing vision that is designed to shift the perception of their audiences. However, where Walcott wrote in a post-colonial context, Highway was speaking to what might best be described as a neo-colonial society. Thus, while Walcott could see himself as expressing the needs and offering solutions to West Indians as a whole, Highway stood as an outsider, exposing to mainstream Canada a marginalised alternative culture. The combination of such parallel works and contrasting social situations offers a test-case for the effectiveness of this type of theatre.

In addition, Walcott possessed a theoretical basis of revolutionary literature about white/black colonial relations that had direct relevance to his subject (Césaire, Fanon), and to which his play explicitly refers – not only through epigraphs from Sartre's introduction to *The Wretched of the Earth* by Frantz Fanon, but in one character's declaration: 'All I have is this [*shows the mask*], black faces, white masks!', which repeats the title of another influential book by Fanon.[3] No such racial analysis exists for the North American Indian, limiting Highway to tribal traditions – so that the epigraph for *Dry Lips* comes from a contemporary newspaper piece by a fellow Cree journalist. This divergence highlights questions about ideological frames for drama. At the same time, neither of the plays is directly political. They work subliminally rather than through direct statement, seeking to manipulate the psychology of the individual spectator, instead of attempting to change political opinion or foster specific action. And the implicit rejection of social protest drama raises the fundamental issue of the potential effectiveness of theatre, as well as the nature of the influence that conventional stage performance might legitimately be expected to exert on society.

Despite his extensive background as a journalist and even a drama reviewer, Walcott has said so little (either in writing or interviews) about the aims of his drama, or its interpretation, that it counts as an intentional denial of external commentary. This implies a rejection of any direct political dimension for a play such as *Dream on Monkey Mountain* – which is indeed borne out by the nature of the few statements he has made. Surveying 'West Indian Art Today' in 1966, while working towards the first performance of the play, he claimed that 'the little art we produce asserts the integrity of the individual, however tragic'.[4] In the programme for a 1970 production of a much earlier play, *Ti-Jean and His Brothers* (1958), he remarked: 'We present to others a deceptive simplicity that they may dismiss as provincial, primitive, childish, but which is in truth a radical innocence. That is what our fable is about' – a description that applies perhaps even more to *Dream on Monkey Mountain*. Where Walcott does discuss politics in art, he argues that both the economic revolution of Marxism and the appeal to an idealised past of black African grandeur are nothing more than 'visionary rhetoric', irrelevant to the West Indian experience, which does not share the revolutionary history of Algeria or even Haiti, and has nothing in common with the condition of black Americans. As a result he dismisses 'protest poetry' as 'smug and barren' in a West Indian environment, and demands writing 'sincere enough to refute a past that was never grand but debased, not to divide our history into pogroms . . . From there it is an easy step to that aggressive self-pity . . . that makes so much of our literature specious.'[5]

Although, as the epigraphs to each half of the play indicate, the revolutionary politics of Fanon's psychology of colonialism serve as a thematic background to *Dream on Monkey Mountain*, Walcott's action effectively rejects Fanon's solution. The characters may fit his analysis of a binary dualism (coloniser and colonised, each defining themselves through the other[6]) in which the 'self is dissociated' – and it is certainly true that the black bourgeoisie, which Fanon attacks for wearing the mask of white culture and reproducing the colonial order in the new nationalist state, is given exaggerated form in Corporal Lestrade. Having 'the white man work to do' in upholding a ('Roman') legal system which is explicitly opposed to 'the law of the jungle', the Corporal comes to see himself as the parody of a white hunter who finds 'nothing quite so exciting as putting down the natives': 'Bwana Lestrade' bearing 'the white man's burden'. Yet this is not only part of the distortion of Makak's dream, but a doubly false image as delirium (caused by a fatal knife-wound) within the dream; and Fanon's political analysis is further undermined by the elements of exaggeration and parody. Dying, Lestrade switches to the other pole of the binary: 'Too late have I loved thee, Africa of my mind . . . I jeered thee because I hated half of myself, my eclipse.' Reborn, naked, into this new racial consciousness, the Corporal becomes both judge and executioner of all white culture and history, including specifically Shakespeare and Marlowe. He also condemns the Trickster figure, Moustique, for having 'betrayed our dream'.[7] However, blackness is an equally delusive state; and his conversion is denied both in terms of the logic of traditional West Indian culture, where the Trickster is a force against repression, and in Walcott's own artistic terms. Walcott is on record as seeing himself as in the tradition of Shakespeare and Marlowe, as well as contemporary white authors (specifically Genet, whose play *The Blacks* was part of the TTW repertoire and is a significant influence on *Dream on Monkey Mountain*; Beckett, who informs the existential despair expressed by Moustique when he dies, and Yeats, both of whom are quoted in Walcott's prefatory 'Overture' to *Dream on Monkey Mountain*).[8]

This counter-image of 'blackness' becomes, in fact, one of the main targets in the play. The vision of a lost African golden age, fostering racial pride as the source of black identity, was first articulated by Aimé Césaire in the 1930s; and it is no accident that Makak's induction of his dream

I see this woman singing
And my feet grow roots . . .

A million silver needles prickle my blood,
Like a rain of small fishes.
The snakes in my hair speak . . .

echoes Césaire's invocation (speaking as a poet who has become rooted like a tree) to the Congo:

the woman who had a thousand names
names of fountain sun and tears
and her hair of minnows
and her steps my climates . . .[9]

This poem comes from Césaire's *Notebook of a Return to the Native Land*, which could also be a subtitle for *Dream on Monkey Mountain*, since Makak's dream is a journey back to Africa. Indeed at this period of his career Walcott is clearly matching his work against Césaire's, since both also wrote plays about the Haitian revolt. But just as Walcott's *Henri Christophe*, first performed in 1968, can be seen as a counter-text to Césaire's 1963 *Tragedy of King Christophe*, so *Dream on Monkey Mountain* rejects the ideal of negritude.

It is significant that the hero of the play takes the name 'Monkey' (Makak); and as such he is not only the tutelary spirit of 'Monkey Mountain', but also the animal defined by its capacity for mimicry – as the farcical opening sequence of 'Everything I say this monkey do, / I don't know what to say this monkey won't do' emphatically points out. Thus, at a very basic level in the play, the search for negritude is an inauthentic copying. Although Makak's dream does carry him back to an 'Africa of the mind' where he attains the title he had been given as a satirical insult in the opening scene, as 'King of Africa' he is forced to execute his only friend, Moustique, whose earlier death at the hands of an enraged mob he had bitterly lamented. As his accuser, the Corporal, claims, Moustique has indeed 'betrayed our dream'. But as the Trickster figure, his betrayal is a positive act: where the dream leads is to madness, in which Makak's humanity is sacrificed for hatred.

MOUSTIQUE. Look around you old man, and see who betray what . . .
in those days long ago you had something there [*Touching his breast*],
but all that gone. All this blood, all this killing, all this revenge.[10]

The ultimate act of violence in the play is the on-stage beheading of the WOMAN, the white goddess whose mask Makak carries and who represents

> the mirror of the moon that this ape look into and find himself unbearable. She is all that is pure, all that he cannot reach . . . if you want to discover the beautiful depth of your blackness, nigger, chop off her head!

This act frees him indeed – but not just from a crippling sense of racial inferiority. It also frees him from the dream of Africa. He immediately wakes to reality, and can remember his name. No longer Makak (the Monkey), he recognises his real being – Felix Hobain, a name encapsulating the mixed ancestry that Walcott sees as typical of the West Indies, and which in itself disqualifies negritude – and realises that in his dream 'the roots of my feet could grip nothing, but now, God, they have found ground'.[11]

Walcott's belief that 'the future of West Indian militancy lies in art' can only be incorporated in art, not political action – and on one level *Dream on Monkey Mountain* is an analogy for his own writing and for the development of his theatre company. And in fact the characters were based on specific actors. As Walcott observed: 'the play was written with [Errol Jones] in mind, or rather, grew round him'. The scenes developed out of improvisations with the company, while one of the central characters, Basil the undertaker who is the extension of Baron Samedi, was added only at the last minute to offer a role to an actor who was accompanying the troupe to Toronto.[12] Just as for the characters in this play, the problem for the TTW in attempting to create a drama for their people was

> How to be true? If one went in search of the African experience, carrying the luggage of a few phrases and a crude map, where would it end? We had no language for the bush and there was a conflicting grammar in the pace of our movement.

Lacking any defining revolution in achieving statehood (the violent breaking of the colonial moulds that Fanon saw as key to establishing authentic identity, in bringing each individual the 'certainty that he embodies a decisive moment of the national consciousness') West

Indian identity could be articulated only in art. This would be achieved by 'the forging of a language that went beyond mimicry, a dialect which had the force of revelation and which began to create an oral culture of chants, jokes, folk-songs and fables'.[13] In its exact correspondence with these aims, the play itself becomes not only a model of identity for West Indian spectators, but an attempt to promote the consciousness it represents.

The tripartite structure, with the dream-action divided into two halves, each comprising three scenes, and enclosed by prologue and epilogue, is deliberately aligned with the form of 'the true folk tale', which for Walcott 'concealed a structure as universal as the skeleton, the one armature from Br'er Anancy to King Lear. It kept the same digital rhythm of three movements, three acts, three moral revelations'. This is combined with the symbolism that pervades the play. The original setting, with its spider webs over the dark tower of the mountain, and the bars of the jail-house, portrays life (or perhaps false culture) as a prison – 'attempting to escape' being a synonym for 'revolution' – from which the dreamer is set free once he rediscovers his true self; and the moon, which had illuminated the dream, is turned around to become the sun: the daylight of reality. The characters are traditional emblematic animals (Tiger and Mouse, who is transformed into 'General Rat', as well as Mosquito and Monkey) and Voodoo figures (Baron Samedi), who also exist on other levels, with Makak not only being an ugly and broken-down old charcoal-burner, but also a crucified Christ flanked by two criminals, whose 'resurrection' takes place at dawn on a Sunday, marked by singing 'from the Church of Revelation'. The performance begins and ends with the drawing of a circle which (as in Yeats' *Plays for Dancers*) is both a literal marking out of the playing area, a metaphor for the revolving treadmill of history, and a magic circle. The psychological impact is heightened by deliberate naivety, and by the use of rhythm in dance and choral singing, while the appeal to the subconscious is explicit in ritualised action and the whole dream context. And indeed West Indian reviewers not only commented on the effectiveness of the 'subliminal techniques' but asserted that the play might help 'free ourselves from colonial neuroses'.[14]

As a play, *Dream on Monkey Mountain* was undoubtedly successful, performed on tour throughout the West Indies in 1967 and in

1968, as well as on the TTW's home stage, in Jamaica in 1971, the Virgin Islands and elsewhere from 1973 to 1977, and re-mounted in 1985 – in addition to being staged several times across America, garnering an Obie in New York, and being filmed for television – and in retrospect it has been acknowledged as one of the clearest accounts of the question of Caribbean freedom and identity. However, its effect on the West Indian psyche is harder to demonstrate. Certainly this was not immediate, since the negritude that Walcott tries so hard to neutralise was a growing force in West Indian politics. Barely three years after the first performances of *Dream on Monkey Mountain* the rising tide of the negritude movement led to violent street demonstrations, attacks on Walcott himself as not being radical (or black), and led to his first break with the Trinidad Theatre Workshop, as well as conditioning political attitudes in Trinidad so that for the next five years only 'revolutionary' drama was critically acceptable. Even so, with benefit of hindsight, when *Dream on Monkey Mountain* was staged in 1985 the response indicated that Walcott's play was one of the conditioning factors that by then had led to the rejection of Black Power politics, and to a general recognition that the 'Back to Africa' movement was a destructive illusion.[15]

Tomson Highway's *Dry Lips Oughta Move to Kapuskasing* was no less successful in Canadian terms. It won four awards, including the Best New Play of 1988/89 when it opened as a co-production between Highway's own performance group, Native Earth, and Theatre Passe Muraille, one of the experimental (white) Toronto theatres. It then moved to successively more establishment stages, including the National Arts Centre, ending up as part of a subscription series in the Royal Alexandra: possibly the most bourgeois theatre in Canada. Yet unlike Walcott, Highway could in no sense be seen as expressing the aspirations of his (almost exclusively non-native) audience; and while his play drew on common cultural symbols, these were deconstructed rather than affirmed.

To understand the effect of the play, some of the social background needs to be taken into account. George Ryga, who had grown up next to a Cree reservation in Northern Alberta, described the 'demoralisation and degradation' of the native community in the 1960s as being about as total as any society can experience anywhere in the world. These people had been worked over by the church; they had been worked over by the Hudson's Bay Company. There was nothing left. There was no language left any more.

The situation in the Brochet Indian Reserve in northern Manitoba at that time would have been the same; but Highway is a whole genera-tion younger. In between – partly fuelled by the Black Power move-ment that Walcott had fought against, which also led to the abortive American Indian uprising at Wounded Knee in 1973 – there has been a conscious attempt to revive tribal culture among Canadian Indian communities, while arguably Ryga's plays had contributed to the de-velopment of governmental initiatives for natives in the early 1970s. And subsequently official projects introduced western theatre as an educational tool. One example, which has particular relevance to some of the thematic concerns in *Dry Lips*, was a public awareness pro-gramme mounted in response to a 1986 North-West Territories Task Force on Spousal Assault. A white Edmonton theatre director, who found that the Dene tribal language had no words for 'drama', 'actor' or even 'theatre', was employed to create performances that would act as a catalyst for group discussion of the problem.[16] Tribal meetings formed the basis for workshops, from which communal scripts were produced; and the only audiences were those in the native reservations.

A rather different example, in some ways paralleling the per-formance context of Highway's work, was offered by Vancouver Head-lines Theatre's *No' Xya'* [*Our Footprints*, 1983], which developed out of 'Power Play' workshops, modelled on Augusto Boal's 'Theatre of the Oppressed'. The script was written by the (white) artistic director of the Headlines company, but in collaboration with members of a tribal council and a core group of native performers. Paralleling a land-claims case being heard before the British Columbia Supreme Court at the time, it was directly relevant to Indian concerns; while the production made striking use of native masks, ceremonial costumes and dances, as well as the symbolism of totem-poles. Initially designed for the local Indian community, it was then taken on tour through British Columbia and across Canada, with a tribal chief who had been one of the main witnesses in the Supreme Court case leading the discussions with the audience that followed each performance. However, the semi-documentary, issue-oriented topicality of this kind of theatre is far from Highway's aims. His plays are quite distinct from protest drama; and like Walcott (who rejects the external forms of carnival and even folk-dance as 'prostitutions of a tourist culture'),[17] he deliberately avoids reproducing the traditional tribal images.

There is nothing folkloric about the way Highway presents his Indian characters, who are shabbily dressed in ordinary clothes, frequently drunken and living in poverty. Indeed, part of his message is the convergence of Indian and mainstream society. Thus in *Dry Lips* the most prominent elements of the 'reserve house' setting are not artefacts of Indian art or native cultural objects, but 'a life-size pin-up poster of Marilyn Monroe', and for another location a jukebox with 'magical, glittering lights'. In Highway's view, 'white culture in Canada is very much changing and transforming as a result of living with native culture; likewise Cree culture, native culture'; and – very much like Walcott – he sees his drama as 'searching for this new voice, this new identity . . . this magical transformation' of society. Working through Native Earth, which is dedicated to developing a professional group of Indian performers and providing a vehicle for new native work, Highway is very much the proof of his own assertions. At the same time, he takes a public position that sets him apart from both the white society he addresses and the Indian society whose values he expresses. In contrast to the generally aggressive heterosexuality of his characters, in interviews surrounding the production of his plays Highway stresses his homosexuality, asserting 'what I appreciate about my sexuality is that it gives me the status of an outsider. And as a native, I am an outsider in a double sense. That gives you a wider vision . . .'.[18]

His first major success was *The Rez Sisters* ('Rez' being slang for 'Indian reservation'); and it is very much a companion-piece to *Dry Lips*. The tone is broadly satiric, combining physical farce with a poetic evocation of the Indian sense of community, against a background of serious social problems. *The Rez Sisters* was designed (in Highway's own words) to rehabilitate 'a people for whom simple human dignity has long been owing', and presents a group of seven women from the semi-imaginary Wasaychigan Indian Reserve, which has become the standard setting for Highway's plays – giving them the sense of a running serial. Or rather, since the characters from one do not reappear, although they may be mentioned in the dialogue of the other, the plays become a set of different perspectives on the same material, thus implicitly demonstrating the complexity of a human situation that is otherwise overlooked (at least by the urban population) as too basic or socially reduced to warrant attention. Using comedy to break through stereotypes, Highway shows the seven Indian women undertaking an epic journey – from their reserve in the wilds of northern Ontario, by bus to Toronto – the place where the play was being performed – to play Bingo. This incongruous obsession for a distinctly non-native game, and their down-to-earth, if highly idiosyncratic, personalities, achieved a degree of identification that led not only Indian but also white audiences to feel, as another Canadian playwright, Carol Bolt, put it, part of 'an extraordinary, exuberant, life-affirming family'.[19] To that extent *The Rez Sisters* was successful in creating a more inclusive sense of community through dissolving barriers of incomprehension and promoting emotional sympathy.

However, Highway's aims were considerably wider: the development of a comprehensive national mythology, in which the original inhabitants of Canada – the now marginalised Indians – would serve as active agents of social renewal, and thus regain their cultural centrality. In fact, one sign of this is his avoidance of any direct political statement. Highway's underlying target may be the patriarchal still-colonialist attitudes of (white) society; but he never deals explicitly with the conflict between white and Indian. Indeed, up to this point, none of his plays have even included a direct relationship between the two. Even in *The Rez Sisters*, where the native women reach the industrial city of Toronto, and take part in a distinctively non-native communal pastime, none of the other players surrounding them is presented on stage or even mentioned; and the place of the white Bingo Master is taken by an Indian mythological figure (the Trickster). Instead, Highway demonstrates the effects of this neo-colonial victimisation on the subjugated in order to foster awareness among those responsible for subjugating them; and the change he works for is not political but conceptual:

Canadian society can gain a lot by looking at native theology. Myths define society and we need to break down the ones that oppress people, whether they're women, or homosexuals, or minorities.[20]

Defining an alternative mythology, based on the experience of the exploited, is most explicit in *Dry Lips*. Here the focus is on official religion – Christianity – and on the Canadian national game of ice hockey.

The Wasaychigan reserve is even more central in *Dry Lips Oughta Move To Kapuskasing*. 'Wasaychigan' means 'window' in Cree, and for Highway the name has some of the same resonance as Wessex in Thomas Hardy's novels – a mythical transformation of a recognisable, real place – and building on this, here it is clearly a microcosm. In the earlier play the 'Rez' women set out for the big metropolis of Toronto. By contrast the only place Dry Lips (the ironic name of the woman organizing an all-female, native ice-hockey team) can be conceived of going to is Kapuskasing. Like Toronto, Kapuskasing is an actual place, a small Ontario backwoods settlement. It represents the most isolated and out-of-the-way community imaginable, making the inhabitants of the reservation isolated even by the standards of the least significant outsiders; and in fact no one can leave. The one person who plans to go elsewhere is accidentally shot and killed on the eve of his departure; and this is clearly symbolic since the dead man is a young activist, whose aim is to revive a purely Indian culture by retrieving a magical drum through which the tribe will 'learn to dance again'.[21]

A counter-play to *The Rez Sisters*, in *Dry Lips* seven male characters replace the seven women, and there is an almost complete contrast in tone. In *Dry Lips*, the affirmative comedy of the earlier play has been exchanged for aggressive violence: even though the characterisation still contains a great deal of humour, it tends towards the grotesque. In *The Rez Sisters* the only non-female personification is the spirit-figure of 'Nanabush' (the Ojibway name for 'the Trickster': according to Highway a sort of universal common denominator in Indian legend, whose nature has been interpreted in many different ways by various tribes). There, played by a dancer – Tomson Highway's brother – Nanabush appears not only as the Bingo Master, but (dressed in white feathers) as a seagull and (in a black-feathered costume) as a night-hawk: birds of the soul and of death in Indian mythology. By contrast in the masculine context of *Dry Lips* this Nanabush deity represents the archetypal female, or rather perhaps the object of male fantasies. The same actress takes the parts of all four women characters, as well as a transsexual Jehova-caricature, donning *'a gigantic pair of false rubberised breasts'* or *'an oversized prosthetic bum'* over her bosom and buttocks for all the different female figures.[22]

The single-sex cast of human characters makes each play gender-specific; and in *Dry Lips* the main theme is sexual abuse, which links up with the community theatre projects in the North-West Territories. In the earlier play, one of the Rez sisters has adopted a girl who suffered permanent mental damage after being raped with a screwdriver by a pair of white youths. Highway has stressed that this was based on a true incident, although the details have been changed. In the actual case, the teenage Indian girl had her eyes gouged out to prevent her identifying the rapists, and froze to death before she was found. Not surprisingly, this horrific incident, widely reported in newspapers some years earlier, is used to epitomise the violence and exploitive neo-colonialism of the male-dominated white society. Yet in the plays it is buried as an unstated background, leaving the audiences to realise the connection. It is only an incidental reference in *The Rez Sisters*. And while the vicious sexual violation of an Indian girl becomes the climactic on-stage action of *Dry Lips*, here the rapist is not white, but another Indian. Indeed, although the visceral response to this graphically presented act is intensified by the fact that the victim is pregnant, guilt is deflected since the perpetrator himself is mentally retarded, having been left mute and infantile from foetal alcohol syndrome – and his diminished responsibility is compounded by the double level of the female characterisation: the girl being *'Nanabush . . . as the spirit of the vivacious, young Patsy Pegahmagahbow, complete with very large, over-sized bum'*.[23] In addition, the audience reaction is further complicated by the presence of two other Indians as bystanders who voyeuristically participate in the rape.

The full-frontal nature of this scene, together with the sympathetic treatment of even the most chauvinistic males in the play, led to complaints of misogyny. But the men's reduction of women (at least in their fantasy) to sex-objects, and the dialogue constantly belittling the women's drive to form their own hockey team – the Wasy Wailerettes – is only a response to the destruction of their self-esteem as outcasts on the margins of a society. Decultured, physically degraded and politically powerless, the illusion of masculine authority is all they have left; and even that is threatened by their wives taking over the uniquely male preserve of hockey. However, by the end of the play all the men are united in support of the Wailerettes at their 'big match' (against the no less comically named Canoe Lake Bravettes); and even the most negative of the Indians – one of those defeated at Wounded Knee, who refused to stop the rape because 'I hate them fuckin' bitches. Because they – our own women – took the fuckin' power away from us faster than the FBI ever did' – cheers the team on as 'the most beautiful, daring, death-defying Indian women in the world' and describes their Captain Hera Keechigeesik as 'graceful . . . like a Russian ballerina'.[24]

The male sexism is also closely associated with religion; and it is Christianity that is symbolically responsible for the rape. The attack is motivated by a confusion in the rapist's thoughts between Christ bleeding on the cross and the blood of his drunken mother flooding the floor of a tavern, where he was born under a table (the grotesque scene of his birth being juxtaposed with the biblical rantings of his uncle, symbolically named Spooky Lacroix). In addition, the retarded youth's mother uses a crucifix to beat him with; and it replaces the screwdriver of the story in the earlier play as the instrument with which he assaults the girl. The point could hardly be more explicit, and was spelled out by Highway. 'The missionaries made such a mess of things', he told an interviewer:

> In the rape scene, a woman is raped with a crucifix. On a
> metaphorical level, the scene symbolises the matriarchal
> [Indian] religion raped by the patriarchy, the Goddess raped by
> God. Until the central symbol of the crucifix is not central in
> our society, women will always be second class citizens [like
> the natives].

However, instead of mounting a verbal attack in the play, Christianity is deconstructed through farce. When, kneeling over the body of the dying youth, one of the characters challenges 'God-Al-fucking-mighty!'

to 'come down and show us you got the guts to stop this stupid, stupid way of living', we get a parodistic vision of the deity:

> *a light comes up on Nanabush . . . sitting on a toilet having a good shit. He/she is dressed in an old man's white beard and wig, but also wearing sexy, elegant women's high-heeled pumps. Surrounded by white, puffy clouds, she/he sits with her legs crossed, nonchalantly filing his/her fingernails.*[25]

Christianity is not only uncompromisingly presented as the epitome of patriarchal colonialism. It also embodies the distorting linear thought-patterns of white culture; and the substitution of the transsexual Indian Trickster for 'God the Father' offers a positive alternative.

Trained as a concert pianist, Highway refers to his drama in musical terms, talking about 'applying sonata form to the spiritual and mental situation of a street drunk'.[26] *Dry Lips* is designed for multi-level action, with a fluid interchange of scenes within a single all-purpose setting, while the plot is fragmented and comprises a series of flashbacks (including the retarded teenager's birth on top of a jukebox). Within this structure thematic motifs recur and become transformed like musical variations. As in *Dream on Monkey Mountain*, the level of reality switches from dream to heightened vision within the dream, which is closely associated with 'a huge full moon'; and the action is circular. The dreamer is already asleep at the opening, lying naked and dead drunk on a couch, and the ending returns him to this position. Within this frame of 'external' reality, the rape and murder has been only a nightmare. However, during the action everything has changed. Instead of being on the couch of a married neighbour, with whose wife he has just had sex (we see '*Nanabush, as the spirit of Gazelle Nataways*' planting '*a kiss on Zachary's bum, leaving behind a gorgeous, luminescent lip-stick mark*'), he is in his own home and woken by his wife, '*the "real" Hera Keechigeesik*', who is bringing home their new-born baby. We are left with the closing image of an idealised Indian family group – as he plants the suggestion of her forming a hockey team:

You ever think of playing hockey?
HERA: Yeah, right. That's all I need is a flying puck right in the left tit, nee . . .

*But she stops to speculate.*
. . . hockey, hmmm . . .[27]

For Highway, the circular dream-structure embodies a specific philosophy. It corresponds to 'the way the Cree look at life. A continuous cycle. A self-rejuvenating force. By comparison, Christian theology is a straight line. Birth, suffering, and then the apocalypse . . .' Thus the play's circular action is intended as a positive antidote to the self-destructive degradation portrayed in it; and Highway also emphasised that 'dreams – and the dream-life – have traditionally been considered by native society to be the greatest tool of instruction'. As with Walcott, tangible effects are hard to document. However, even Highway acknowledged that the play might be 'easily misunderstood'.[28] As he said, 'a lot of people missed' the positive significance of Hera Keechigeesik (the name of the one real-life Indian woman, the sleeping man's wife who appears briefly after the end of the dream). This name was meant to signal 'the return of the goddess', Hera being queen of heaven in Greek mythology, and Keechigeesik the Great Sky in Cree legend.[29] However, that such specific references may be too arcane hardly diminishes the overall effect; and *Dry Lips* certainly fed into changes in the climate of political opinion.

The revelations about child abuse by priests teaching in Catholic schools (like the one he himself attended) that began to surface shortly after the play's first performance would probably have happened anyway, given the vogue for 'recovered memory' in North America, which has led to highly publicised reports of familial abuse. Certainly the play attracted considerable attention in Ottawa, and was seen by a number of Federal ministers and civil servants who were responsible for negotiating new land-treaties with the Indians. Since its performance, there have been two violent confrontations reminiscent of Wounded Knee, which were precisely the kind of assertions of a separate Indian identity that Highway rejects. But *Dry Lips* was specifically aimed at a white audience, and designed to cause a shift in the psychology of the dominant society. As with Highway's first plays, *The Rez Sisters* was initially mounted in the Native Earth Performing Arts space, attended almost exclusively by Indians. It had been workshopped on the Manatoulin Island Reserve, and was designed to address a native public. As one Toronto reviewer commented, it came 'out of nowhere' to win a prestigious award, followed by a sold-out national tour.[30] By contrast, though still performed by an all-native cast, *Dry Lips* was developed for a mainstream (white) audience. It was a co-production with one of the well-established Toronto fringe theatres; and the acknowledgements in the published text include an Ontario cabinet minister and an ex-Federal cabinet minister. Shortly after the various performances, a new spirit of conciliation was evident in the renegotiation of Indian land claims, which are still continuing. But Highway's intended effect, creating an amalgam of the Indian existential perspective with mainstream values, will be a gradual process, evident only long after the event.

It is, of course, impossible to prove even that the community theatre mounted in response to the North-West Territories Task Force on Spousal Assault moulded the private behaviour of the communities as a whole, or even the participants, in the expected ways. The aims of both Walcott and Highway were far more wide-reaching; and the social result they were working for through their plays is far more subtle – evident only in the long term, perhaps even after the plays themselves have been forgotten. But this does not mean that they should be rejected as ineffective in comparison to more politically strident, or problem-oriented, drama. The parallels between their work, arrived at independently, should give pause. Both are experienced writers, one a Nobel laureate. Both focus on creating a new national identity, rather than correcting a specific wrong or producing an immediate political result. Both use subliminal means in order subtly to change the essential nature of their society. There is a fundamental divide in twentieth-century drama between playwrights who believe that if you change the political system, the nature of citizens will be revolutionised as a consequence (Brecht); and those who believe that if you can alter the psychology of individuals, then the eventual result will be social revolution (Artaud).

The dream-play approach of Walcott and Highway puts each firmly in the latter camp (Walcott in fact cites Artaud in the fullest overview of his drama).[31] And indeed it is arguable that this may be the only avenue open to standard theatre, unless there are extraordinary political events surrounding the performance – as supposedly with Beaumarchais's *Marriage of Figaro* in 1784. Other contemporary playwrights would agree. To quote a metaphor used by Stoppard, where one of his alter egos uses a cricket bat to illustrate the way plays should be constructed:

> What we're trying to do is write cricket bats, so that when
> we throw up an idea and give it a little knock, it might . . .
> travel . . . you may perhaps alter people's perceptions so that
> they behave a little differently at that axis of behaviour where
> we locate politics or justice . . . you can build bridges across
> incomprehension and chaos . . . If you get the right ones in the
> right order, you can nudge the world a little.[32]

The effect may be almost indiscernible. Neither in the West Indies nor Canada has there been a watershed political event following the performances of Walcott's or Highway's work to which the plays might be linked; and despite the Black Power movement or the occasional confrontation on Canadian Indian reserves, the recent history of both countries has been free from the social upheaval that has erupted elsewhere in the world, and that might fuel an immediate political response to a theatrical performance. Yet in each case a discernible shift in general attitudes occurred after these plays were staged. Although they may not have initiated such developments, it is clear that *Dream on Monkey Mountain* and *Dry Lips Oughta Move to Kapuskasing* contributed – and not only as important public statements seen by a significant fraction of their respective populations. By combining their native heritage with European theatrical forms, Walcott and Highway offered a new and more inclusive definition of cultural identity. And, almost by definition, this has to be transmitted on an individual, subliminal level.

NOTES

1 Although there were occasional, isolated playwrights who appeared in the 1930s (Herman Voaden) or 1950s (Robertson Davies), it was only after the 1967 centennial that a significant number of Canadian dramatists emerged (George Ryga and James Reaney in 1967; Michel Tremblay in 1968; George Walker, David Freeman and David French in 1971–2).

2 Cf. Christopher Innes, *Politics and the Playwright: George Ryga* (Toronto: Simon and Pierre, 1985), pp. 50f.

3 Derek Walcott, *Dream on Monkey Mountain* (New York: Farrar, Strauss and Giroux, 1970), p. 271.

4 Walcott, *Sunday Guardian* (8 May 1966), 8.

5 Walcott, *Sunday Guardian* (15 January 1967), 8.

6 See Frantz Fanon, *A Dying Colonialism* (New York: Grove Press 1967), p. 40; *Sociologie d'une révolution* (Paris: 1978), p. 22.

7 *Dream on Monkey Mountain*, epigraph, p. 211, and pp. 279–80, 286, 296, 299, 162.

8 See Walcott, 'Overture', *Dream on Monkey Mountain*, p. 31: 'I saw myself legitimately prolonging the mighty line of Marlowe, of Milton, but my own sense of inheritance was stronger because it came from estrangement.'

9 *Dream on Monkey Mountain*, p. 227, and Aimé Césaire, *The Collected Poetry*, trans. Clayton Eshelman and Annette Smith (Berkeley and Los Angeles: University of California Press, 1983), pp. 52f.

10 *Dream on Monkey Mountain*, pp. 223, 214, 314–15.

11 *Ibid.*, pp. 319, 326.

12 *Ibid.* ('Overture') p. 18; Walcott, letter to Gordon Davidson (14 August 1969), Rockefeller Archives.

13 *Ibid.* ('Overture') pp. 37, 17; and Fanon, *Towards the African Revolution: Political Essays* (first published 1963); trans. Haakon Chevalier (London: Writers and Readers, 1980).

14 *Dream on Monkey Mountain*, pp. 287, 324 and 'Overture', p. 24; *Voice of St. Lucia* (9 November 1968) 6; *Sunday Express* (28 January 1968), 8. (For an extensive summary of the reviews, see Bruce King, *Derek Walcott and West Indian Drama* (Oxford: Clarendon Press, 1995), pp. 84–104.)

15 Patricia Ismond, *Sunday Express* (17 March 1985), 23. For a discussion of the response to the 1985 production of *Dream on Monkey Mountain*, see King, *Derek Walcott*, pp. 329–31.

16 Ryga, Interview, in *Canadian Drama*, 8, 2 (1982), 162; *Canadian Theatre Review*, 53 (Winter 1987), 15.

17 Walcott, 'Overture' in *Dream on Monkey Mountain*, p. 26 (see also pp. 7, 8).

18 Tomson Highway, *Dry Lips Oughta Move to Kapuskasing* (Saskatoon: Fifth House, 1989), pp. 15, 77; and Highway, cit. Ann Wilson in *Other Solitudes: Canadian Multi-cultural Fictions*, ed. Linda Hutcheon and Richmond Manion (Toronto: Oxford University Press, 1990), p. 354, and in *Toronto Life* (March 1991), 36.

19 Highway, cit. *Winnipeg Free Press* (20 October 1990), 25; Carol Bolt, *Books in Canada* (March 1989), 26.

20 Highway, cit. Michael Smyth, *Winnipeg Free Press* (15 April 1991), 16.

21 *Dry Lips Oughta Move to Kapuskasing*, p. 43.

22 *Ibid.*, pp. 15, 38.

23 *Ibid.*, p. 97.

24 *Ibid.*, pp. 124, 120 and 124–5 (translated p. 133).

25 Highway, cit. *Toronto Star* (24 March 1991), D2; *Dry Lips Oughta Move to Kapuskasing*, pp. 116–17.

26 Highway, cit. Nancy Wigstin, *Books in Canada* (March 1989), 8.

27 *Dry Lips Oughta Move to Kapuskasing*, pp. 10, 16, 127, 129.

28 *Globe and Mail* (15 April 1991), C3; and Highway, cit. *Toronto Star* (24 March 1991), D2.

29 *Toronto Life* (March 1991), 36, 81–2.

30 Highway, cit. *Canadian Literature* (Spring–Summer 1990), 259, and in *Brick* 37 (Fall 1989), 60; *Toronto Star* (28 November 1986), D24.

31 See *Dream on Monkey Mountain*, 'Overture', p. 28.

32 Tom Stoppard, *The Real Thing* (London: Faber, 1982), pp. 53–4.

# 6 The French-speaking Caribbean: journeying from the native land

CAROLE-ANNE UPTON

In 1992 the Nobel Prize for Literature was awarded to a Caribbean poet and dramatist for the first time, in the person of Derek Walcott. The theatre of the French-speaking Caribbean, comprising French Guyana, Guadeloupe and Martinique, has yet to receive such an accolade. International acclaim tends to favour novelists such as Patrick Chamoiseau, Edouard Glissant, Simone Schwarz-Bart and Maryse Condé. This is not to say that a distinctive francophone theatre culture does not properly exist in the Caribbean. In fact, Glissant, Schwarz-Bart and Condé have all successfully written plays as well (*Monsieur Toussaint, Ton beau capitaine* [*Your Handsome Captain*] and *Pension les Alizés* [*The Tropical Breeze Hotel*] respectively). The theatre is by its very nature ephemeral and the French publishing realm is clearly more interested in the worldwide dissemination of prose than of dramatic texts. And yet the theatre is a vital marker of cultural identity, the nature of which has been a key subject of debate in the French-speaking Caribbean for at least the past sixty years, a debate which continues to shape political ideologies.

No two figures have made more of an impact in the creation of post-colonial culture in relation to political theory than Aimé Césaire and Frantz Fanon; both denizens of the young African states, both citizens of France, both natives of Martinique. A third figure, also from Martinique, has emerged since the 1970s to carry the debate of cultural politics/political culture(s) forward, beyond the so-called decade of independence and into the age of Maastricht. That figure is Daniel Boukman. Like Césaire, Boukman is a poet and playwright driven by political conscience. This chapter identifies a line of development through these three writers, which, despite their contrasting conclusions, is characterised by their efforts to situate complex ideological notions of Martinican identity with reference to an external (global) as well as an internal (national) context.

Daniel Boukman may not enjoy the same stature and international renown as Césaire or Fanon, but his work has undoubtedly succeeded in raising political consciousness in a series of more localised societies both within and beyond Martinique. Boukman's plays have been translated into Spanish in Cuba (*Ventres pleins, ventres creux* [*Full Bellies, Empty Bellies*]; *Orphée nègre* [*Negro Orpheus*]) and performed in Arabic in Constantine, Algeria (*Chants pour hâter la mort du temps des Orphée* [*Songs to End the Days of Orpheus*]). They have been adapted for Cuban television (*Ventres pleins, ventres creux*) and for radio by France Culture (*Des voix dans un prison* [*Prison Voices*]). *Les Négriers* [*The Slavers*] was made into a film entitled *West Indies, ou Les nègres marrons de la liberté* [*West Indies, or Freedom and the Runaway Slaves*] by Med Hondo in 1979, following his stage productions of the play in Paris. There have been productions in Martinique and Guadeloupe of *Ventres pleins, ventres creux, Les Négriers* and *Chants pour hâter la mort du temps des Orphée.* Several ephemeral Creole translations have been generated for performance there by the Poulbwa company under Robert Dieupart, but these have never been published. From 1962 until 1981 Boukman lived in Algeria as a teacher and journalist in self-imposed exile, having refused the call-up for French military service. He was awarded the Prix Carbet in 1992 for his published *œuvre*.

His relative isolation from the theatre during his period in Algeria might account in part for the uneven production history of his plays. While certain works have made a significant impact both within and beyond Martinique, others have never been staged. However, such mixed success is undoubtedly more directly attributable to the qualities inherent in the various pieces, on both a thematic and a practical level.

*Les Négriers*, for example, reinvents the familiar iconography of the Middle Passage in a contemporary socio-political attack on the condition of Caribbean migrant workers in Paris. Its theatricality is striking, vibrant and direct; almost a multimedia piece ahead of its time, this is certainly Boukman's most successful play. Similar techniques, involving masks, mannequins, puppets, dance, mime, slides, song, poetry and the presentation of statistical data are employed in *Et jusqu'à la dernière pulsation de nos veines* [*To the Last Beat of Our Hearts*] but to a degree that makes any fluent staging seem virtually unimaginable. Furthermore this involved docudrama deals with a specific historical situation – the Palestinian occupation and liberation – the universal appeal of which, though overtly signalled in the text, remains at best secondary.

Both of these works, whatever their respective dramatic merits, look beyond the shores of Martinique for a political framework in which to situate a Martinican vision. *Et jusqu'à . . .* makes a bold attempt to draw parallels with a historical moment elsewhere in the world. The Sephardic youth movement in Israel is called the Black Panthers, we are told, because 'la situation de la jeunesse juive afro-asiatique rappelle celle des Noirs des Etats-Unis d'Amérique'.[1] [The situation of these young Afro-Asian Jews is reminiscent of that of the Blacks in the United States of America.] Primarily an outward act of solidarity in support of the Palestinians, there are moments in this play when the general is invoked over the particular in a broad political embrace which is also clearly designed to invite reciprocal sympathy. Globalising references to the Third World set out the Martinican cause against the French oppressor as firmly as the Palestinian against the Zionist:

> Le leadership sioniste a transformé les juifs dans l'Etat d'Israël en un peuple de grands seigneurs suivant le modèle classique avec tous les traits distinctifs du colonialisme usurpateur et de l'oppression européenne contre les peuples du Tiers-Monde.[2]
>
> (The Zionist leadership has transformed the Jews in the State of Israel into a people of overlords in the true classic style with all the distinctive characteristics of usurping colonialism and European oppression of the peoples of the Third World.)

The ideological connection implicit in this Martinican view of the Palestinian question leaves the play without an obvious audience. It is suspended between the universal and the specific, abstracted from both the cultures it implicates, yet unable to transcend their limits.

Boukman's statement that 'mon pays est actuellement une colonie française'[3] (my country is currently a French colony) expresses a political opinion rather than a statement of fact. The three French territories in the Caribbean present a curious anomaly in relation to the independence paradigm of most former European colonies. The colonial exception to the post-colonial rule, French Guyana, Guadeloupe and Martinique have remained, apparently willingly, attached to the French *mère-patrie* right up to the present day and throughout the period of independence that swept the other Caribbean islands around the 1970s. Since 1946 Martinique has enjoyed material benefits unique amongst the Caribbean islands through its official status as one of the Départements d'Outre-Mer (DOMs). As of 1992, the Maastricht Treaty brought the DOMs, including Martinique, within the framework of the European Union. The ambiguity surrounding their present and future relationship with Europe runs deeper than economic and social legislation. This recent act of integration has exacerbated the questions first publicly addressed by Aimé Césaire in the 1930s[4] concerning the very nature of identity – black? white? Martinican? West Indian? French? Or European?

Culture is both the means and the matter of such a debate, as Daniel Boukman has demonstrated in his latest play *Délivrans!* [*Deliverance!*] which addresses the tensions inherent in the Martinican diglossia of Creole and French. In the DOMs, once political integration has been accepted, there can be no possibility of establishing 'une identité souveraine et emblématique' in the words of Vinesh Y. Hookoomsing, 'établie selon les normes définitionnelles en cours (peuple, nation, état, territoire, indépendance, etc.)'.[5] [A sovereign and emblematic identity, established according to the usual norms of definition (people, nation, state, territory, independence, etc.).] Self-definition can only be expressed through a sense of cultural, geographic or anthropological entity which is almost entirely directed through literary channels. The theatre, as the most accessible form of literature, thereby assumes a political responsibility to both question and affirm an ersatz 'national' identity.

*Négritude, antillanité, créolité;* these are the three defining movements which have dominated the discourse of cultural politics in Martinique for the last sixty years or so. The 'mouvement de dépassement'[6] by which each ideal has been superseded by the next suggests a centrifugal refocusing of the perceived diasporas – from the black peoples of the world, to the Caribbean peoples of the islands, to the Creole-speaking population within the Caribbean. The constant in this shifting process is the identification of an 'Other' who remains outside the defined circle of 'Sameness'. That 'Other' – whether defined racially, anthropologically or linguistically – has always included metropolitan France. The 'Same' has always reached outwards to include a greater critical mass than Martinique itself.

There is an organic link with Africa, a large proportion of Caribbeans being the direct descendants of displaced African slaves. Caribbean history is by definition spatial, haunted by echoes of the Atlantic Triangle, the poignant metaphorical voyage 'home' in search of the self, for which Césaire's famous *Cahier d'un retour au pays natal* [*Notebook of a Return to My Native Land*] is the ultimate paradigm. This celebrated spiritual poem was written in Paris while Césaire was preparing to return to Martinique. It charts a journey of the mind through mythical and actual contours of the island and culminates in the proud acceptance of black identity through negritude, literally in spite of the years of white oppression through the slave trade. This seminal text is littered with signs of a conscious generalisation from the particular of Martinique to the universal of the black diaspora, including American, African and Caribbean blacks who are united in negritude by shared origins and a shared consciousness born out of slavery and oppression.

> Et mon originale géographie aussi; la carte du monde faite à mon usage, non pas teinte aux arbitraires couleurs des savants, mais à la géométrie de mon sang répandu, j'accepte.[7]

> (And my original geography also: the map of the world drawn for my own use, not dyed with the arbitrary colours of men of science but with the geometry of my spilt blood, I accept.)

For Césaire and his successors committed to cultural self-definition in the French Caribbean, the recourse to an international sense of solidarity seems paradoxically to represent a way of at once accepting and resisting French metropolitan values. Upholding Jacobin ideals of universality in a claim to international sympathies, shadowing the global authority of France and to a certain extent appropriating the aesthetic values of the French canon in the validation of their work, these writers reject the principle of domination by the centre in their assertion of the vital quality of difference at the periphery.

The relationship between cultural activism and political identity is close and complex. Although the notion of difference from the centre is now widely accepted in the case of the DOMs,[8] it is important to note that the promotion of a distinctive culture or set of cultures still does not necessarily equate with a call for political independence. While it is undoubtedly true that 'nationalism in Martinique and Guadeloupe is political activism based on cultural identity',[9] the spectrum of politico-cultural resistance to full assimilation in the 'vieilles colonies' ranges from regionalism to independence, with calls for various degrees of non-independent autonomy occupying the majority ground.

In the legislative elections of May 1997, two of the four constituencies in Martinique returned RPR (right-wing) representatives to the Assemblée Nationale in Paris. The third seat was retained by the PPM (Parti Progressiste Martiniquais), the party founded by Césaire and seeking favourable forms of decentralisation from a Socialist government. A growing level of support for independence outside of Fort de France finally led to the charismatic Alfred Marie-Jeanne being elected as *député* for Saint-François, representing the 'Régionalistes' alliance including autonomists, nationalists and independentists. His Mouvement Indépendantiste Martiniquais (MIM), founded in 1972, had boycotted presidential and legislative elections in the 1970s and never achieved a significant percentage (more than 5 per cent) of the vote during the 1980s. It should perhaps be noted here that the 1997 voting turn-out was in some cases less than 40 per cent; in the past the independentists have rather dubiously claimed a low turn-out as a victory, interpreting it as a widespread boycott of the French legislature. The current situation (in mid-1997), as France enters a new political era, is that the recently appointed Socialist government has no representative from its own or associated parties in Martinique. The PPM is undoubtedly the most favourably disposed towards Socialist policies, but the debate over the precise relationship between the 'hexagone' of mainland France and the DOMs, which has never really abated, seems set to resurge with renewed vigour as the millennium approaches.

The timing of Boukman's return to writing for the theatre in 1995 is perhaps more than mere coincidence. His long period of absence from it since 1974 overlaps substantially with Césaire's moratorium on the independence debate under Mitterrand's presidency beginning in 1982. Now that that period is at an end, and with Alfred Marie-Jeanne elected to the Assemblée, it seems that the politicised cultural resistance that peaked in the 1970s may well be about to re-emerge in a key public role.

The 1970s saw the publication of three quite distinct theatre works by Daniel Boukman: *Ventres pleins, Ventres creux* (1971); *Les Négriers* (1973); *Et jusqu'à la dernière pulsation de nos veines* (1976). The early *Chants pour hâter la mort du temps des Orphée* (1970) re-appeared in 1993 in a new edition, and his latest play *Délivrans!* was first published in 1995. The intervening period was devoted largely to poetry, latterly in Creole. His earliest work, *Chants pour hâter la mort du temps des Orphée*, sub-titled *Madinina, île esclave* [*Madinina, Slave Island*], brings together three dramatic *récits* composed between 1959 and 1967: *La voix des sirènes* [*Siren Voices*]; *Orphée nègre*; *Des voix dans un prison*. The central piece is dedicated to Fanon and has enjoyed the most attention from theatre companies and critics alike. It is a scathing repudiation of negritude and a vitriolic attack on Césaire, who, as the negro Orpheus, is metaphorically 'killed off' in the play. As Boukman elaborated in an interview in 1971:

> Mes Antillais ne sont pas les Nègres abstraits de la négritude.
> Ils ont des problèmes concrets à résoudre. Ils sont les petits-fils
> de l'Afrique, certes, mais les hommes ne vivent pas avec leurs
> grands-pères! . . . C'est bien beau, aujourd'hui, la négritude,
> mais quelle est son efficacité réelle, dites-moi, face aux
> problèmes économiques, sociaux et culturels qui assaillent
> le Tiers-Monde sous-développé?[10]

> (My West Indians are not the abstract Negroes of negritude.
> They have concrete problems to solve. Sure, they are the
> grandsons of Africa, but men don't live with their grandfathers!
> . . . . It's all well and good, today, negritude, but what is its real
> effectiveness, tell me that, faced with the economic, social and

cultural problems with which the developing Third World is assailed?)

The action of the play, such as it is, revolves around the corpse of Orpheus (that is to say Césaire), as it lies centre-stage. A host of representative and allegorical figures appears, to engage in the debate over whether he should be revived or laid to rest forever. Amongst those paying mournful tribute are Occidental Death, the voice of colonial repression; a Banker, clearly in the service of western enterprise; and an indoctrinated old Christian woman seeking another miraculous resurrection. On the opposite side are various workers, persuaded to kill Orpheus in a *prise de conscience* by the Militant, an autobiographical figure. Negritude appears in the only personification possible, as a beautiful black woman, spouting a convincing mock-Césairean poetry. She eventually drifts away as the workers have their victory and begin to take action in a pantomimic battle with imaginary weapons over the corpse.

Orpheus stands, or rather lies, accused of having accepted the stereotypical image of the Negro created by the west, whose generic and harmless prowess in matters sexual, spiritual and artistic is exalted to the exclusion of all potentially subversive qualities such as reason or militancy. In true Brechtian fashion, his soft hands reveal him as an intellectual, the doyen of French academe, divorced from the concrete problems of the Martinican workers. He is further accused of having betrayed his people, 'objectively if not intentionally'[11] for his own political advancement, by subjugating political action to a Black revolt which was purely spiritual and precluded social action, to the immense satisfaction of the colonial powers. Directed towards Césaire, the one-time communist mayor of Fort de France and communist deputy for Martinique, this is both damning and prophetic.

By 1956, after some ten years of grappling with the tension between the class-based universalism of the Parti Communiste Français and the race-based particularism of negritude, Césaire broke with the PCF and two years later established the Parti Progressiste Martiniquais. On the election of a socialist government in 1981, the PPM entered into a close relationship with the ruling left, based on the increased autonomy it would bestow on the DOMs through a commitment to regionalisation. With a comfortable measure of 'difference' officially acknowledged in policy-making, and Césaire still at the helm of the controlling PPM, the modern version of negritude inevitably left the ranks of the West Indian proletariat and entered the western European hegemony.

If *Orphée nègre* is an indictment of the ideology and the manipulation of negritude, it is just as surely a homage to the art of its founder. Ironically, the paradox inherent in Césaire's own adoption of a highly erudite European aesthetic as the means to oppose cultural assimilation (for example, his reworking of Shakespeare in *Une Tempête*) is paralleled in Boukman's use of Césaire's techniques to oppose the latter's discourse. The language and imagery of the three pieces is reminiscent of the *Cahier* and the dramaturgy is unmistakably that of Césaire's play *Et les chiens se taisaient* [*And the Dogs were Silent*]. As A. James Arnold puts it, 'sans Césaire, en un mot, cet ouvrage est littéralement incompréhensible, le travail d'un écorché vif en révolte mortelle contre celui qui lui a donné, poétiquement parlant, le jour'.[12] [Without Césaire, in a word, this piece is literally incomprehensible, the work of someone who has been flayed alive in mortal revolt against the person who, poetically speaking, gave him life.]

Césaire's ideas have been refined with increasing selectivity down through the generations of his successors. Like Boukman and the Guadeloupean Maryse Condé,[13] many now reject the racial basis of negritude, whilst honouring the poetic and dramatic skills of its founder and even acknowledging its political value at a given moment in history. (Even the Militant in *Orphée nègre* is momentarily effusive in his gratitude for its past achievements.)

The title *Orphée nègre* refers ironically to Sartre's famous prefatory essay *Orphée noir*[14] which gave negritude its first blessing by a white European intellectual and which so offended Frantz Fanon in his *Peau noire, Masques blancs* [*Black Skin, White Masks*].[15] Boukman's play is dedicated to Fanon, the first Martinican to refute and refine Césaire's ideas on negritude. The play contains several tributes to Fanon's thought: the ironic 'Muses, réjouissez-vous: Orphée nègre est bien l'image de l'autre Orphée'[16] [Muses, rejoice: the negro Orpheus is quite the image of the other Orpheus]; the otherwise inexplicable cameos of a little girl playing with a white doll and dreaming of being whiter than any French person, and the mad black Caribbean whose aspirations are painted white. The wife of 'un Bourgeois' cringes on imagining the lustful gaze of 'un grand nègre' in a cafe, but the ultimate tribute comes from 'La Négritude' herself, in a double-edged comment on the significant but incomplete achievement of Césaire and the need for Fanon to salvage the black soul from the wreckage wrought by negritude:

> Ma négritude
> c'est aussi l'arracheur
> des masques blancs
> sur les peaux noires
> et dans mes mains
> des lambeaux de chair
> et d'âme.[17]

(My negritude is also that which tears white masks off black skin and in my hands shreds of flesh and of the soul.)

The conclusion, predictably, is Fanon's; the play ends in a call to arms in the face of concrete suffering. If *Orphée nègre* is incomprehensible without Césaire, it is utterly unthinkable without Fanon. Césaire could write himself on to the stage;[18] this is the play that Fanon might have written, had he lived. *Orphée nègre* might sound like an abstract exercise in literary criticism and political theory. Its intertextuality is, I would argue, like Fanon's ideology, deeply rooted in a concern for the everyday reality and future survival of his fellow Martinicans. Having exposed the misconception that all negroes are alike, Boukman the militant articulates in Marxist or rather Trotskyite terms the specific and concrete problems of Martinique, advocating violent action in place of esoteric philosophy.

Nevertheless, through the generalisation of the opposition in personifications like 'La Mort Occidentale' the conflict remains fundamentally generic and anti-colonial. The piece is dated 1962: its revolutionary fervour should be read in the context of the wave of independence in Africa immediately preceding its appearance, and the inspiration such a parallel offered to the Caribbean territories. The precise nature of the presumably international support being adduced is not spelled out when the Militant states that 'Nous ne sommes pas seuls sur le chemin'[19] [We are not alone on our path], but whereas Africans are 'frères', Europeans and white *békés*[20] are both bourgeois and colonials. Hence the black diaspora is not entirely dismissed as a base for transatlantic solidarity, but rather reclaimed in terms of a class war which is by historical definition colour-divided in the wake of colonialism.

Brecht, the ultimate guru of the anti-colonial dramatist, is never very far from the techniques of the piece, techniques which were to be much more eloquently developed in Boukman's *pièce de résistance, Les Négriers* (1969).

The three pieces which make up *Chants pour hâter la mort du temps des Orphée* prioritise the verbal in their theatrical language. *La voix des sirènes, Orphée nègre* and *Des voix dans un prison* are essentially dramatic poems complemented by visual devices such as projections and shadow-play, with occasional music. *Les Négriers* on the other hand is a veritable *coup de théâtre*, where the verbal and the non-verbal are in perfect equilibrium. With the help of still and film projections, placards, shadow puppets, extensive use of lighting and sound effects, dance, song, mime and acrobatics, and a split stage area with a range of sets and costumes, the piece advances with pace and fluidity through three highly episodic sections.

The basic premise of the play maintains that the stream of emigrant workers from the French Caribbean to mainland France constitutes a new slave trade, this time in a different direction. The analogy may not be altogether original,[21] but the image remains striking nonetheless, particularly when fully exploited, as here, for its theatrical impact.

The play enacts a constant 'voyage sans retour'[22] [journey of no return], from Martinique to Paris, against the backdrop of that other one-way passage from Africa to Martinique in the slave-ships of old. The time–space continuum is collapsed so that more than 350 years of history appear in the frame of a contemporary snapshot, whilst the two legs of the Atlantic Triangle are deliberately superimposed, so that they become almost indistinguishable. Any linear chronology is skilfully dissolved as the new slave-traders, consisting again of the anonymously representative figures of 'La Mort', 'Le Parlementaire', 'L'Assistante

Sociale', 'le Représentant des Patrons' and 'L'Abbé' (Death, the Parliamentarian, the Social Worker, the Executive Representative and the Abbot) reappear in different historical guises from the founders of the seventeenth-century General Transatlantic Company to the committee of the modern DUBIDON.

The satirical acronym (meaning something like 'a load of bull') is Boukman's version of the BUMIDON,[23] a state agency operative between 1961 and 1981 for the encouragement and management of emigration from the West Indies to France. According to Alain Anselin, it operated a consistent quota of 2,500 sponsored emigrants per island per year, excluding the near-equivalent numbers emigrating outside the auspices of the scheme. Boukman cites 15,000 applicants in one year alone, a figure which is endorsed in one study[24] with some qualification as the maximum annual total of migrants from Martinique and Guadeloupe combined. Edouard Glissant, writing in 1981,[25] maintains that over forty years the Martinican population was reduced by some 100,000 and increased by the influx of as many Europeans (in a then population of 350,000). He estimates there were 150,000 Martinicans living in France and cites the PPM coinage of 'genocide by substitution'. The intention behind this aspect of French labour policy was twofold: first to satisfy the needs of the expanding metropolitan economy with a cheap, largely unskilled labour force, and second to control the population explosion in the DOMs through a combination of contraception and emigration. Boukman vividly presents what he sees as the fascistic implications of this kind of demographic control, when the neo-feudal overlords threaten to sterilise the whole population of the islands. The actual BUMIDON programme underwent revisions into four separate Plans over its twenty-year existence. In the play, its sinister ideological basis is revealed when it is remodelled as the militaristic DONBIDU, engaging openly in coercion after the failure of the first Plan of the DUBIDON to achieve its statistical targets by enticement. The programme is regarded as life-threatening for the islands if not for individuals; the whole scheme is after all overseen by the character of Death, who represents French capitalism.

Once again the play amounts to a revolutionary call for West Indian independence. Having exposed the abolition of slavery not as an act of humanitarian benevolence by the white oppressors but as a result of violent revolt by runaway slaves ('les nègres marrons'), he calls upon the contemporary labour force of the West Indies to follow the example of their forbears and seize freedom by force. 'Si le système colonial se prolonge aux Antilles, les mitraillettes parleront'[26] [If the colonial system continues in the West Indies, machine guns will do the talking].

In presenting the contemporary enemy as a straightforward reincarnation of the slave-traders of bygone centuries, Boukman appears to be engaging the same binary opposition between black and white that underlies negritude. The play is certainly advocating a *prise de conscience* of the West Indian history of exploitation that will lead to the end of white oppression. The persistent juxtaposition of images of modern emigrant labourers and African slaves from the past suggest an Orphic descent worthy of Césaire into the black soul of history, where the mother-country is not France but

> Afrique ma mère
> visage aux millions de plaies.[27]

> (Africa my mother / Millions of sores on your face.)

The question of emigration is profoundly linked to that of collective identity and is seen as a duplicitous strategy of assimilation, both cultural and economic. In common with the dramatists of negritude, Boukman is broadly concerned here with consciousness-raising and the reinstatement of a pre-colonial black identity. Where Boukman characteristically departs from negritude is in his advocacy of a violent response to social and economic realities, including racism. Spiritual solidarity is not enough.

The recurrent tension between the general and the specific throughout the culture and politics of the DOMs is present in this play too, but less obtrusively than in some of Boukman's other works. His migrants are at times Martinican, at times more widely 'Antillais'. In reality it suited the French for a variety of economic and administrative reasons to draw immigrant labour from the DOMs rather than Africa or the Iberian peninsula. Boukman, however, has Death calling in workers from the Caribbean islands, Africa, Asia, northern Europe and the Americas. It is primarily the images of African slaves and of the wise Ancestor that broaden the implications of the situation, evoking a plight shared by a greater number than the people of Martinique. By this device, Boukman's anti-assimilationist Martinicans reclaim a greater kinship with Africa than with the descendants of the Gauls.

The last third of this biting satire moves a little further from the universal towards the particular. The universal types are replaced with more culture-bound representatives of political tranches when the Assimilationists appear, alongside the Legalists (autonomists). The former are balletic and the latter enter 'comme un peloton de coureurs en petites foulées'[28] [like a pack of runners in tight little groups]. Both imitative of French rather than Caribbean culture, both are portrayed as physically and ideologically feeble in the face of brutal reality. The assimilationists, happy to be more French than the French (to paraphrase De Gaulle), see no need for reform. The position of the legalists is equally ineffectual. They call – or rather sing – for autonomy (*l'auto-motion*) as a French DOM, with terms to be agreed through peaceful negotiation. The Parliamentarian is clearly sympathetic to the latter – his dream of being king of the (French) island offers a glimpse of neo-colonialism rarely seen in Boukman's theatre of independence. This figure has sold out, perhaps a farcical shadow of the neo-colonial icon of Henri-Christophe, the former slave turned power-crazed king of Haiti from 1811 to 1820, and the subject of Césaire's play *La Tragédie du Roi Christophe* [*The Tragedy of King Christophe*] (1964).

If the peoples of the black diaspora are identified here again as political soul-mates against capitalist exploitation, it is also clear that Boukman's proletarian solidarity stops short of any alliance with the European workforce, whose motives he mistrusts. A metropolitan worker in a brief cameo asserts that 'La solidarité prolétarienne s'arrête aux portes des acquisitions de la classe ouvrière menacées par ces étrangers.'[29] [The moment these foreigners threaten at the entry gates of the working class, proletarian solidarity stops dead.] A revisionist politician replies that these so-called foreigners are brothers in arms, and that History will empower them one day in 'la discipline la paix et la légalité républicaine' [discipline peace and republican legality]. Freedom will be a gift from the evolutionary socialists to the Martinican workers, just as it was from the feudalists to their slaves, at least according to the official history. This, together with the satirical references to 'Papa François', give the play a very topical resonance which cuts close to the bone of Césaire's autonomist PPM and its faith in François Mitterrand's socialism.

The European homogenised perception of the 'nègre' to which Boukman so vehemently objected in *Orphée nègre* is still apparent in the racist prejudice of the French in *Les Négriers*. His understandable counter to the phenomenon is to be equally undiscriminating in his generalised portrayal of Europeans as weak, disingenuous and self-interested. By the end of the play machine guns have become the only meaningful form of discourse left available to his characters, entrenched as they are, on both sides of the power divide, in a perceptual stalemate.

The course of history has not followed Boukman's radical predictions. In 1981 the BUMIDOM was transformed to run a rather half-hearted and ultimately ineffectual programme of return migration. Emigration continues and only a minority of unsuccessful émigrés return to the 'pays natal'. With Mitterrand's presidency there began a period of socialist optimism in Martinique under the controlling PPM. Césaire issued a ban on discussion of the independence question, encouraged by the prospect of greater autonomy under the decentralisation and regionalisation policies proposed by the centre in the early 1980s. Assimilation intensified. Fanon had come to be known only as a street name in Fort de France. There was no bloody coup.

In terms of cultural activism, the early 1980s saw the full emergence of a new movement, *antillanité*, which had been gathering momentum since the 1960s. Its ideology rejects universalism as a way of addressing the particular problems and distinctive character of the Antilles. Faced with oppression by the Other, it says, the peoples trans-shipped through slavery have sought instinctively to return to the One of origin. But the Return is no longer possible, since the experience has changed them into something other than they were. Instead of looking back, the approach aims to address the givens of the here-and-now, in order to consolidate a uniquely West Indian identity upon which to build from a people in the present to a nation in the future.

The clearest proponent of antillanity, Edouard Glissant, uses the metaphor of the outward journey from the native land to express what he sees as the essential obstacle to Martinican self-definition. The Detour is a psychological process by which Martinicans have repeatedly, he claims, focused their attention and energies outside of the 'pays natal'.[30] In exorcism of that impossible Return, it continues to prolong the spiritual, emotional and material dispossession of the people. He explains the phenomenon thus:

> Le Détour est le recours ultime d'une population dont la domination par un Autre est occultée: il faut chercher *ailleurs* le principe de domination, qui n'est pas évident dans le pays même. . . . Le Détour est la parallaxe de cette recherche.[31]

> (The Detour is the last resort of a population where domination by an Other is obscured from view: one has to look *elsewhere* to see how domination works, since it is not apparent within one's own country . . . The Detour is the parallax of this search.)

By this process, the Martinican emigrating to France, the motherland which confers citizenship upon him, finds himself adrift. Whereas Boukman in *Les Négriers* focuses on social and economic disadvantage, Glissant is concerned primarily with a kind of psychological paralysis of emigrants from the DOMs. Upon the sudden discovery that metropolitan French climate, culture and customs are foreign to him, finding himself victim of widespread and indiscriminate racism, the West Indian in France is suddenly aware of his difference. With France as the *mère-patrie*, however, he has no sense of a distant *patrie* or homeland of his own to which he might return. The universal ideal of republican citizenship breaks down before the fact of his difference, leaving him a set of equally spurious generalisations with which to console himself, such as 'proletarian internationalism, minority rights, global revolution'. Boukman, as we have seen, seems to retain a limited faith in such concepts, at least across the Third World or the proletarian black diaspora. Boukman and Glissant converge in their criticism of the romanticised image of France which is promulgated in Martinique and which can only lead to the dead end of disillusionment.

The name of Daniel Boukman could be added to Glissant's list of illustrious West Indians who have turned their attention away from the native land, alongside Marcus Garvey (Jamaica to the United States), Padmore (Trinidad to Ghana), Césaire (Martinique to Black Africa) and, most conclusively, Frantz Fanon (Martinique to Algeria). Despite their achievements elsewhere, these West Indians have all used the *pays natal* as a point of departure for their respective physical or psychological voyages of no return. This voyage has always been made from the specific to the universal, from the Different to the Same. According to Glissant, Césaire and Fanon have both attempted to incorporate Martinique into the 'landscape of a shared Elsewhere'.

Ironically enough, Boukman was away, following Fanon's footsteps to Algeria, during the whole period when *antillanité* was being proposed. Unlike Fanon's, his journey there was more of an escape than a quest. Military service was introduced in the DOMs in 1959. Boukman refused to be recruited into the army of a distant power that could have sent him, along with many of his compatriots, to fight the French cause in Algeria. He has yet to return to Martinique, despite his expressed desire to do so. Glissant speaks of the importance of the psychological return:

> Il faut revenir au lieu. Le Détour n'est ruse profitable que si
> le Retour le féconde: non pas retour au rêve d'origine, à l'Un
> immobile de l'Etre, mais retour au point d'intrication, dont on
> s'était détourné par force.[32]

> (We have to return to the place. The Detour is a fruitless ploy
> unless the Return makes it fertile: not the return to the dream
> of one's origins, to the static One of Being, but the return to the
> point of implication, from which one had turned away by force.)

Boukman's physical return to Martinique might yet lie ahead, but his latest play, *Délivrans!* marks not only a welcome return to the theatre but seems also to signal an emotional return to his native land. In contrast with his previous theatre work, this short piece contains little or no evocation of international solidarity. Rather, it sets its sights directly upon an internal conflict between the Creole and French-speaking populations of Martinique. Presented as a 'serious farce', *Délivrans!* is a theatrical exorcism of the spirit of French culture which has possessed Martinicans ever since assimilation began.

The violent overthrow which Boukman advocated during the years immediately following the Algerian war, Castro's rebellion in Cuba and the independence of many African and indeed Caribbean states, is replaced in this post-communist play by a spiritual flight towards independence of mind for the Caribbean people. The oppressive Other has now taken up residence within the hearts and souls of French Martinicans; the new battle takes place within.

For the first time the setting is recognisable as a Martinican household, even if it is one adorned with the trinkets and tokens of Francophile alienation. Previously, Boukman's settings were either quasi-mythical (*Chants*) or remote (*Ventres pleins, ventres creux; Et jusqu'à . . .* ). Even the anti-illusionistic *Les Négriers* sets more of the action in France than in Martinique. *Délivrans!* employs many of the distinctive stylistic features of Boukman's earlier works: shadow-play, mime, song, dance, giant apparitions, snap tableaux and stylised lighting and sound effects. The projections, however, are gone, as is the documentary element, often statistical, which gave pieces such as *Les Négriers* and *Et jusqu'à . . .* their characteristic tone of political didacticism. There is a sea-change in atmosphere, away from the aggressiveness of episodic agit-prop to a more measured form of protest, the whole woven (though still without a trace of naturalism) into a broadly linear narrative framework. The sociological evidence adduced is in the nature of ironic observation, the kind of anecdote that abounds in accounts of the absurdities of everyday life in the French DOMs.[33]

From his home in Martinique, the main protagonist, M. Gaëtan Cupidon, listens avidly to the French weather forecast of snow on the mountains and traffic reports for Ile-de-France. This petty bourgeois 'fonctionnaire' is successor to the anonymous 'Parlementaire' of *Les Négriers*, whose 'mission civilatrice' is perhaps all the more sinister for having penetrated further into the social fabric of the islanders, and whose missionary zeal is fuelled more by doctrinal faith than by mercenary self-interest.

His wife is the hopeless returnee of whom Glissant speaks, who cannot but sing the praises of France on her return to the islands, whatever the truth of her experience of metropolitan life might be. Significantly, her regular journeys are not just to Paris but to her 'dear Vichy', a name which evokes sinister images of a compromising collaboration with the oppressor. (Martinique, of course, had shown better judgement in resisting the Vichy regime, for which it was rewarded with departmentalisation in 1946.)

However, the dénouement of *Delivrans!* is where the Detour bears glorious fruit in the Return, in the figure of their prodigal son, Athanase. This return is far from the one his parents had envisaged. In three years time Athanase would be fully qualified for local government, Madame Cupidon tells us. 'Alors, il effectue son retour au pays natal, s'installe dans son honorable fonction. Il occupe son rang, il épouse une jeune fille de bonne famille.'[34] (Then he will make his return to his native land, take up his honourable office. He will get promoted, marry a well-bred young woman.) At the end of the play the parents play a cassette message they have received from Athanase, who has just passed his civil service exams in Paris. As the message progresses, Athanase himself appears at the window in a marvellous vision of homecoming. Much to the horror of the Francophile parents, his message is sung in Creole. This is his ideological bequest, framed in terms of a will. In it, he first expresses revulsion at his own assimilation and then celebrates his re-acceptance of the homeland, as opposed to the mother country. In the closing words of the play, he finally renders explicit the meaning of the central image of the whole piece, the escaped parrot.

> Alô
> andidan fondôk kô'mwen
> man gadé man wè
> man kouté man tann . . .
> l'éspri'mwen
> èvè nanm'mwen épi tjè'mwen
> ansanm ansanm
> gran gran gran
> wouvè zèl'yo
> épi
> kontèl an toutwèl
> man pran lavôl . . .
> Atanaz jako-répèt
> mô!
> DELIVRANS!
>
> [And so
> I looked into the very depths of my being

> I looked I saw
> I listened I heard . . .
> my mind
> and my soul and my heart
> in unison
> spread wide their wings
> and like a turtle dove
> I soared away . . .
> Athanase
> the docile parrot
> is dead!
> DELIVERANCE!]³⁵

Throughout the play, Monsieur Cupidon is obsessed with teaching his pet parrot Démosthène to speak in the 'language of Bossuet'. When it finally finds its voice, it speaks a rebellious and fully-fledged Creole, though like all the characters in the play it clearly understands French. The parrot metaphor is strongly reminiscent of Sartre's Preface to Fanon's *Les damnés de la terre* [*The Wretched of the Earth*], where he describes natives returning 'home' after a period of European nurture:

> These walking lies had nothing left to say to their brothers; they only echoed. From Paris, from London, from Amsterdam we would utter the words 'Parthenon! Brotherhood!' and somewhere in Africa or Asia lips would open '. . . thenon! . . . therhood!' It was the golden age. It came to an end; the mouths opened by themselves.³⁶

In fact, the rejection of the Pavlovian technique of assimilation that Démosthène – and moreover Athanase – demonstrates is the culmination of a resistance that has been growing steadily. Démosthène is the latest in a series of parrots to escape the Cupidon household, despite Monsieur's paranoia about opening the windows for fear of contamination by the savage Creole world. We witness the release of Démosthène, a dramatic and symbolic coup staged in a dreamlike sequence by the fantastical animal figures of West Indian folklore just before Athanase's return.

The anonymous types of Boukman's earlier plays are here replaced by characters with significant names. The play is after all about language, the appropriation of the signified through the appropriate sign. The incongruity of the parrots' grandiose Graeco-Latin names – Thémistocle and Virgile before Démosthène, as well as that of Athanase himself – also includes a referential irony. These names, all chosen by the upholder of French orthodoxy, Monsieur Cupidon, do not only represent icons of western rhetoric. Their original bearers also happen to have used their skills of oratory, combined with an independence of mind, for political ends. Themistocles was a founding Athenian statesman and the general responsible for the defeat of the Persians at Salamis, who later fled from Greece to the Persians in Asia Minor. Virgil, the celebrated Roman poet of the *Aeneid*, was deeply concerned with national revival following civil war. Demosthenes was the greatest Athenian orator in the cause of Greek liberty against the threat of Macedon. The most ironically named of all is Athanasius, whose fourth-century namesake was bishop of Alexandria, renowned for his defence of orthodoxy.

The parrot is of course the perfect metaphor for a play about the appropriation of language (though requiring some ingenuity in the staging). The validation of an indigenous language is presented as the essential means to cultural liberation. This idea lies at the heart of the latest development from *antillanité*, which is most notably explored in *Eloge de la Créolité* [*In Praise of Creolity*] (1989) by Jean Bernabé, Patrick Chamoiseau and Raphaël Confiant. *Créolité* seeks an alternative to monolithic universalism in the regrouping of the various races and cultures that constitute a pluralistic West Indian populace. The single factor common to all West Indians, the theory maintains, is their Creole language.

In terms of the dissemination of ideology, the opposition of a localised patois to an internationally recognised language is always problematic. It is the now all-too-familiar dilemma facing post-colonial African writers such as Ngugi wa Thiong'o. Since the 1970s, Boukman's work has been produced from time to time in Creole translations, well before the appearance of *Délivrans!*, which is written partly in Creole. Bridget Jones identifies the paradox in Boukman's Creole theatre: 'une mise en accusation par le créole du pouvoir français atteint le public antillais concerné, mais se cantonne à l'intérieur d'un groupe linguistique restreint'[37] [any indictment through Creole of the French government touches the West Indian audience concerned, but confines itself to a limited linguistic group]. The pan-Caribbean audience to which Boukman aspires cannot, it seems, be reached by creolophone drama.

And yet the case of creolity is even more complex. There is debate over which orthographic form it should take, a debate which broadly corresponds to a political *prise de position* between the radical independentists and the moderate regionalists. The radicals, with whom Boukman's sympathies apparently lie, reject the many shades of interlectal variants between French and 'pure' Creole, in favour of maximising Difference. To them the only admissible form is a phonetic transcription of a pre-assimilation Creole which is rarely spoken in a post-assimilation culture. This retrogressive return to the original One, to borrow Glissant's terminology, seems strangely at odds with an ideology designed to be progressive.

In *Délivrans!* the politically unenlightened servant, Hortense, who tries to prevent the release of Démosthène and remains incapable of taking up an authentic position, speaks a hybrid mixture of French and Creole. By contrast Athanase, the redeemer, speaks an undiluted Creole. Boukman's *porte-parole*, it is Athanase who offers a radical Creole paradigm for a future independent Martinique. (Perhaps Hortense is to be regarded as a victim of class. If so, this marks a radical shift in Boukman's ideology. The voice of self-determination no longer belongs to the proletariat with their machine guns, but to the educated intellectuals with their Creole language. The introduction of popular folkloric elements as a catalyst in the process of liberation might be interpreted as an attempt by Boukman to pre-empt such criticism.)

A key element in *créolité* is the opposition of the Other not by the Same, but by 'le Divers', as conceptualised by Glissant. The movement aims to be open and flexible, in order to encompass difference within the Caribbean islands in a way that the race-based negritude never could. It promotes solidarity between all the islands of the Caribbean, including the non-francophone territories as well as the other creolophone DOMs of Réunion and Mauritius. But the inevitable tension between the generalised and the particular is hardly alleviated by the declaration of 'une spécificité ouverte'[38] (an open specificity); surely specificity implies the demarcation of limits?

The exposition of Boukman's harmonious vision of Caribbean diversity in *Délivrans!* takes the form of a folktale told by the old Creole woman, Man Dédé. She tells of how Ti-Jean (of African origin) was sent for to restore harmony by force when the competing claims on the land of all the various indigenous plants had brought anarchy and chaos. The use of ecological discourse to reflect a localised identity is a mainstay of *créolité*. Coincidentally, it was also the hallmark of Césaire's *Cahier . . .* and the poetics of negritude.

*Délivrans!* has yet to receive its première. Perhaps the most notable Creole success enjoyed by Boukman's theatre to date has come in the form neither of his original writing nor even the translations of it, but of *West Indies*, the film adaptation of *Les Négriers* by Mauritanian Med Hondo. Whereas Boukman's play, set largely among the French, is written entirely in their language, the film version features a considerable amount of Creole dialogue. To further complicate the issue, it employs a range of contemporary Creole dialects as endorsed by Boukman's moderate opponents. Med Hondo explains the decision thus:

> Nous avons retenu le créole parlé dans les agglomérations,
> par opposition à celui des campagnes, plus pur. C'est celui de
> l'immigration, où se mélangent les accents de la Guadeloupe,
> de la Martinique. L'Ancêtre, dans mon film, parle le créole du
> paysan. Il nous est totalement incompréhensible.[39]

> (We went for the kind of Creole spoken in the urban areas,
> as opposed to its purer rural counterpart. It's the language of
> immigration, with a mixture of accents from Guadeloupe, from
> Martinique. The Ancestor, in my film, speaks peasant Creole.
> To us, it's totally unintelligible.)

The production history of the film embodies that very 'métissage' of cultures in a global village which *créolité* aims to support. With funding from France, Algeria, Ivory Coast, Senegal and Mauritania, it was shot in Paris and premièred in Venice and Montreal. The film's title *West Indies* consciously encompasses in its subject-matter all the former colonies of the Caribbean, not just the DOMs.

Film is now well established as an international medium, at the level of both production and distribution. For Glissant, however, cultural independence can only be achieved from within, by the actions of the islanders themselves. The theatre has a vital role to play in the process of consciousness-raising in terms of a specific and politicised community.[40] It must correspond to actuality; not merely reflect the status quo, nor regress into a folkloric nostalgia. He warns against the danger of blocking progress through the ossification of a historic form of Creole in the name of ideological purity. The popular theatre must look forward from historical roots to engender a new sense of community. Its task is to 'reprendre à partir du premier bateau négrier qui débarqua sa première cargaison et, de là, combler le hiatus. Cela sous-entend que soit dénoncée au départ et en permanence l'exploitation économique'[41] [pick up from the moment the first slave ship unloaded its first cargo and, from there, fill the hiatus. That implies the immediate denunciation, once and for all, of economic exploitation]. *Les Négriers* exemplifies the practical application of such a theory.

Boukman, like Césaire and Fanon before him, has made the journey away from his native land of Martinique both mentally and physically. Across the work of all three politico-cultural activists we can discern a pattern of 'le Détour' by which they have each sought to address the problematic status of their own island by identifying it as part of a wider cause. However, there is evidence of the circle of solidarity being tightened. From Césaire's broad race-based diaspora of negritude, via Fanon's psychoanalytical approach, Boukman has brought us through a Third World class-based anti-colonialism to a position where resistance is to be drawn from within the hearts and minds of West Indians themselves, in line with the new ideologies of *antillanité* and *créolité*. The new revolution is to take place in the mind rather than on the streets. Its manifestation might be more subtle, but the new dawn it aims to engender is just as bright. Perhaps, having benefited from the parallax view, Boukman's return to his native land in *Délivrans!* will herald a new era in the theatre of resistance.

The characteristic search for external solidarity marks a contrast with the anti- or post-colonial anglophone theatre, which has generally sought to establish national culture through the use of indigenous aesthetics to explore localised themes. Consider the examples of Trinidadian Errol Hill's *Man Better Man*, Jamaican Trevor Rhone's *Smile Orange*, or even the more cosmopolitan Derek Walcott with plays like *Ti-Jean and His Brothers*.

One can only speculate on the reasons for this. Perhaps Glissant is right in suggesting that the particular style of French domination is subtly hidden from the view of its subjects, requiring an 'outside eye' to picture it clearly. One factor is surely central and that is the continuation of French control in the DOMs some twenty years or more beyond the independence of the majority of non-francophone islands. Nationhood, and with it a particular national identity, is still only a theoretical construct for the people of the DOMs. Depending heavily on France for their socio-economic stability and wary of the disastrous model of independence in Haiti, many Martinicans remain unconvinced of the desirability of political independence, although its supporters do seem to be increasing in number.

The recent status of the DOMs under the Maastricht Treaty of the European Union as an 'Ultra-peripheral Region of the Community' would appear to consolidate their integration with Europe. The ambiguity surrounding such a move is reflected in the voting figures: an overwhelming 70.13 per cent majority in favour of ratifying the treaty in the Martinican referendum, occurring in the context of a 75.47 per cent abstention rate.[42]

Cultural assimilation is the hallmark of the French colonial system. Opposition to such a practice, which is seen as a threat to the ontological identity of its subjects, is less ambiguous, as the work of Fanon, Césaire, Glissant and Boukman, along with many others, reveals. And yet in aesthetic terms these writers have often epitomised the very values of that French culture which their ideology rejects. Formally at least, they reflect the success of the strategy of assimilation.

Boukman cites, as inspiration for his satirical farce *Ventres pleins, ventres creux*, Aristophanes and Rabelais.[43] Monsieur Cupidon is worthy of Molière in his obsessive folly. The poetic language of *Chants* is evocative of Rimbaud. His episodic agit-prop is more reminiscent of Brecht than of anything West Indian. His innovative theatrical style, with its technical (and electrical) exigencies, requires a context for production which is far removed from the impromptu versatility of most traditional Third World theatre. Like Césaire before him, Boukman is ostensibly a product of the very culture he renounces.

Walcott has been vociferous in claiming his right to access the great literatures of the world, whether they emanate from colonised or colonisers. Unlike Boukman and his compatriots, Walcott was never subject to the policies of enforced assimilation that have so repulsed anti-colonialists in the DOMs.

The British system of colonialism by indirect rule at least tolerated indigenous cultural practice where it was not perceived as threatening to the status quo. It made no attempt to integrate its colonial subjects as British citizens. In education and administration France sought actively to reproduce its own by exporting French culture wholesale to its colonies in a policy of homogenisation which naturally required the eradication of local practices including language, religion and theatre.

The universalism that underpins French republican values and is so boldly enacted in the policy of colonial assimilation is difficult to oppose. The scales will always be weighted against any strategy of resistance that sets localised 'Difference' against the universal 'Same'. The dilemma posed is how to resist such a powerful universalism when its tenets preclude the possibility of difference. Negritude, which set out to assert difference, has now been all but subsumed within the hegemonic orthodoxy. As assimilation continues its relentless march, the spaces in which difference can be identified are reduced, so that the 'shared elsewhere' to which so many Martinican activists have been driven becomes increasingly hard to find. It is being replaced by a complex conglomeration of diversity in the shared here-and-now of the West Indies.

Martinican dramatists like Boukman cannot return to the native land they once left, for such a land no longer exists. In their conscious efforts to appropriate a theatre of resistance that looks forward instead of back, inward instead of outward, striving for harmonious West Indian integration rather than bitter confrontation, they are however moving perceptibly towards a consolidation of the complex multiplicity of modern identity. According to Bridget Jones, the small-scale Creole productions of Boukman's plays in Martinique by companies like Cyclone, Volcan and Fer de Lance have been of greater benefit in raising the political consciousness of those taking part than of their audiences. Such an appropriation of a popular theatre of proactive self-definition can be seen as an important step in the process of cultural reclamation that Glissant describes. This theatre might not enjoy the grandeur of scale nor the international acclaim of Césaire's literary drama. However, the relative scarcity of productions of Césaire's plays in Martinique, compared to their popularity with directors like Jean-Marie Serreau in Paris, for example, suggests that in returning to the scale of the native land, Boukman and his contemporaries are moving closer to establishing a living theatre which is capable of addressing the particular concerns of 'home'. The impact of local productions is designed to be immediate, addressing targeted and popular audiences at union meetings and the like, and rejecting the spectre of bourgeois dilettantism associated with the French classical theatre. The gradual narrowing of the circle of solidarity to which Martinican writers have appealed in the past, through race, class, history, geography and now language, perhaps signifies the gradual deconstruction of the myth of French universalism, which has long been the obstacle to specific cultural identity in the DOMs.

NOTES

1 Daniel Boukman, *Et jusqu'à la dernière pulsation de nos veines* (Paris: L'Harmattan, 1993), p. 44. All translations are my own unless otherwise stated.

2 *Ibid.*, p. 75. These lines are attributed to a documentary source.

3 Boukman interviewed by Guy Hennebelle, 'La négritude en question', *Jeune Afrique* 531 (9 March 1971), 60.

4 The first and last issue of *Légitime défense* appeared in 1932, advocating radical resistance to political and cultural assimilation. Césaire's famous *Cahier d'un retour au pays natal* first appeared in 1939.

5 Vinesh Y. Hookoomsing, 'La créolité en question', *Notre librairie 119 – 25 ans de découverte* (octobre-novembre-décembre 1994), 43.

6 I am grateful to James A. Arnold for this term, which appears in his useful article 'Les héritiers de Césaire aux Antilles', *Présence africaine* 151/152 (nos. 3 and 4, 1995), 145.

7 Aimé Césaire, *Cahier d'un retour au pays natal* [*Notebook of a Return to My Native Land*], trans. Mireille Rosello with Annie Pritchard, French–English bilingual edition (Newcastle-upon-Tyne: Bloodaxe Books, 1995), pp. 124–5.

8 The famous Article 73 of the Constitution of the Fifth Republic enshrines this 'difference' in statutory terms: 'Measures may be taken to adapt the legislative system and administrative organisation of the overseas departments to their particular situation.' This clause was

added in 1958, and since 1960 proposals from Martinique of laws for adaptation have been admissible at the centre. The decentralisation laws of the 1980s further entitled Martinique to contest the application of any proposed French legislation.

9 Robert Aldrich and John Connell, *France's Overseas Frontier – Départements et Territoires d'Outre-Mer* (Cambridge University Press, 1992), p. 175.

10 Hennebelle, 'La négritude en question', 59.

11 Boukman, *Chants pour hâter la mort du temps des Orphée* (Paris: L'Harmattan, 1993), p. 89.

12 Arnold, 'Les héritiers de Césaire', 146.

13 See especially Maryse Condé, 'Pourquoi la négritude? Négritude ou révolution?', *Les littératures d'expression française: Négritude africaine – Négritude caraïbe* (Paris: Editions de la Francité, 1973), pp. 150–4.

14 Originally the Preface to the *Anthologie de la nouvelle poésie nègre et malgache de langue française*, ed. L.S. Senghor (Paris: Presses Universitaires de France, 1948). English translation by S.W. Allen, *Black Orpheus* (Paris: Présence Africaine, 1976).

15 Frantz Fanon, *Peau noire, Masques blancs* (Paris: Editions du Seuil, 1952). English translation by Charles Lam Markmann, *Black Skin, White Masks* (London: MacGibbon and Kee, 1968).

16 Boukman, *Chants*, p. 78.

17 *Ibid.*, p. 82.

18 *Et les chiens se taisaient* (1946, original version); *La tragédie du roi Christophe* (1963); *Une Saison au Congo* [*A Season in the Congo*] (1965, original version); *Une tempête* (1968).

19 Boukman, *Chants*, p. 89.

20 The local name for the former white plantation-owners, now the hated land-owning minority of Martinique.

21 See, for example, Condé, 'Pourquoi la négritude', 154.

22 Daniel Boukman, *Les Négriers* (Paris: L'Harmattan, 1978), pp. 33, 79.

23 Bureau pour le Développement des Migrations des Départements d'Outre-Mer. Boukman's misinterpretation of the original acronym is telling. According to him it stands for 'Bureau de la Main d'Oeuvre Immigrée des Départements d'Outre-Mer' (Hennebelle, 'La Négritude en question', 60). For a fuller account of the operations of the BUMIDOM see Alain Anselin, 'West Indians in France', in Richard D.E. Burton and Fred Reno, eds., *French and West Indian: Martinique, Guadeloupe and French Guiana Today* (London: Macmillan, Warwick University Caribbean Studies Series, 1995), pp. 112–18.

24 Boukman, *Les Négriers*, p. 21; Aldrich and Connell, *France's Overseas Frontier*, p. 110.

25 Edouard Glissant, *Le discours antillais* (Paris: Editions du Seuil, 1981), p. 498.

26 Hennebelle, 'La négritude en question', 60.

27 Boukman, *Les Négriers*, p. 32.

28 *Ibid.*, p. 62.

29 *Ibid.*, p. 43.

30 Glissant, *Le discours antillais*, especially pp. 28–36, 74–81.

31 *Ibid.*, p. 32.

32 *Ibid.*, p. 36.

33 See, for example, Aldrich and Connell, *France's Overseas Frontier*, pp. 68–9; Clarisse Zimra, 'Négritude in the Feminine Mode: the Case of Martinique and Guadeloupe', *Journal of Ethnic Studies* 12:1, 57–8.

34 Boukman, *Délivrans!* (Paris: L'Harmattan, Théâtre des 5 Continents, 1995), p. 10.

35 *Ibid.*, pp. 32–3. The published text includes a French translation of Creole sections, and it is on this that my English translation is based.

36 Frantz Fanon, *The Wretched of the Earth*, trans. Constance Farrington (London: Penguin, 1990), p. 7.

37 Bridget Jones, 'Quelques choix de langue dans le théâtre antillais (1970–1995)', in J. P. Little and Roger Little, eds., *Black Accents: Writing in French from Africa, Mauritius and the Caribbean* (London: Grant and Cutler, 1997). I am indebted to Bridget Jones for her generous help with source material for this chapter.

38 Jean Bernabé, Patrick Chamoiseau and Raphaël Confiant, *Eloge de la créolité* (Gallimard: Presses Universitaires Créoles, 1989), p. 27.

39 Louis Marcorelles, '*West Indies*, un film de Med Hondo: La galère de l'histoire', *Le Monde* (20 septembre 1979).

40 Glissant, *Le discours antillais*, pp. 393–415.

41 *Ibid.*, p. 409.

42 See Emmanuel Jos, 'The Declaration of the Treaty of Maastricht on the Ultra-Peripheral Regions of the Community: an Assessment', in Burton and Reno, eds., *French and West Indian*, pp. 86–97.

43 Hennebelle, 'La négritude en question', 61.

# 7 'Binglishing' the stage: a generation of Asian theatre in England

JATINDER VERMA

*Binglish*: 'black English', 'being English', 'beastly English', 'bastardly English', 'be English' . . . all these nuances are implicit in this term for that particular negotiation between English and Indian languages and sensibilities that is under way in contemporary England. It is within such negotiation that I believe Asian theatre needs to be sited and understood.

Asian theatre in England – as a distinct body of work – is of relatively recent vintage. The main impetus for the movement stems from the first mass migration by Asians from Kenya between January and February 1968. It is this migration which led to the emergence of the homogenising term 'Asian', a term which was used increasingly to lump Indian, Pakistani, Bangladeshi, Kenyan-Indian and other diasporic migrants of Indian sub-continental origin under one catch-all word. While Asian presence in England is considerably older, Kenyan-Asians, unlike their cousins from the Indian sub-continent, were predominantly more middle class and relatively more integrated into the metropolitan economy. Kenya did not achieve independence until 1964 and so education, commerce and the polity were more closely influenced by Britain. Senior school examinations, for example, were conducted by the Cambridge Educational Board, with the result that school curricula closely resembled those in force in the 'mother country'. Equally, there was an emulation in Kenyan-Asian society of the range of professional and amateur theatre activity under way in England. Indeed, to a large extent, the forms of theatre activity in Kenya were essentially derivative of English popular theatre.

One of the earliest consequences of this different type of migrant was that where theatre activity in one or other of the Indian languages (most often, Urdu, Punjabi and Gujarati) was increasingly becoming the norm among earlier Indian and Pakistani migrants, among Kenyan-Asians theatre almost exclusively took English as the medium of communication; a practice echoed by other diasporic Asians. (Indeed, currently, the overwhelming majority of Asian theatre companies in England have been founded by Asians from the diaspora, as opposed to the 'authentic' sites of India, Pakistan, Bangladesh or Sri Lanka.)

For the Kenyan-Asian, migration to England led almost literally to a condition of being 'twice-born': once, sixty years ago, as migrant-workers and settlers from British India to eastern Africa; the second time, as African-Indian migrants to England. This condition has led – in the inevitable process of establishing an identity in England – to a discourse with Indian and Pakistani cultures, and to a near-total absence of any with Africa. The Kenyan-Asians (along with those from the rest of the diaspora), therefore, more so than the Indian, Pakistani or Bangladeshi migrant, have been *inventing* an identity in post-imperial England.

What are the textures of this invention of identity in theatre practice? And, indeed, is the search for identity the only *raison d'être* for theatre practised by this community of migrants? To answer the latter question first, 'identity' has been the inevitable sub-text of Kenyan- and other diasporic Asian theatres. I say 'inevitable' with severe qualification: had England not been racially conscious, had Asians been perceived as an integral part of the theatre resource of the country, then perhaps there would have been no impulse to seek self-identification through the theatre. Sadly, this was not the case in the 1960s, nor, to a great extent, is it the case now. It needs also to be borne in mind that the Kenyan Asians were migrants with the most recent memory of colonial rule. Kenyan society up to Independence in 1964 was rigidly stratified along racial lines, with mutually exclusive White, Asian and African residential and educational areas. Under the conditions of life in late-1960s England, this memory had to be rapidly negotiated; indeed, for all effective purposes, suppressed, if only because schools and residential areas were broadly multi-racial.

Such suppression of memory, coupled with the incessant need to answer the question 'where you from?' (most often posed by whites), began the process of invention: the search for 'roots'. India and Pakistan, depending upon one's religious affiliation, became the inevitable (and simpler) repositories of origin. Memory, in my experience, is a seductive, tricksy devil which does not always need actual experience to form a feature of the imagination. I grew up in Kenya, as did my family – with the sole exception of my father, who left the Punjab when he was 17 and never returned. Yet the word 'Ganga' evoked images in me as a child in Kenya of a wild, turbulent, sacred river – though none of the family had ever seen that great river of India until recently. Images that had no correspondence in rivers of Kenya. Equally, as a Hindu-Punjabi, my attitude and relations with Asian Muslims was mediated through the received stories of the Partition of India and Pakistan into two separate nations in 1947. Is memory myth, then? Perhaps. It certainly endures long after the immediate experience, passing like the game of Chinese whispers down the ages. Such memory seems to draw one ineluctably to the elephantine embrace of the sub-continent, tugging the Asian into a constant flirtation with England *and* – for the diasporic Asian – with India/Pakistan.

This process is clearly evident in the work of the longest-established Asian theatre company in England: Tara Arts. Founded in the wake of the racist murder of a young Sikh boy in London in June 1976, Tara spent its initial years exploring the trinity of spaces (East Africa, India and England) which were the inheritance of its founder-members (predominantly Asian migrants from Kenya). Two productions in this period offer useful examples: *Yes, Memsahib* (1980) and *Scenes in the Life Of . . .* (1982). The former traced the genesis of the Kenya colony at the turn of the century; analogising the treatment of migrant Asians there with that being experienced in contemporary England. The latter production traced the growth from childhood in Kenya to adulthood in England of a young Asian woman. Both were essentially documents of particular moments in history. Both sought, tentatively, to locate a particular set of Asian experiences in more ambiguous territory. Yet, by the mid-1980s, Tara's work began to express a more straightforward dialogue: that between English-Asians and Indians.

In part, this was the consequence of a self-conscious drive to elicit the company's theatrical identity: in other words, to discover in theatrical terms that which made Tara distinctive – beyond the socio-political badges of colour, race, legal status. Tara's search was premised on classical Indian aesthetics, the central premise of which – and it is one which is shared by classical Chinese, Japanese and all south-east Asian theatres – is eschewing the photographic sense of 'reality'. As the earliest treatise on the theatre – the *Natya Shastra* – puts it, drama must be 'a delight to the eyes as much as the ears', working on the paradox that theatre 'is like a dream: it is not real, but really felt'. This discourse with classical Indian dramaturgy contributed to Tara's rejection of the dominant convention of the modern English stage – the spoken word. Gesture became speech, as much as a phrase of music a sentence – or the passage of time. It is in this sense that the word, in Tara's productions, took on the texture also of dance and music.

From the late 1980s, Tara began a more overt dialogue with England through texts; more specifically, the 'tradaption', as Robert LePage has called it, of European texts, viewing Gogol, Büchner, Molière, Shakespeare, Sophocles, Chekhov, Brecht through Asian eyes and ears. The result was that such texts, the familiar canon of English theatre, became 'other', providing a neat equation with the status of Tara as an 'Other', an 'Outsider' theatre company within the matrix of English theatre.

This attempt to transform texts encompasses two attendant ideas: translation and quotation. In the work of Tara Arts as well as Tamasha (which originated from Tara), Kali, Hathi, Mehtaab, Moti Roti, Man Mela, Yelele and Maya – to name just a few of the companies currently in existence – both ideas provide important clues to the texture of invention in Asian theatre, as much as pointing up differences of application and approach.

In 1988, Tara Arts produced Gogol's *The Government Inspector*. The production brought together several elements of Tara's development; primarily, its creative discourse with India (achieved through the director of the production, Anuradha Kapur from the National School of Drama in New Delhi, as well as a performer and a musician from Kerala) and its approach to the transformation of texts. Dispensing with the broadly naturalistic structure of Gogol's original play, techniques derived from Indian theatre were employed to re-invent the play. Locating the story in a mythical small town in post-Independence

India – a town which was blissfully unaware of Independence and so remained in thrall to 'Blighty' (England) – the primary techniques employed were the use of a story-teller as both narrator and character; the use of rhythm and movement as elements in characterisation; an epic structure that displaced time-and-space continuities; and the creation of a spoken text that embraced song, verse, soliloquy and dialogue. The latter was a deliberately theatrical language, comprising archaic Anglo-Indianisms alongside quotations from Chekhov, Eliot, Kipling, Tennyson, Kalidasa, Shakespeare, Salman Rushdie and Bollywood cinema. This quotational texture seemed to offer the closest correspondence to the lives of the Asian performers, who were products of migration and colonisation and, therefore, inheritors of a highly eclectic sense of 'culture' . . . a culture composed of fragments of memory, text and song. Transformed in such a way, Gogol's satire became not only an attack on material corruption but, more self-referentially, an attack on one of the abiding legacies of Empire – the colonisation of the mind. The grotesque nature of the satire took on a peculiar poignancy (especially when performed before Asian audiences) when, at the end, the story-teller turned to the audience and said, 'Laugh not, for then must you laugh at yourselves.'

The apotheosis of this transformational texture was reached in my production of Molière's *Tartuffe* for the Royal National Theatre (1990). (The event in itself was significant for two reasons: I was the first of the current generation of Asians to be invited to direct at the National; and I chose for my cast members of Tara Arts – hence, an all-Asian cast was seen for the first time at the Royal National.) Locating the production in India, it was set in a period of Indian history equivalent to that in which Molière originally wrote the play (the seventeenth-century France of Louis XIV). To quote from my production note-book:

> I am setting out to translate a seventeenth-century French farce through an all-Asian company of performers. This entails a double translation: once from the French original to English; and secondly to an English spoken by Asian actors, who have their own history of the acquisition of English speech. In other words, who are themselves 'translated' men and women – in

that they (or their not-too-distant forbears) have been 'borne across' from one language and culture to another. In order then to lay bare the full dimension of 'translation', I must take account of the specificity of my performers (their history): by conveying Molière's original play-text into a form that allows the performers to make creative connections between their ancestral traditions and their English present . . .

The form that this translation took was broadly derivative of Indian popular theatre conventions; most notably, *bhavai*, from Gujarat – a form that closely corresponds with *commedia dell'arte*, which influenced Molière. Molière's story was presented 'as a gift from the West' to the Emperor Aurangzeb by a French traveller, Françoise Bernier (a friend of Molière's who travelled to the court of this emperor between 1660 and 1676); and 'translated' by the emperor's court poet. I deliberately employed Indian languages, at times directly 'translated' by one of the two story-tellers. And these intersected a simple, almost prosaic English speech. Live music scored the entire production text. The bogus priest, Tartuffe, became an Indian *fakir* – a religious mendicant. This heaping together of fragments of diverse cultures is what I characterise as a Binglish process. Coming at the start of the last decade of this century, the production proved seminal in introducing Asian theatre on a national scale – a theatre that could be comic, inventive and provocative, and a theatre which introduced Asian audiences to the Royal National. A runaway success in London and around the provinces, the production eventually undertook an extensive overseas tour, representing the changing face of contemporary English theatre.

Tamasha's production of *Women of Dust* (1992) provides a variant on the idea of translation. The play, by Ruth Carter, relates the story of migrant women workers from Rajasthan, working on building projects in Delhi. A product of research in India, the production attempted to translate, for English audiences, the experience of these women. A realistic stage setting was infused with speech that attempted to recreate, in English, the particular rhythm of Rajasthani dialects. This transformation of the lives of Rajasthani migrant workers into English did not aim to establish a correspondence between the particular Asian performers and the particular stories of these women in contemporary

India, nor to problematise the act of translation. Rather, the production sought simply to document these particular lives in a manner accessible to a broad, English-speaking audience. It offered, in other words, a slice of life of the 'other'.

Such presentation of the Other, contrasting with Tara's correspondence with the Other, has become a defining feature of Tamasha's production history, a feature that achieved its best-known expression in the 1997 co-production with the Royal Court and Birmingham Repertory Theatre of Ayub Khan Din's *East is East*. The play, set in late-1960s Salford, told the story of a mixed-race family: Pakistani father, white working-class mother. The cross-cultural tensions and misunderstandings were conveyed with gentle humour against a realistic set recreating a terraced house in the Lancashire town. The text interrupted an idiomatic English with idioms derived from Punjabi and Urdu. This was echoed in the taped music design, with 1970s rock sitting uncertainly beside 1950s Bollywood songs. This enormously popular production seemed to tap in to the mood of the late 1990s: self-confidence among certain sections of the Asian population mingled with a desire within the wider population for some insight into Asian life in contemporary England. That it was possible also to locate the production clearly within recent English theatrical history was an added bonus: *East is East* seemed to be firmly within the territory paved by Shelagh Delaney's *Taste of Honey* and the other crop of working-class plays from the Angry Decade.

This form of presentation of the Other appears in stark contrast to Mehtaab, the first theatre company to receive Arts Council support for non-English work. Mehtaab's production of *Kali Salwar* (1996) – based on a short story by Saadat Hassan Manto about a prostitute whose customers are predominantly English soldiers serving the Raj – was entirely in Punjabi, pitching this production firmly into the territory inhabited largely by overseas productions touring England. Yet Mehtaab's producers and performers are all English Asians. What Mehtaab seemed to be doing was to go beyond flirtation with Indian languages into another text that, by definition, would exclude some and include others, and, in so doing, translate (transport) its Punjabi-speaking Asian audience into a memory of pre-Independence Punjab. In this enterprise, the company seemed to be fulfilling the same need that Bollywood cinema caters for: a means of entering, for a while, the Indian sub-continent without the interference of the migratory experience.

Subsequent to this production, however, Mehtaab has entered into that flirtation with Indian languages that is, by the late 1990s, the unifying feature of all Asian theatres (as evidenced by the company's latest production, *Not Just an Asian Babe*). It is with such flirtation that we enter squarely into *Binglish* – that invention of text and form which seems to point Asian theatre in both directions at once: towards the memory of ancestral lands in India and Pakistan *and* towards the reflection and refraction of contemporary England. Binglish has been the site for the invention of a distinctive Asian theatre identity – whose characteristic is *not* its uniformity, as has been noted in this brief glimpse of the work of just three of the contemporary Asian companies.

### Summary
I have sought to argue that Binglish has the texture of translation: the translation ('bearing across', according to the *OED* definition) of Asian experiences, histories and stories and sensibilities to England (the erstwhile 'mother country'). Equally, that this texture is varied in approach and application across each of the companies currently operating; that it can be a presentation (documentation) to and for England; that it can be a vehicle for transporting a particular audience to the sub-continent; and that it can be a means to seek a creative correspondence between memory and contemporary English experiences.

As the millennium draws to a close, English-Asian identity is showing no signs of losing its ambivalence: it is at once insular and international. Generations are growing up that seem on the one hand to be entirely 'English' in culture: idiomatic Yorkshire, Brummie, Cockney, some *sans* any Indian language and whose sense of music bears little relation to Indian music, with its preponderance of melody and rhythm. On the other hand, these same generations seem to be more confident, more willing to assert their 'Indian' identities – as is borne out by the contemporary Asian music scene. Global communications, coupled with the explosive pace of economic and social change in the urban areas of India and Pakistan, have conspired to re-kindle a fascination with the ancestral 'mother country' that, for a time, seemed to be waning (if only because, viewed from England, India and Pakistan seemed far from 'modern').

Yet, this ambivalence is, to a large extent, at the expense of memories of other homelands – East Africa, South Africa, Mauritius, Fiji, Trinidad, Guyana. Perhaps over the next thirty years or so these other memories will come to take their rightful place in the make-up of the unique theatrical enterprise which is Asian theatre in England: a microcosm of the world on a tiny spit of land on the northern fringes of Europe. And, in so doing, Asian theatre may go beyond the translative exercise, in a manner achieved by the current giants of English literature: Salman Rushdie, Arundhati Roy and Vikram Seth.

# 8 Popular theatre for the building of social awareness: the Indian experience

JACOB SRAMPICKAL SJ AND RICHARD BOON

There has long been a tradition of popular theatre, in its various mani-festations, seeking to make positive interventions in Indian society and politics. In urban and semi-urban areas street theatre, a form predom-inantly in the domain of the ideologue, is an established vehicle for political agitation and protest, and has achieved a high degree of tech-nical accomplishment as an art form. However, in rural areas, the use of theatre as a tool for the building of social awareness has been primarily the responsibility of the numerous Social Action Groups (SAGs) that have mushroomed since the mid-1970s. Given the Indians' inherent taste for theatre, it is hardly surprising that SAG workers should have seen its potential as a means for educating and conscientising the rural masses. Several SAGs operate more than one theatre group, and their daily performances in the villages are seen as a vital means of devel-oping awareness of social and political issues among the poor. In this chapter we examine both the current and the potential value of this kind of work as one contribution to rural development in India, basing our arguments on field-work and research undertaken by Father Jacob Srampickal, himself a practitioner in the area.

Development in India has occurred through three distinct, but complementary, areas of social work. The first consisted prim-arily of relief-oriented, project-development initiatives wherein non-governmental and voluntary agencies targeted disaster-stricken and economically backward areas with capital projects such as the building of houses, roads and wells. In the second, mass literacy was identi-fied as the single most important tool for development, and particular emphasis was placed on the provision of adult literacy classes and informal education centres for the dispossessed; here, there was an acknowledged debt to the pioneering work of the Brazilian education-alist, Paulo Freire.[1] Freire's influence – in particular, his emphasis on education through cultural revolution – was a key characteristic of the third focus of social-work activity: the decision by the voluntary sector to concentrate its energies on the development of a dual programme of literacy *and* education in awareness of wider social issues. Predictably, perhaps, it is in this area that successive governments, which had been happy enough to initiate programmes of development in the first two categories, have clashed with the voluntary agencies. It is also in this area that theatre can make most impact. India's problems are well known: poverty on a massive scale; a savage divide between rich and poor, enshrined in the caste system; corruption throughout the system. Any theatrical intervention which seeks in any way to tackle such enormous and deep-seated difficulties faces a huge task riddled with problems and contradictions; but it is also arguable that theatre is uniquely placed to engage with ordinary people and to stimulate the processes by which they might begin to transform their lives.

### The SAG theatre

The origins of the SAG movement lie in the 1960s, when a large number of educated young men and women, motivated by what they saw as the failure of the government's developmental policy and the inef-fectiveness of political parties generally, formed action groups in rural villages. With financial support from funding agencies in Europe and the United States (and also, though to a very minor extent, from private sources such as the Gandhi and Nehru Foundations in India), they con-centrated their energies on the most oppressed sections of rural soci-ety: women, tribal groups, landless labourers and fishing communities. Much of their activity continues to consist of the creation and devel-opment of adult literacy programmes, self-employment schemes and cottage industries, and always with a particular eye on the needs of women; the key characteristic of their work, however, has always been the passionate belief that individual projects must be put – and be seen to be put – in the wider context of a constant struggle towards greater economic and social justice. Making people aware of the social, eco-nomic and political issues which lie behind their immediate problems is what distinguishes SAG work from simple project-based initiatives, and it is in this area of conscientisation that theatre has come to play an important, if as yet under-developed, role.

All SAG work, including theatre, is overseen by cadres who may have responsibility for three or four villages; they are effectively the village teachers, charged with initiating, co-ordinating and monitoring a range of developmental activities. Those activists who specialise in theatre – the animators – have usually been trained by their city-based counterparts or by cultural workers who have specialised in folk forms such as *tamasha, nautanki* or traditional dances. It is the responsibility of the SAG theatre workers to pass on their training to the villagers; those selected (mainly men) generally have some natural acting ability, and may already have some experience of theatre. They are paid Rs 600 (US$20) per month. The inclusion of performers from the villages is crucial, for at the heart of this kind of theatre-for-development is the notion of *participation*, of the democratic empowerment of the people for whom the work is intended.

Put at its simplest, SAG plays – and they are a widespread phenomenon in India – are short, open-ended pieces, performed in villages and usually addressing topical and local areas of concern. The plays seek to explicate specific social issues affecting their audiences, and to promote formal discussion of those issues with a view to bringing about change for the better. This, then, is an essentially didactic form of theatre, but one which, at its best, seeks also to offer a sense of celebration and festivity in the form of song, dance, drama and plenty of humour.

Let us cite a concrete and not untypical example of a theatre performance in a village. The performers (seven in number) have gathered at the village SAG headquarters at 6.00pm. They cycle out to a village, about 6 kilometres away, arriving by 7.00pm. After refreshments, which the villagers provide, they tour the village playing drums and inviting the people to come to the plays. The women, who are still cooking, hurry. By 8.00pm the performers are ready.

They begin to gather their audience by singing appropriate songs and telling jokes. Once a reasonably sized group (comprising mainly women, children and some elders) has come together, the performance begins. The subject at issue is the abuse of religious power. The play concerns a poor villager, who is told by a local Brahmin priest that he must pay a large sum of money to the local goddess in recompense for his (accidental) killing of a cat. When he reaches the temple to offer his gifts (rice, cereals and chicken) the Brahmin's henchman seizes the villager, collects the offering and tells him he is rid of all his sins. It is a simple play, only 25 minutes long, but it provokes both laughter and recognition; religion is an enormously powerful force in all aspects of village life, and, when it is abused, is one of the main instruments by which people may be kept in a state of ignorance and disempowerment. The play over, one of the performers enters to ask if similar incidents happen in the village. The response is divided: some are willing to debate the issues raised, but others insist that the group go on with more plays. The group succumbs to the latter demand and three more plays are staged, all of a similar nature, until the audience has had its fill. As some fall asleep and others drift away, the group itself retires; members cycle back to SAG headquarters and then to their homes. They meet the following afternoon, prior to going to a new village, to evaluate their work. At this point changes and additions are made to the plays, under the supervision of the director of the centre. The group continues its work in this way on an almost daily basis. New plays are practised and performed as the director feels new issues need to be handled.

Assessing the effectiveness of the SAGs' theatrical activity is a hazardous task, partly because of the limited nature of what has so far been achieved, but also because, as may be seen from the example given above, audience reaction is seldom either consistent or predictable. Even if it were so, one can seldom say with certainty that any particular effect in a community is due to a single cause. Further research may provide more answers, but it is also clear that whilst SAG theatre undoubtedly contains the seeds of a genuinely effective force for change, its potential has yet to be fully realised. As will be seen, it is possible to demonstrate in particular cases that tangible benefits have accrued to communities as a result of the theatrical interventions of SAG groups. But these examples tend to be isolated and limited in their effects. In fact, our original intention while looking at the theatre activities of various SAGs was to study the effect of theatre exposure in one particular village over a lengthy period. However, very few of the areas visited provided evidence of systematic theatre programmes

which were organised with proper follow-up procedures developed over a sustained period of time. Most SAG groups will return to a village whenever they can, sometimes after as long as a year, rather than on a structured or planned basis. Even when they do return, fear of simply boring their audiences leads them to come with completely new plays; already there is evidence here of a recurrent and debilitating tension in SAG theatre work: the tension between the didactic and the entertainment aspects of the plays produced. The difficulty arises in part because theatre groups are too few, requiring individual SAG groups to work with more than a hundred villages. Inevitably, under pressures like these, many groups never penetrate beyond the periphery of communities, and awareness-building through theatre has little chance of developing in a systematic way.

The notion of the effectiveness of this kind of work is, then, one that has to be treated with caution, at all levels of involvement. But it is important to recognise that assessing the value of SAG theatre work is a complex and difficult exercise, and one which extends beyond the immediate point of contact between performer and audience, as obviously crucial as that is. What must also be considered is the wider context; in particular, the internal organisation of SAG theatre groups, including the value of the work for the participants themselves, and the practical, economic and political circumstances in which the work takes place, especially as regards the difficulties engendered by the caste system and the attitudes of local government powers. Only then can a realistic evaluation be made of the efficacy of the work at the point at which it most matters: in the lives of the people themselves.

Much of the information that follows was gathered from a particular group of villagers that had been exposed to a number of plays by an action group.

### On the field-workers and actors

The cadres who run the action groups may have some knowledge and theoretical awareness of the educational possibilities of theatre, but they often have little background or training in its practice. When a SAG begins a theatre project, they join in with selected members from the villages, many of whom, as we have indicated, may be experienced actors. The function of the cadre is to see that the social education

incorporated into the plays is appropriate and not misleading. There are occasions, however, where their presence can be harmful: they may attempt to force their viewpoint on the group as a whole, regarding themselves as privileged members of their groups, being better educated and, moreover, paid workers of the SAG. With this kind of attitude their influence on a group can be detrimental, especially within the context of a theatre workshop, in which democratic processes are essential, not only as a matter of practicality but also as the embodiment of the kind of ideals of social equality and justice the plays seek to advance. However, the better animators and cadres can and do contribute positively to the groups in which they work, and then their presence as catalysts is more than justified. In workshops conducted by better-equipped animators, many cadres have performed very well, becoming good organisers, especially in the crucial area of collaborating in the preparation of plays to be staged in the villages, a key area to which we will return later. Experience has shown that activists who are prepared to submit themselves to the essentially democratic process of creating a theatre project not only become better performers but also produce better and more effective theatre.

Much the same may be said about the actors themselves. Performing in a play is not merely an act that enhances their confidence, or provides the chance to articulate to an audience ideas they truly believe in; as is almost always the case in more radical forms of political theatre, the process of making the play is for its participant actors a valuable learning experience in itself, developing skills in analysing the issues involved, studying characters and scrutinising social situations critically. As Brecht demonstrated, actors who are able to learn, and to show that they are able to learn, produce audiences which are able to learn.

### On upper-caste and government reactions

Most of the SAGs work with the lower castes, who live in segregated parts of the villages: these are the poorer, dirtier and less attractive areas. The plays are normally performed in the courtyards of lower-caste homes. Typically, the upper castes quickly hear of a theatre group's arrival: their children flock to see the plays, whilst the men stand apart and watch the performances surreptitiously. Often they may ask the

SAGs to ignore the lower castes and come to their part of the village. However, when the play turns out to be a direct or indirect attack on their own exploitative behaviour (such as land-grabbing, for example), the upper castes can react violently. The electricity supply may be cut off, and stones thrown at the actors and the crowd. Several groups have been chased away by hired men in landlords' pay. Direct confrontation with the animators of the SAGs is rarer, for landlords are fearful of playing into the groups' hands by being seen inadvertently to acknowledge the validity of the plays' arguments. Local government officials are often in league with the landed gentry and the exploiters, and the threat they pose can be more insidious, for the SAG quota of foreign-aid funding is dependent on their good report. Several groups have softened their work as a direct response to this kind of financial pressure. One such group is READ (Rural Education and Development), a SAG run by Christians in Bihar. Kurien, its director, describes their plight:

> We can hardly do anything in this part of the villages. For we
> are in the bad books of the Circle [local government] Officer.
> Our FCRA [funding obtained under the auspices of the Foreign
> Contribution Registration Act] has been confiscated, since we
> tried to expose the laws of the jungle they follow. And without
> depending on foreign money we have not learnt to run SAGs
> successfully.[2]

Local government officials penalise SAGs that do not toe the party line. A number of SAGs, shorn of their financial support and stalled by legal action, have ceased to be active. Similarly, rumours spread that SAGs are disrupting the peace, spreading violence, or even acting as agents of foreign powers. In such circumstances theatre can have explosive repercussions; consequently, plays on milder topics of social reconstruction become routine, and those with more radical agendas are directly or indirectly driven from the repertoire.

### On the people themselves

This, clearly, is the most important area of consideration. To study the effectiveness of popular theatre generally and SAG theatre groups in particular, fieldwork was undertaken in several villages in Bihar which had been exposed to a variety of plays. Typical among these was

*Aadhunik Ramlila. Ramlila* is the mythological story of Ram and Sita, gods in the Hindu pantheon, and how they fight against the forces of evil in the shape of the demon king, Ravan. In *Aadhunik Ramlila*, the mythological and the modern are intertwined, as Ram and Sita become ordinary, simple villagers struggling against an iniquitous social system represented by a wealthy landlord (Ravan). Here, the power of religion in the villages is turned to advantage: the story is immediately familiar to the audience, so enabling its re-contextualisation as a modern social parable. The play was able to address a wide variety of social problems of immediate relevance to its audiences, and to do so in such a way as to prompt discussion regarding what the underlying causes of those problems might be.

One of the villages where *Aadhunik Ramlila* was performed is Madwaha, close to the READ training centre, with a population of about 1,600. Of these about 700 (85 families) are low castes who live a hand-to-mouth existence. None has any land or income other than from casual labour. The people spend some time working in the fields of the higher castes for meagre wages. Bonded labour was once prevalent, but has since been abolished through the efforts of READ. Only about 10 per cent can read and write. Among the children, about 20 per cent attend schools, others help their parents in the fields. The children are often married off when they are around 15. The READ team has consistently tried to persuade the villagers to concentrate on issues such as cleanliness, sending their children to school, attending the evening adult literacy classes and abolishing child marriages. More generally, it has encouraged villagers to become more sensitive to how they are exploited by the higher castes and landowners, to unite in the fight against corruption, and to press their demands for communal benefits from the government.

It is clear that the SAG initiative in Madwaha has enjoyed demonstrable success. What is less clear is how important the theatrical component of that initiative was, and how far the work had managed to penetrate beyond the immediate problems of daily life to a deeper social analysis of why those problems existed in the first place. Everyone had enjoyed *Aadhunik Ramlila*, and felt that the play presented topical problems in a realistic way, but when it came to the question of whether people could come together in their own lives to oppose an exploitative situation, there was silence. Finally, a middle-aged man spoke:

> We appreciate the work done by READ and the drama troupe. They have made it very clear to us that exploitation is mainly due to our lack of education and unity. However, if anyone of us raises our voice against the higher castes they will dismiss us from their fields and someone else will get our work. And then we will starve.[3]

Clearly awareness has been raised, and indeed life in the village has improved in visible ways. General hygiene is better. The children look cleaner. The tube well and the surrounding area is kept dry and clean at all times. The pond, where everyone bathes and washes clothes, could not be cleaner. In the village proper, a number of places where marsh used to develop in the rainy seasons have been reclaimed. There are now youngsters who resist early marriage (although in the case of girls the parents are still adamant that they need to have their first marriage ceremony when they are around 12; they go to their husbands only when they are about 18. For many reasons this was found to be extremely hard to change). School attendance has risen from 12 per cent in 1979 to 20 per cent today. That the contribution of the theatre work to the initiative was significant is evident, particularly among the youth, where there is a growing understanding about the kinds of problem faced by the village. A number of them have shown keen interest in doing plays with similar themes, although READ has not yet been able to organise a stable group.

Generally, however, the problem remains of a lack of carefully planned, forward-thinking action. Issues such as a minimum wage, the misuse of the law, and exploitation by money-lenders, local political figures and government leaders, have been analysed through many of the plays, and many villagers today are willing to seek further guidance in these matters. But with regard to action for greater change initiated by the people themselves, hardly anything has yet been done. Insufficient numbers of activists are again at least partly to blame, but, crucially in our view, what needs also to be addressed is the question of whether the SAG popular theatre initiative is reaching its full potential.

### The potential of SAG theatre

A major advantage of SAG theatre groups over the street-theatre groups of the cities is the possibility of post-performance discussion and follow-up action. The SAGs can be sure that when they return to a certain village they will confront the same people and the same situations. Even if the theatre groups can themselves do no more than perform their plays, it is quite possible for the local field-workers or the SAG animators from central headquarters to undertake responsibility for some form of follow-up action. Theatre may then intervene again, and offer a means of continuing review and analysis of progress. To a large extent, this depends on ensuring the continuing production of plays on relevant themes. The strength of a SAG play resides primarily in the topicality of its theme: any such work depends on and is tested by a group's ability to improvise a piece on a current burning issue and to make the audience aware of the various implications of that issue. Here, there is already evidence of positive progress. Over the years, several groups have proved that it is possible to engage village audiences at a profound level by exploring more serious themes in their plays. Sociopolitical themes have become popular. Plays dealing with varying types of repression of the poorer classes, with the use of religion to exploit people, with low wages for workers and so on have all been successful and popular. Sentimental religious and patriotic plays have given way to plays dealing with the harsh social and economic conditions under which the great majority of people live, and with the injustice and corruption which sustain those conditions.

However, the situation is not helped by ideological differences within and between SAG groups, differences which operate at political and theatrical levels. As we have suggested, voluntary agencies have travelled a long way from the days of charity and welfare schemes. There has been a visible shift towards broader development issues and conscientisation. Similarly, the tools they use have changed from Gandhian idealism to Marxist rhetoric and to Freirian participatory methods. Now they use theatre. For how long this trend will continue is an open question. In fairly recent history, two prominent theatre movements, IPTA (1941–56), and Samudaya (Bangalore, 1971–8), have collapsed under the weight of ideological conflicts. This may not augur well for the future of the theatre in SAGs.

Moreover, it has to be acknowledged that in several groups theatre is not seen as a powerful means of helping the people either to explore their social and political problems or to enhance their participation in social re-construction. Some see it purely as an entertainment medium, useful for gathering people together for a bigger meeting or, at best, as a starting-point for a 'proper' discussion . This is to underestimate the potential of theatre as an educative force. But such perceptions remain a serious problem, not least for audiences; the reality of village life itself is intense, and villagers have to work hard every day to make both ends meet. If they do not work, they do not eat; hence it is difficult for them quite simply to find time for workshops or study and discussion sessions. Some are simply not interested in theatre ('the harp and fiddle can wait, let us get on with matters of significance', is a not untypical attitude), or have been alienated by previous experience of poor-quality work. Factionalism within villages is another problem: if animators make contact with one group, another may keep away.

That SAG theatre has made genuine attempts to highlight the immediate issues the people face is undeniable. That much they have inherited from street theatre, but too often they have not progressed sufficiently beyond mere protest into a fuller and more analytical – and therefore more socially useful – form of practice. It is upon this that we now wish to concentrate. There are several important areas to be considered.

The first is the question of localism. SAG theatres have largely failed to present plays improvising on events in the particular villages for which they are responsible. Plays based on borrowed scripts and general themes of oppression have their place (see below), but improvising plays on local events is often more effective. It helps the audience to identify with the characters and concentrate on the issues. Opposition will inevitably follow, but that in itself can further focus issues and develop responses. Thus not only production of the play, but also its after-effects, can help to unite and empower the community.

At the same time, the wider context needs to be taken into account more fully. There are some action groups which develop plays based on factual events in their own village or which make use of borrowed scripts that have particular relevance to specific situations. The plays are duly staged and analysed. But hardly any attempt is made to relate the events in the play to the national and indeed international oppression of the poor. It is important for local audiences to understand how an apparently isolated event in their village is linked to overall patterns of oppression in the wider country and indeed across the world. Hence after a play is staged it is necessary to draw parallels with events happening in other villages, districts and states. This can be done more easily in the case of the right kind of scripts borrowed from outside, for these have already been proved as the expression of the experiences of other groups in comparable if not identical situations. Without this 'macro' approach, there is hardly any possibility of the movement acquiring a mass character, or of individual villages learning to understand how their immediate problems relate to the wider socio-political context.

The key area which needs attention here is the question of how well-qualified SAG groups themselves are to present and analyse complex material. One of the most significant criticisms levelled against SAG plays is that the attendant analytical discussion of issues raised is imperfect and weak, with key ideas not sufficiently understood by the villagers. A common error is the failure to penetrate beyond the superficial. Typical examples are those plays which deal with oppression. Within the fictional world of the play, the oppressor is exposed, convicted and instant justice is meted out: a landlord or a money-lender is found guilty. Yet little attempt is made, either within the play or through subsequent discussion, to find out why the villains are what they are. Deeper analysis can lead to identifying the system of oppression working in the village and beyond. The greater historical, economic and political factors underlying a particular situation need to be explored. This is how the poor may come to understand, very much along the lines demonstrated by Freire, that the real causes of poverty and under-development are not the ignorance or wickedness of individual rich men, but the inherent injustice of a social, political and economic system which not only keeps them powerless and exploited but which indeed depends on them being so. The first step to empowerment is the realisation that the real problems are not lack of proper drinking water, illiteracy, superstition, large families or malnutrition, but the exploitation, inequality, injustice and corruption from which they flow. The former are only symptoms of the latter. For precisely this reason, plays which attempt to deal with single issues are also problematic. For example, alcoholism and malnutrition result largely from exploitative working conditions, yet too often SAG plays treat them as isolated phenomena and prescribe solutions accordingly. Such problems are not analysed in relation to their society, but put down to individual weakness, the 'solution' requiring the afflicted character to undergo a 'change of heart', which amounts to little more than wish-fulfillment. Similarly, some SAG plays have a tendency to treat problems as if they were caused by the 'backward' behaviour of the people themselves. Economic and social relationships are not considered, and blaming the victim only makes him or her more insecure and fatalistic.

This lack of proper understanding of the realities of the lives of the people is at the very root of many of the weaknesses SAG work currently exhibits. We have already noted that problems can arise when cadres and animators live away from the villages for which they have responsibility. Those problems are exacerbated when the target audiences come from – as they often do – lower-caste communities. Such communities suffer from an absence of self-worth, and are denied even basic human dignity. Their position is essentially the result of a centuries-old subjugation under the caste system, so it is hardly surprising if they do not easily respond to outsiders, and find it very hard when the outside animators expect trust, let alone critical responses, from them. Yet positive results can be achieved, and sometimes through simple means. For example, Kizhakekala and Vadassary, studying the myths and stories prevalent among the Harijan communities in the Dharaut village of the Gaya District of Bihar, have pointed out that whereas the community believed itself to have been cursed by a fall from grace, there were in fact good historical reasons for their demeaned status, reasons which owed nothing to inherent failings on their part. Plays which show Harijans in high positions, holding responsible jobs, confronting unjust authorities or even simply operating in the company of people in high positions like local government officials begin to build in the audience a sense of worth and dignity, an essential prerequisite to further development.[4]

The importance of SAG groups simply promulgating a positive outlook among village communities should not be underestimated.
SAG theatre has perhaps become too preoccupied with themes of grim
oppression. Plots have become clichéd, with stock situations, obvious
humour and two-dimensional characterisation. An agit-prop style of
revolutionary treatment has been their forte, but the presentation of
too many desperate situations, in too simplistic and limited a form, can
serve only to emasculate revolutionary potential and strengthen fatalistic attitudes. Apathy towards theatre begins to develop. Creative and
innovative efforts at re-working the village structure, and the possibility of hope, could perhaps enliven the spirit of the people. Too few
SAG theatre workers understand the richness and variety of theatrical
form, with its capacity for celebration, festival and the means to reflect
different aspects of the colourful complexity of community life. The
medium could be used to explore the richness of village life: the fears,
anxieties and dreams of the villagers, and the vibrancy of their cultural
traditions. Such forms of celebratory theatre can help to develop people's
self-esteem and lead to individual and collective empowerment.

As we have already suggested, even (perhaps especially) in fictional narratives people weaned on a culture of dependency tend to seek
solutions, rather than open critical analysis. A number of SAG groups
(especially the roving troupes) unfortunately pander to this, presenting
polished, well-finished plays, structured primarily as performance, and
presented at night, on stage, under disciplined conditions. These present a single view: that of the outsider. Such efforts do not help to raise
critical social consciousness. The audience is disempowered, explicitly advised and implicitly trained to watch silently. The performance
proceeds much as it would in a conventional theatre. Some groups
encourage question-and-answer sessions at the end of their plays, but,
with the kind of actor-audience relationship that has already been
established these tend only to confirm what has already been commun-
icated, not to interrogate it. Villagers might be in total disagreement
with the arguments of a piece, but because those arguments have been
presented by apparently all-knowing activists, their views are left
unexpressed.

If a truly open process is to be utilised, then that process must
begin at the point when projects are initiated and developed; if SAG

plays are primarily meant to educate, then the nature of their preparation should surely be vital. Yet few groups seem fully to have realised that the process of play-making is one of self-education for the participants, and a crucial time for analysing social issues and building social awareness. Improvisation, which is often the key element of this play-making, is taken too lightly. Except under the particular circumstances outlined above, there is little point in plays being prepared from completed or even published scripts in isolation, behind closed doors, away from the people.

It must be stated emphatically that the very essence of this kind of developmental theatre is the full involvement of the people in every aspect of play production. Unfortunately, not many SAG activists have understood how essential audience participation is. The worst cases, again, normally involve activists who live away from the people and who 'parachute in' with their 'message', a form of communication which treats the public as mere consumers of information, reinforces the notion of passivity and legitimises the culture of silence. Thus they perpetuate a 'top-down' format. In too much SAG theatre, programmes are planned by the staff, themes are chosen by the animators, and the scripting is done by the fieldworkers. At no point is the local community invited to participate as part of a 'bottom-up' process. The problem is exacerbated by the growing professionalism of touring SAG troupes, some of which now own their own transport and possess an electricity supply, a PA system and stage facilities, all of which have been made essential to their theatre. This kind of professionalism is in itself a barrier to audience involvement, and prevents theatre from taking root in the village, particularly as it often goes hand-in-hand with the lack of follow-up action. Participation is the key, and must be made the primary goal of the work, and there must be an acknowledgement that the long years of oppression and exploitation may have dampened the villagers' enthusiasm for theatre, especially theatre which they see as attempting, through content, style or form, to dictate to them. The resultant passivity, suspicion and fear need to be taken as challenges. The effort of SAG theatre in such instances of apathy should be to create an atmosphere conducive to sharing and dialogue.

One significant means of creating that atmosphere would be to recognise more fully than is currently the case the cultural traditions of the audiences which are being addressed. In this area, SAG theatre cannot claim to have touched the issues that are crucial to the people. Culture – that which represents a society's awareness of its own values, aims, visions and dreams – should provide an important incentive for and means of development. If theatre can concentrate on the villagers' identity as a group seeking justice and equality, then it could rightly be said to be a true reflection of their culture. Folk forms are a key element here, but there are different opinions in SAGs regarding their use. While some groups present plays in folk forms, others select only a few folk elements. Yet, in either case, it is evident from the tradition of folk theatre that it was most often performed by specialised groups, and that years of training alone make a good folk performer; these are not skills which can be easily or quickly learned. Establishing a folk theatre group, attempting to 'borrow' a tradition, has often ended in vulgarising the form. Few SAGs realise that not every form can be adapted and that each has its own historical background and significance. Many well-meaning social activists have even tried to adapt elements of religious rituals. For example, as part of a social awareness play, a group of people suffering from an epidemic was advised by a goddess to turn to the doctors. The villagers, satisfied that it was the goddess herself who spoke, did so. At least one observer condemns this use of superstition by the SAG production as inappropriate, and offers the following illustration of the dangers of such a tactic. The Young Farmers' Club in a village in Tamil Nadu wanted to erect a shed for their association in the temple premises, but met with strong opposition from the trustees of the temple. At one of the temple festivals, a SAG persuaded a dancer to perform. In the course of his dance, he lay on thorns, burned himself and performed other acts causing himself pain. Although the audience knew him to be a common drunkard, they were tremendously impressed by his performance, and believed he was possessed by the spirit. Apparently in a trance, he declared: 'Annam [a local god] has come, and said that the farmers are my people and those who do not let them build their shed will be punished.' What the organising SAG had not realised was that the temple trustees could as easily have persuaded the same man to say the opposite for a better price![5]

The point is that whilst the desired outcome was achieved, the means by which it was achieved was not only disreputable but offered no possibility of a real lesson being learned or indeed applied elsewhere, and to this extent was counter-productive.

Bordanev condemns the use of folk media for disseminating the development message:

> Development thinkers' obsession with goal achievement and not with human growth may take up these folk media as another set of instruments for changing people's way of thinking, feeling and behaving. And this is not the purpose and function of the traditional media. I am afraid, as soon as the people realise that their folk arts are being used for subliminal propaganda they will let them die.[6]

The observation is valid not only in the case of using folk theatre for disseminating development messages, but also of using it for any purpose other than allowing it to play its established role in society. Folk theatre has always echoed the needs of people and it should continue to do so. Adaptation of its contents, if validated by this criterion, can be justified and may indeed prove very effective. It would have been better if development communicators had convinced the folk performers of the appropriateness of the development message, and given them the freedom to present it in a manner the performers considered suitable. Moreover, not many groups concentrate on using the simple resources the people already have available to them. Ordinary people may not be proficient, all-round practitioners of folk theatre, but there will be some who are good at story-telling, or singing, dancing and so on. These abilities have not yet been explored sufficiently. If the local people have not been involved in the preparation of the plays then these resources will remain unused.

Theatre can be a powerful cultural expression, as it has the potential actively to involve a wide range of physical, emotional and imaginative capacities. It can bring together many facets of cultural creativity: the socio-political, religious, ritualistic; mythological and story-telling; dance, music, satire, mimicry, role-playing and the festive celebration of a community. If the catalysts make it a point to explore these inherent capabilities they will surely contribute to education through cultural action.

### Conclusion

SAG theatre needs itself to develop, both qualitatively and quantitat-
ively, if it is to realise its full potential as a means of conscientising
the poor and disempowered in rural India. We believe that it has already
shown that it is able to operate as a uniquely powerful means of addressing and prompting action on a whole range of problems faced on a daily
basis in the villages. But if it is to move on, more needs to be done at
the level of creating a greater awareness of the deeper-lying problems
of Indian society generally. It is only when people begin to understand
how the difficulties of their own lives originate in and are determined
by greater social, political and economic forces that truly meaningful
change can take place.

More committed groups need to come to the fore, which means
more animators and more performers. Central organisation needs to be
tightened and developed. Funding remains a problem, but if the work
can secure the confidence and goodwill of the people for whom it is
intended then it need not rely forever on foreign aid, and with financial
independence will come greater freedom from political interference.
SAG theatre can be politicised, as is already the case with urban street
theatre, but only if, through the quality and integrity of its work, it
develops widespread grass-roots popularity. Crucially, villagers need to
feel that a SAG theatre group is *their* theatre group, worthy of their
whole-hearted support. Cadres and animators must connect more fully
with the lives of the villages, engaging people's interest and trust, and
securing their co-operation and – vitally – participation. Only then will
the process of empowerment begin, as people begin to feel responsible
for and confident about changing their lives.

NOTES

1 Paulo Freire, *Pedagogy of the Oppressed* (Harmondsworth: Penguin,
1972). Freire's theory of conscientisation has had a huge impact on
development work around the world. The theory rests on the belief that
the act of becoming literate is also a process of analysing and becoming
critically aware of social and political circumstances. It places great faith
in the ability of ordinary people to understand, learn and change.
'Development' is not simply a matter of economics, but a process of
liberation and acculturation.

2 Quoted in Jacob Srampickal, *Voice to the Voiceless: The Power of People's Theatre in India* (New Delhi: Manohar, 1994), p. 207.

3 *Ibid.*, p. 208.

4 K. Kizhakekala and J. Vadassary, *The Charmars: Their Beliefs and Practices* (Patna: St Xavier's, 1985).

5 D. Dabreo, 'Giving Voice to the People', unpub. ms., 1988.

6 Quoted in John Lent, 'Increasing Importance of the Folk Media in Third World Nations', *Vidura* (October 1981).

## 9  The promise of performance
## True Love/Real Love

PAUL HERITAGE

O gringo vem aqui e não conhece a realidade
Vai para Zona Sul para conhecer agua de coco[1]

(The gringo comes here and doesn't know the reality
Goes to Zona Sul to know coconut water)

In her introduction to *Acting Out: Feminist Performances*, Peggy Phelan[2] marks the difference between True Love and Real Love in the persistently disruptive promises of feminist performance:

> Like all promises they won't be kept. And that's the point. For by not keeping them these artists allow us to be loosened from our enthralment with the future they promise (a future itself enfolded and articulated within a narrow narrative model) and, more important, the failure of these promises allows us to disengage from a particular romance with our future selves . . . True Love becomes less heroic and Real Love more palpable. Performance can't rely on the future: it lives and loves and fails and wins and whines in the pressing present.[3]

My own relationship with theatre in Brazil has had to negotiate similar bonds and boundaries[4] between True Love and Real Love, which began but has not ended with the work of Augusto Boal. In the bleakness of Britain in the late 1980s, Boal offered a romance with theatre and its infinite possibilities that seemed to be disappearing in a culture of despair and disengagement. His brief appearances to give workshops, and the eventual publication of *Games for Actors and Non-Actors* to supplement our tattered copies of *Theatre of the Oppressed*, began to stimulate interest in a theatre praxis that was ludic, functional and confident in its social role. But as in all long-distance relationships there was always something missing. Hence my arrival in Brazil.

Part of my desire to work in Brazil over the last seven years has been the seduction of seeing Augusto Boal's Theatre of the Oppressed come home. While Brazil represented to me all that was exotic, I was in some sense looking for the domestication of a reading and a practice that had always been haunted by a sense that it must work better 'over there'. Whatever difficulty I encountered, whatever obstruction or non-function in the methods of Theatre of the Oppressed that arose in a youth club in Manchester could easily be dreamed away by the rather imprecise thought that somehow it must work better in Brazil (or probably South America as I found it rather difficult to distinguish my imaginary Brazil from my imaginary Argentina or Peru). Boal and the Theatre of the Oppressed had become my True Love. Disengaging from the comforting warmth of this romance has not been easy or perhaps even possible.

My imaginary Brazil was bananas and Boal, *favela*[5] and football, street children and samba, Chico Mendes and Carmen Miranda. Somewhere there were rain forests and perhaps perpetually there was Carnival. Orson Welles tried to make a film about Brazil and never finished it, but the exclamatory title he chose in 1943 seems as appropriate for the startled impressions of today's visitors to Brazil: *It's All True!* In some ways I have seen all the myths I expected and more. It would be foolish to expect that in writing about Brazil after seven years and nine visits there is any less mythology colouring my vision. If anything, Brazil's own cultural myths are now so vivid for me that I fantasise more and not less about what I see there.

Within the first few pages of his latest book *Teatro Legislativo*,[6] Boal sets out the objective of both his writing and his theatre: 'I hope it should be useful.'[7] The book reflects the interactive nature of his theatre, as he has written it in a form that expects and solicits readers' responses. Described as a 'Beta Version' of the text, *Teatro Legislativo* is intended as a preliminary attempt to write up the latest experiment in participatory theatre that Boal commenced when he was elected to Rio de Janeiro's municipal assembly in 1992.[8] The objective is to collect information and suggestions from those who have used the book and have experiences to relate, so that the revised version when it is published can reflect the diverse ways in which the experiment is being followed. While the experiment and its description in the book are very specific to the situation of Boal and the Centre for the Theatre of the Oppressed in Rio de Janeiro, clearly it is hoped that the final version will include examples from across the four continents and more than thirty countries in which Boal has worked.

Boal's hopes for a functional theatre pre-date the creation of the techniques and strategies that in the 1970s became known as the Theatre of the Oppressed. From his first work with the Arena Theatre in São Paulo in 1957, Boal has been concerned with the ways in which it is possible for a socially engaged theatre to function and what we can expect it to achieve. Programme notes accompanying these early shows proclaimed theatre as an instrument in the fight for national liberation. The re-thinking of theatre was apparent in every aspect of Arena's work, from the redefinition of the audience–stage relationship through performances in the round,[9] to the development of Brazilian dramaturgy with a weekly Saturday seminar to promote and encourage new writing for the contemporary stage. Similarly, Boal's proclaimed 'nationalisation' of the classical repertoire was intended to bring Brazilian gestures, idioms and corporeality to internationally renowned plays. The military coup of 1964 brought the function of theatre into even sharper focus, as activists and radical intellectuals looked to cultural means of engagement and protest. It sometimes seems as if Boal is still recognised in Brazil for this work that took place in the 1960s, and the fifteen years of exile from 1971 to 1986 have not always been recognised by those who remained behind. There is both continuity and obvious change in the work that Boal developed outside Brazil during those years. But dictatorships and exile break cultural and personal histories, and at times it can appear as if Boal's achievements beyond Brazil have had an adverse effect on the reputation he has in his own country.

In 1994 Boal was awarded the Pablo Picasso Medal by UNESCO for a lifetime of achievement in the arts. His position in twentieth-century theatrical heritage is memorably inscribed in Richard Schechner's striking claim that Boal has 'created the theatre Brecht only dreamed of'.[10] But it is not a theatre that goes unchallenged. Indeed, Boal recognises this himself when he describes in *Teatro Legislativo*

Boal's books are based on past experiences filtered through anecdotes, his writing and teaching seem caught in a perfect future tense rather than an imperfect past. His stories are not so much accounts of actions in history as parables for our theatrical lives to come. He continues to represent for me the heroic True Love that I have sought in the promise of performance. While the overt and clarion claim of this writing has guided the practice of so many community and development theatre workers for over a decade now, it seems to make it all the harder to see where and how theatre works.

The present and everyday social crises that are so clearly visible and pressing in Brazil are powerful sites to locate and test ideas about the functions of theatre. When asked to write a chapter for this book I could have selected many different fields of study from Brazilian theatre in action, from projects with street children in Recife to prison theatre groups in Brasília,[13] and I have chosen to look at a small example from Rio de Janeiro, already pre-inscribed as one of the world's most dramatic cities. Although like my journeys to Brazil since 1991 this chapter has begun with Boal and the Centre for the Theatre of the Oppressed, my search for Real Love takes me to a different kind of romance in the *favela* of Vidigal. But the work there is only intelligible for me because of the passionate promise that Boal installed in my vision of what theatre might be able to achieve.

### Nós do morro [Us from the Hillside]

Eu só quero ser feliz,
Andar tranqüilamente na favela onde nasci
E poder me orgulhar
E ter a consciência que o pobre tem seu lugar[14]

(I only want to be happy,
To walk peacefully in the *favela* where I was born
And be able to be proud
And have the consciousness that the poor have their place)

The first *favela* that I visited in Rio de Janeiro climbs up from the back streets of Copacabana. The dramatic geography of the 'Cidade Maravilhosa'[15] ensures that as mountain meets sea, 'luxo' (luxury) must rub shoulders with 'lixo' (rubbish). The narrow strips of expensive real estate that border the beaches of Ipanema and Copacabana are contained by the mountainsides that have become home to thousands of 'faveladas',[16] their numbers augmented by the collapse of the Brazilian economy in the 1970s. At least one million people live in more than 570 *favelos* that stretch across the formal metropolis of Rio de Janeiro.[17] Like almost everything else in Brazil, the *favela* is as strong in myth as it is in reality and the images that you encounter are irresistibly linked to what you are prepared to see. I first entered a *favela* with CTO-RIO to visit a group that was working in a new crèche being built by the community there. At the entrance to the main street that ran down from where we arrived was a man and his guitar. The guitar was turned upside down and on the back of it he was preparing the cocaine that he was about to sell to a well-dressed couple waiting in their imported car. 'Luxo' meeting 'lixo'. But what struck me most forcibly was the corrupted use of the guitar.

In an essay entitled 'Liveness: Performance and the Anxiety of Simulation',[18] Philip Auslander cites as a cultural fact that 'in our current, mediatised culture, live performance is largely a marginal activity'.[19] The *favela* is both physically and socially a marginal territory, so the importance of live performance within the *favela* might be seen to both prove and test the efficacy of Auslander's proposition. From samba to funk, from pagode[20] to rap, popular music is more than just a mediatised product that is bought on disc or heard on the radio. The close association of the Samba Schools with the *favela*, the conflicts performed and fought out in the 'baile funk',[21] the street corner pagode band and the improvised transformations of life into rap, resist the idea that live performance has lost its impact or significance within this culture. Clearly none of this activity is independent from technological reproduction, but nor is the enterprise of mass media unaffected by what is produced within the *favela*. However, the degree to which they may or may not be interdependent is perhaps less important at this stage than the continued presence of live performance. The guitar is still used for more than as a counter for a drugs deal.

Theatre does not occupy a natural or easy space within these communities, as the experience of both CTO-RIO and Nós do morro has shown. Cultural and political histories have divided aesthetic forms and societies, so that the activity of live theatre has not formed a part of the life of the *favela*, although in its mediatised form theatre is served at least three times a day as easily digestible soap-opera on television. But the story of how theatre has come to occupy a physical and cultural space in the *favela* of Vidigal offers a chance to think through the questions raised by the assertively defensive title of this collection of essays. How then does theatre matter in Vidigal?

Nós do morro began as a newspaper and is now a theatre building and company. The journey from one to the other has been led by Guti Fraga, who has lived in Vidigal from 1976. He came to Rio de Janeiro to study journalism at university and acting at drama school, and found accommodation on the hillside of Vidigal: 'I was always poor but until I moved to Vidigal from where I was born in the interior of Brazil, I had never lived so close to such poverty.'[22] Guti's first attempt to produce work based in the language and life of the *favela* began with journalism in the creation of two newspapers: *O Jornal comunitário* [*The Community Newspaper*] and *O Jornal morral* [*The Newspaper of the Hillside*]. The former consisted of wooden panels on to which were fixed headlines, stories, news items. These panels were displayed in key points of the community. The principles of producing a newspaper for and from within the community are the same ones that lie at the heart of the theatrical work today. Indeed, residents who worked as journalists are now, twenty years later, writing plays for the theatre company.

A special edition of *Jornal morral* to greet the Pope's visit to Brazil in 1982 produced powerful results. All equipment was destroyed and the copies of the paper were burned. Guti Fraga: 'I stopped being a journalist when an article that I wrote about the Pope led to an attempt to kill me. My career as a journalist began and ended there, and I found work as an actor instead.' Between 1982 and 1986 he worked as actor and stage manager in the company of Marília Pêra, one of Brazil's best-loved and most famous actresses. Though seemingly so far from the work that he now does, it is Marília Pêra that Guti cites as the inspiration for the formation of Nós do morro, in the discipline of theatre that she taught through her own practice. Thus in October 1986 he invited Frederico Pinheiro, who lit Marília Pêra's productions, to work with him in setting up a theatre group. Fernando Nelo da Costa, an artist who lived in Vidigal, joined them as designer. The same team still has artistic responsibility for the company eleven years later.

Any attempt now to recall and register the histories of the plays and performers that have formed this project will inevitably serve the narrative of the particular teller of the tale. My tale is supposed to be about how, where and why theatre works. When I hear the various stories from those who have participated in making and seeing this theatre, there are striking moments that stand out from the years of everyday activity, though it is probably in the quotidian and not the exceptional moments on which the strength of Nós do morro is built. The moments I choose to emphasise are those that construct the idea of the theatre that I want and need to love.

The impetus for the formation of Nós do morro came from a local priest: an unconscious mocking of the mythical birth of European theatre in the bosom of the Church. Father Hubert Leeb, an Austrian missionary from the Vietnam war who was banned from celebrating mass by the Catholic Church, had established a community centre in a church in Vidigal during the 1980s. He invited Guti Fraga to establish a theatre project which progressed from the patio of the church to the inside of the church itself. It would be impossible to quantify how many people in Vidigal had been to a theatre before this project began. Most newspaper accounts pay tribute not only to the abilities of the group in performance but to their powers of persuading the inhabitants of the *favela* to go to the theatre. In order to encourage people to come to see the first play they gave two invitations to each household in the 'morro'. When people arrived for the performance they had to swap the invitation for a ticket at the makeshift ticket office. The intention was to initiate an audience to the cultural habits of a theatre-going activity that was necessarily alien. Before each performance Guti gave a speech explaining how the scenery and lighting had been created (the lights, for example, were constructed out of tin cans), and introduced people to the language of theatre. The project was as much a training for the audience as the actors, unaccustomed to watch anything in silence: not because of indiscipline or because of a disruptive nature but because no cultural activity known to them was received without direct reactions. Even today the plays about the *favela* are never received in

silence, as the close association and identification between the characters portrayed and members of the audience elicit active commentary
throughout the performances.

During 1987 Nós do morro performed every weekend for over
eight months and invited guests gradually gave way to paying customers. The first play was based on improvisations by a group of twenty
people from Vidigal working with Guti. This was formed into a play
entitled *Encontros* [*Meetings*] which dealt with situations that were a
part of the life of the participants but avoided the subjects that were
inevitably linked to the *favela* by the media. 'There was nothing about
drug trafficking, violence, death, injustices, fights with the police, etc.
We see this on the television and experience it in our everyday lives.
Our intention was to recreate a little of the world which could be
anybody's and provoke the dreams of the spectators.'[23] This attitude
remains the same a decade later and marks the polemical difference
from the theatre of Boal. It is an attempt to create theatre that is in no
sense useless, but makes no direct allusion to its usefulness as commentary or agitation. It is the 'user' of theatre rather than its 'use' that
is brought sharply into focus. And the users of theatre must clearly
include those who watch as well as those who do.

The repertoire of the company in the years since then has regularly included similar plays based on improvisation workshops. For
Guti and the other directors, they act as a register of individual and collective social histories. It is common for Brazil to be called a country
without memory, and the lack of official structures within such a marginalised community as a *favela* makes the act of registering histories
all the more difficult and all the more necessary. Individual stories of
violence or of resistance start to gain a wider resonance in the collective story-telling and remembering that forms a part of this process.
Without it, individual acts of barbarism are experienced as terrible and
chaotic incidents that are out of control because they are a part of no
pattern. The physical fabric of the *favela* is in itself provisional and subject to constant disruption and destruction, unlike the official urban
environment which is generally experienced as stable and permanent.
While modern and historic cities are integral parts of the national pat-
rimony, the *favela* is that part which must be removed if all that is

deemed wholesome and healthy is to survive. The survival of the lives of the residents in any form of cultural registration is at odds with the very environment in which those lives are lived.

But while such community-based theatre projects are commonly focused on plays that perform the lives of the participants, Nós do morro alternates plays about the *favela* with classical works of Brazilian literature, from which many of the participants are excluded by a combination of educational and cultural factors. One of the earliest examples of this was the performance of Martins Pena's nineteenth-century comedy *O inglês maquinista* [*The English Machinist*] in 1988. Slavery is the central question of a play which is based on the opposition between Brazilian traffickers anxious to maintain their illegal trade with Africa and English merchants who see the end of slavery as a way of increasing the profits of their commercial interests in Brazil. It is not difficult to see ways in which the play offers parallel readings for contemporary Brazilian society and the illegal traffickings of other merchandises which serve the interests of privileged and powerful groups. But while the production opened up questions of social interest and was performed to coincide with the anniversary of the death of one of Brazil's national black heroes from the time of slavery, the work of Nós do morro has rarely brought political issues to the front of the stage. The production received attention in the press at the time because of the skill of its presentation and the dedication of the participants, thus beginning a tradition of press articles about the group that contrast the activity of theatre with the media expectations of the *favela*.

The company was eventually required to leave the church where they had established their work and moved to a disused school building. The crumbling edifice offered no protection against the destructive rains that periodically devastate the *favelas* and the building was infested by rats. Guti watched as the members of the company adapted themselves to the environment: 'People become accustomed to shit and learn not to expect better.' So he approached the director of the Colégio Almirante Tamandaré, a school within Vidigal that was still functioning, and asked if they could move in beneath the pillars of the school building that created a natural cavity on the slopes of the hillside. There they stored their materials and built walls to keep out the landslides and the rain. It was this space that would eventually become the 50-seat studio theatre that now bears the name of the company. For the new venue the group developed a project which began as a show for children, mounted every week at 5.00 o'clock in the school playground on a stage constructed from classroom desks. Over the years the hour changed, and the audience on the patio grew to include both adults and children. It was more than just a cultural event; it was a cultural manifestation. The *7 o'clock Show*, which began promptly at 8.00 o'clock every Saturday during 1992–3, calls attention for the scale of its impact and the foundations – both literal and abstract – that it laid. In its final format the show was performed regularly for an audience of more than a thousand people, playing host to visiting groups from the neighbouring *favelas* of Bonsucesso, Nova Iguaçu, Rocinha, Padre Miguel and others.

The format was based on the variety shows that dominate the weekend schedules of most of the Brazilian television channels. Attention was deliberately drawn to the 'borrowed' cultural form in the constant presence of a mock hand-held television camera that accompanied all proceedings. The *7 o'clock Show*, presented by Guti, provided an open space for the various bands that formed part of Vidigal: samba, rap, pagode, rock. People could tell stories, make announcements, celebrate a birthday or make a proposal (social, political or romantic). Music was interspersed with games, competitions, interviews, 5-minute sketches and even advertisements. The audience paid the equivalent of the price of a bottle of beer to enter and won anything from sacks of rice or beans to free haircuts during the show. Apart from the box-office receipts, the future studio theatre was being subsidised with donations of paint and building materials by local businesses that used the show to advertise. It was a performance event that integrated the audience and its performers, attracted young people as well as their parents, made links between commercial and community concerns, and created a stage to make announcements and protests or participate in celebrations. And when the bus companies on which the communities depend for their connection to the city failed to improve the services, it was the *7 o'clock Show* that managed to open up a dialogue that established new practices. The power of live performance was beginning to be felt in ways that few of the initial participants had expected.

Every show had a moment when Guti would call for silence and what he referred to as a 'theatre scene' would be performed. These were frantically improvised in the hours before the show and based on current events, characters, and gossip in the community. The actors that now lead the company reflect on these performances as part of their artistic baptism in a form that demanded instant impact based on acute powers of mimicry and invention. Guti insisted that this was the moment when the audience could not talk. At the beginning people used this opportunity to go to the toilet or to get a drink, but over the two years the public learned the silence and attention that was necessary for the actors to perform. And it is that experience that formed the training of both performer and audience for the work that the company went on to do in the theatre as it took shape in the concrete and crumbling earth beneath the school.

The diminutive studio theatre, with its difficult approach up steps improvised from concrete and tree roots in the hillside behind the school, was inaugurated in 1995 and seats fifty people with a stage of only 5 × 6 metres. The money that was raised by the success of the 7 o'clock show was put towards the construction of the theatre and indicates perhaps where the interest of the company lies. For many popular theatre practitioners and theorists the move probably seems regressive. From large-scale outdoor popular theatre for the crowds, the company moved to a new performance space which was based on an apparently bourgeois model of an indoor theatre, with fixed seating for an audience looking down on a framed stage which, within the economies of scale, kept a distance between the actor and the spectator. And the first play to be performed there made the move seem all the more emphatic as an ornate red velvet curtain was raised to reveal painted Romantic backdrops of nineteenth-century Rio de Janeiro. The play they chose to inaugurate the theatre was *Machadiando* and it has become the work that has given the company its highest profile in the city of Rio and beyond.

Awarded the equivalent of a Brazilian Oscar with the highly prestigious Prêmio Shell in 1996, *Machadiando* (based on three short stories by Machado de Assis) was performed every weekend for more than eighteen months, with periodic breaks for carnival and holidays.[24] The group spent more than a year reading, discussing, adapting this nineteenth-century author who was completely unknown to the actors before Guti proposed the project. No one believed that Vidigal could understand Machado de Assis, let alone present his characters and his tales within the 'morro'. The achievement of the production is not just that the actors managed to read and adapt and present this work but they did so in such a way that the members of the community of Vidigal also came to appreciate and demonstrate their affection for the work of one of Brazil's most distinguished 'classical' authors. The actors, as they speak about the experience today, talk of the personal changes that took place over the two years as they learned to see these characters when they looked at themselves in the mirror. Had they changed the image of their reality or the reality of their image? For Luciana Bezerra, the winning of the Prêmio Shell was like gaining a new identity card and becoming a citizen. As I write now in June 1997 the *Machadiando* is about to come back into the company's repertoire with special performances in the august and presidential splendour of the Museu da República in the centre of the city. 'Lixo' meets 'luxo'.

Bárbara Heliodora, now in her seventies and Brazil's most redoubtable theatre critic, having climbed up to Vidigal for the first time in 1996, wrote a letter to the company in October of that year that expresses something of the bizarre meeting that was taking place in Brazilian theatre; I translate:

> You cannot imagine the pleasure that I had in watching *Machadiando*; your work enchanted me not only for the singularity and sincerity with which you presented the three stories that form the play, but also in the living example you give of the conviction that theatre is a privileged school of citizenship and democracy . . .
>
> To encounter your tiny theatre in the heights of Vidigal, to see all the work that has gone into its construction and the continuity of the productions is a great joy, especially to see work based on Machado de Assis and his era, a delicious way for all those involved to know a little more about Brazil. It seems very wise to me to alternate the consecrated authors of Brazil with new authors that express the reality of the group itself. . . . Congratulations to all those involved in Nós do morro, a reason

for pride for all of us who live in Rio de Janeiro, who generally only hear about things that worry us . . .

The final phrase delicately hides and reveals the real shock of the encounter for all those who live outside of the hillside communities and thus experience the *favela* only through the Brazilian media. The amount of coverage that Nós do morro has received in the press has in itself become a news story. A journalist for a newspaper published by the Brazilian Institute for Youth recently commented that one of the positive results of the group's activities is that it is now easier to find the name of Vidigal in the cultural pages of the city's newspapers than in the pages devoted to crime stories.

Undoubtedly one of the fascinations for journalists who have made it up the hillside of Vidigal to see *Machadiando* since it was first performed is the staging of a seemingly impossible encounter between the two halves of such a divided city. The text of the play is a blend of light romantic comedy and detailed observation of the life and manners of middle-class Rio de Janeiro at the end of the nineteenth century. The actors are young 'favelados' who are separated from the characters they present by almost every imaginable social division. Even the elaborate period costumes they have painstakingly created seem to defy the bodies that wear them. Or perhaps it is the other way round, and the performers' elaborately dressed bodies challenge the social costumes and customs from which they are historically and actually excluded. Boal talks in *Teatro Legislativo* of how we are only able to see 'absence' on the stage. If we use an actual telephone in a scene the audience will not see it, whereas if we represent it with a telephone made from an impossible material, size or colour then the absent real telephone will be seen and registered. At the *Machadiando* it seemed as if we were able to see the absent 'real' of the actors' lives because of the vivid representations of the nineteenth-century bourgeoisie.

How are we to understand the nature of such performances in the context of the questions this collection of essays seek to demand of the act of theatre? Theatre that describes and reveals the social problems of the community seems to fulfil more directly a functional and utilitarian role. The sort of theatre that re-constitutes the immediate world of its performers and its audience is more usually celebrated as

on the negative aspects, it is true that violence and deaths have been a disturbingly regular feature of the 'baile funk'.

*Abalou* does not deal directly with the negative side of the 'baile'. In a way characteristic of all the work of Nós do morro, the company depicts comic and romantic encounters by a set of characters none of whom is totally villainised by the play. But for the actors who play these parts there is a clear distinction between the culture of theatre and the culture of the 'baile'. Luciano, 'funkeiro' in the play and previously in everyday life, described to me graphically the increasingly limiting options that existed for him when he was regularly going to the 'bailes'. The close association of the narcotics trade in the *favelas* with the organisation and running of the 'bailes' means that both the violence and the money of drugs become inseparable from the pleasures of the dance. For Luciano it is the activity of theatre that offers him alternatives. It is once again in the act of doing theatre and not in the noticeable moralising or direct politicising of its message that Nós do morro seeks to make its theatre work.

In the same essay that is quoted at the beginning of this article, Phelan writes about constatives and performatives as parts of language: 'Constatives describe events; performatives enact them. The performative is linguistically distinguished from the constative because within the former the signifier and the referent are mutually enfolded within one another: the signifier performs the referent within the performative *because* the referent is the speech act itself' (p. 16). Performance work that is *about* social problems (for example, life in the *favela*) could be said to describe the event and so the play as written text remains constative. *Abalou* attempts to describe the daily lives of those who perform in and visit their theatre, but it is the performance of it by Nós do morro – an act of faith and a promise – that is the revelation. Its meaning is enacted in the event of utterance that goes beyond the words that are spoken.

At the age of 20 Lúcio Andrey is performing the central role in *Hamlet* for the company, a project that has already begun in workshops[26] but will not finally be performed until 1998. He is both the signifier and also a multiple referent, being, at least, the boy from the *favela*, an actor and a character called Hamlet. Thus he mutually enfolds these meanings – 'the signifier performs the referent within the performative *because* the referent is the speech act itself'. But the multiplicity of these meanings cannot prevent singular readings that might in themselves be said to be mis-readings. Thus the newspapers and the television news that arrive to cover the event of Shakespeare in the *favela* might see only 'the boy from the favela' who has to make up his mind 'to be or not to be a bandit'. They do not see the actor because they imagine that the lines he speaks at any moment are about the 'reality' of a boy from a *favela* (a real that is a fantasy-construction by the media). Nor do they see Lúcio who may or may not have been faced with this imagined dilemma. They do not even see the complexities of the character of Hamlet, but choose to hear only a faint echo of a line they think they know from the play. Only an acknowledgement of the complexity of the multiple referents at the moment of performance offers the possibility of locating the performative nature of this act and the promise it holds for us of a theatre that is at work in complex ways that go beyond a constative act of description.

For some of the performers in the company that act of performance has already brought a different future, as the young actors are sought by television and film directors to take part in 'novelas', mini-series and feature films. Lúcio Andrey has been with the company for more than seven years. He used to play as a junior with the football club Flamengo and began his artistic career because the Brazilian film director Walter Lima Jr needed a boy who could keep a ball up in the air for a film about street children. From that first experience he went on to join Nós do morro, and his father has had to swap his dreams of a son playing football at Maracanã for the realities of his son's career as a rising actor. As a result of his involvement with Nós do morro, over the last two years Lúcio has taken part in three full-length films, four shorts, the soap opera *O Campeão* [*The Champion*] and a mini-series for Globo Television. But there is an irony in this success as Lúcio himself acknowledges:

> Because I live in Vidigal, all the producers think that I can only play bandits. They have to understand that I am not a bandit. I am an actor who lives in Vidigal.[27]

Described variously in the press as the record-holder for playing bandits and the 'campeão de pivete' (champion of young thieves), Lúcio has, in becoming a professional screen actor, begun to play the social roles that he had avoided in his life in the *favela*. And he is not the only one. Nós do morro has been very successful in finding screen and television work for the participants. The achievements of the group and Guti's own professional connections have brought curious directors looking for new actors. This is good money for the actors' families, many of whom were initially sceptical about the worth of the project. Young sons and daughters are often an essential part of the income of the family in these communities and the long hours they spend rehearsing reduces their capacity to be earning elsewhere. Most of them will have had paid work from the age of 9 and still work at some time during the day, hence the necessity of evening rehearsals. Thus the income and the professional experiences they acquire in cinema and television are greatly appreciated, but the young actors will be expected to perform the marginal roles that are associated with every *favelado*: street children, prostitutes, thieves and bandits.

In addition to his acting work, Lúcio is also studying to be a primary school teacher. Four of the most experienced members of Nós do morro now give classes within the company in addition to maintaining their own performance work. They teach new members so that, in Lúcio's words, 'they too can feel capable to be actors or perhaps just to be someone'.[28] A few, like Lúcio, manage to go to acting school if they can win a scholarship to pay the fees. Luciano, another actor with the group who has appeared in numerous films and television series, has now spent a year at CAL, one of Rio de Janeiro's most prestigious acting schools, and recognises the difficulties of the transition. But far from leaving behind his community in order to make the change, he has very much taken it with him and acknowledges that he continues to derive his strength from the work of Nós do morro. He recognises that few of the middle-class students from CAL have the opportunities he has to perform with a group that has its own theatre, doing work that is now very much in the public domain. And he has taken as his professional name, Luciano Vidigal: 'I want to pay homage through the art that I do to this place where I was born and where I live.'[29] The self-definition as actor that has been so powerful for Luciano, Luciana and Lúcio has not been achieved by ignoring the way in which they are named as 'favelados'.

From the hillside of Vidigal these young actors can look down across Ipanema to where Augusto Boal has lived since he returned from exile. Boal justifiably continues to be celebrated as a Brazilian artist of international repute for the work that he has practised and imagined in re-forging the potential interaction of political, personal and artistic lives. His work is valued because it is utilitarian, but it is loved because it promises an heroic vision of what theatre could achieve. Perhaps no less romantic is the story that I have constructed of Nós do morro, but Lúcio and Luciano's stories are only a part of the promise of performance: the 'narrow narrative' that perhaps we would like theatre to deliver for all these participants from Vidigal. There is also the story of Flavinho, who was at the heart of the project for five years, part of the team that hewed the theatre out of the rocks underneath the school. Guti asked him to leave Nós do morro when he discovered that he was also involved with the local drug traffickers.

Throughout the years Guti has kept the company as distant as possible from all contact with the drug trade that controls so much of what happens in the *favelas*. To an outside visitor the sound of gunfire that periodically competes with the animated sounds of the actors at work is usually all that seems to penetrate, without comment, the very real world of illusions that are created in their theatre on the hillside. Three weeks after he was told he had to leave Nós do morro, Flavinho was found dead on a rubbish tip. His body was not discovered for at least three days and only Guti and the other actors were there at the cemetery to bury him. Killed because he was important to someone or perhaps because he was no longer necessary to anyone. To return to Phelan's criteria for Real Love, perhaps here we have a glimpse of a theatre that 'lives and loves and fails and wins and whines in the pressing present'. Flavinho's death is a part of the 'pressing present' in which Nós do morro perform. And it is the failures that reveal the promise of performance.

NOTES

1 From *Rap da Felicidade* [*The Rap of Happiness*], by MC ('Master of Ceremonies') Cidinho and MC Doca, Rio de Janeiro, 1994. Zona Sul is

the southern district of Rio de Janeiro that includes Copacabana
and Ipanema.

2 'Reciting the Citation of Others; or, A Second Introduction', in Linda
Hart and Peggy Phelan, eds., *Acting Out: Feminist Performances*
(University of Michigan Press, 1993), pp. 13–31.

3 *Ibid.*, p. 24.

4 An immaculate phrase conceived by Phelan in the same essay.

5 The word *favela* is not easily rendered in English. Perhaps 'slum' or
'shanty town' are the closest approximations, but both evoke their
own specific image of urban poverty, and *favela* seems the only word
appropriate for these improvised communities that lie outside and inside
so many Latin American cities.

6 Augusto Boal, *Teatro Legislativo: versão beta* (Rio de Janeiro: Civilização
Brasileira, 1996). All quotations are taken from this, the Brazilian edition,
and are given in my own translation. *Legislative Theatre*, translated by
Adrian Jackson, will be published by Routledge in 1998.

7 *Ibid.*, p. 10.

8 See Paul Heritage, 'The Courage to be Happy: Augusto Boal, Legislative
Theatre and the 7th International Festival of the Theatre of the
Oppressed', *TDR* 143 (1994).

9 *Teatro de arena* is the Portuguese phrase used to describe theatre-in-
the-round.

10 Cited on the back cover of Augusto Boal, *Games for Actors and Non-
Actors*, trans. Adrian Jackson (London: Routledge, 1992).

11 The 'jokers' in the classic model of Forum Theatre. It is the name Boal has
used to describe the five members that constitute the Centre of the
Theatre of the Oppressed (CTO) in Rio de Janeiro.

12 Boal, *Teatro Legislativo*, p. 15.

13 See James Thompson, ed., *Perspectives and Practices in Prison Theatre*
(London: Jessica Kingsley Publishers, 1997).

14 *Rap da Felicidade.*

15 Meaning 'Marvellous City'. This is the familiar name by which Rio de
Janeiro is known in Brazil. It is used with irony and affection, enduring in
tourist campaigns and advertisements as well as popular music and poetry.

16 People who live in *favelas.*

17 Paulo Casé, *Favela, Arenas do Rio* (Rio de Janeiro: Relume Dumará,
1996), p. 53.

18 Elin Diamond, ed., *Performance and Cultural Politics* (London:
Routledge, 1996), pp. 196–213.

19 *Ibid.*, p. 196.

20 A form of Brazilian popular music closely related to samba.

21 Nights of funk music at clubs or in halls in the *favelas* and in the more
peripheral areas of the city. For the description and history of 'baile funks'

I am indebted to Hernano Vianna, *O mundo funk carioca* (Rio de Janeiro: Jorge Zahar, 1997 (second edition)), and the account given to me in personal testimony by Luciano Vidigal.

22  Personal interview with the author, 28 June 1997.

23  Guti Fraga, second section, *O Globo* (23 July 1987), 2.

24  *Machadiando* is almost impossible to translate. It is created from the name of the author, Machado de Assis, who wrote the three stories on which the play is based. The literal translation might be something like 'Machado-ing', giving the idea that the group is not so much 'doing' Machado de Assis as 'being' Machado de Assis.

25  A word used to describe a person, feature or thing that comes from Rio de Janeiro.

26  Including a series of workshops in April 1997 given by Cicely Berry, OBE (Voice Director of the Royal Shakespeare Company) during a visit sponsored by the British Council.

27  Lúcio Andrey, *Jornal do Brasil B* (1 April 1997), 1.

28  Personal interview (2 July 1997).

29  Personal interview (2 July 1997).

# 10 Making America or making revolution: the theatre of Ricardo Halac in Argentina

GEORGE WOODYARD

In the twentieth century the balance between democracy and military dictatorship in Argentina has been precarious at best. John Simpson and Jana Bennett, writing in *The Disappeared*, report that 'between 1930, when the military first intervened in government in Argentina, and the overthrow of Isabelita Perón in 1976, there had been six coups and 21 years of military dictatorship'.[1] In that 36-year period, only one civilian administration lasted for a full term. That Buenos Aires, a city that is strikingly beautiful and essentially European in its ambiance, should be subject to such political vagaries is one of the ironies of the western hemisphere. Since the nineteenth century a great number of essays, novels and plays have dealt with the whimsies of Argentine politics, including the famous treatise of Domingo Faustino Sarmiento, *Civilización o barbarie o vida de Juan Facundo Quiroga* (1845), which pointed to the root problem in reflecting the bloody dictatorship of Juan Manuel de Rosas from 1835 to 1852 with its legacy of exiles and political murders. The massive European migrations of the late nineteenth century, however, invoked a new and promising image of seemingly unlimited land and opportunity. As millions of Italians, Spanish, Germans and other nationality groups flooded into Argentina, nearly dwarfing the existing population, the ethnic, linguistic and cultural mixture produced an inordinately rich potential for economic growth and development. Regrettably, the political stability that could have supported such expansion failed to develop at the same pace, and violent changes in the government came to characterise the twentieth century as well. Various excellent histories of Argentina document the period in detail, so the focus here will be the relationship between periods of major social upheaval and the Argentine writers and artists, in particular Ricardo Halac, who confronted and interpreted myriad arbitrary governmental decisions and processes.

In the first years of the twentieth century, the so-called 'Golden Decade', Florencio Sánchez (born in Uruguay in 1875) developed an important new theatre that reflected the concerns of a people in the midst of massive social and economic change. His *Barranca abajo* [*Down the Gully*, 1905] set a pattern of realistic portrayals with facile psychology that was to characterise the Argentine/River Plate theatre for twenty years. In 1930 the social protest theatre of Leónidas Barletta and his Teatro del Pueblo (People's Theatre) with its leftist political orientation opened a new line of independent theatre activity. David William Foster has observed that the 'Barletta group was not . . . just another theatre that would attempt to produce experimental or avant-garde plays outside the professional network . . .'. One of its major goals, he points out, was 'to take the theatre outside its upper-middle class context to the people'. This movement coincided with the national bankruptcy produced by the world-wide 1929 financial crisis and the incapacity of President Irigoyen to govern, leading to the military coup of José F. Uriburu in 1930. Foster notes that the period of independent theatre continued until the mid-1950s, and that 'Barletta and his colleagues were eminently successful, so much so that to this day Argentine theatre remains one of the most innovative and exciting national dramatic movements in Latin America and probably the world.'[2]

The generation of writers, and especially the playwrights who emerged in the late 1950s and early 1960s, shouldered the burden of resisting where possible the injustices of a system gone wrong. Whereas the nineteenth-century migrations offered the promise of a great nation-state, by the end of the Second World War, with the United States having replaced Great Britain as the world power, Argentina was clearly on a downward slide. Most of the playwrights born to this generation – such as Roberto Cossa, Osvaldo Dragún, Griselda Gambaro, Ricardo Halac, Eduardo Pavlovsky and Ricardo Talesnik – found themselves denouncing injustices while advocating processes of social and political change. The result, needless to say, was the frequent clash between government policies and writers of the committed left.

One of the important playwrights to confront the issues of this generation is Ricardo Halac, born in 1935 to immigrant parents from

Damascus. His grandparents were Sephardic Jews from Syria, Turkey and Morocco. Halac studied economics at the University of Buenos Aires but left without completing the degree. His models were Marx, Shakespeare as seen through Bertolt Brecht, and Arthur Miller. His objective, from the beginning, was to reach his audience with a message that it was necessary to denounce and resist an unjust society. As a political activist he was committed to raising the level of consciousness within the general public. His work, and his art, were designed to serve a political objective, to work against the decadence within a country that had great potential. His early plays, written between the fall of Perón (1955) and the birth of the Cuban Revolution (1959), were designed, in his words, to 'make America' (which was failing) and to 'make revolution' (which was spreading).[3]

With the collapse of the government of Juan Domingo Perón in 1955 and his subsequent exile to Madrid, the country embarked on a new wave of frenetic political activity. In 1961 Ricardo Halac opened the path for the new generation in Argentina with *Soledad para cuatro* [*Solitude for Four*],[4] the work that is normally cited as the first in the neo-realistic aesthetic (or 'realismo reflexivo', as it is generally known in Argentina).[5] With some resonance of *Death of a Salesman* (1949) by Arthur Miller and *El puente* [*The Bridge*, 1949] by Carlos Gorostiza, this play captured the essence of a generation suffering from the moral bankruptcy and the identity crisis brought on by massive social, economic and political upheavals.[6] One of the theatres rejected his early work, Halac says, because, 'although it criticised reality, it was pessimistic and it did not speak of the youth that wanted to change the future'. At this point, Halac found himself to be more in tune with the Peronista left than with the Communist Party, even though it was a less revolutionary position, as his colleagues and critics observed. The leftist *peronistas* were primarily workers operating with the original people's organisations rather than adhering to the theoretical models imposed by the dogmatic left. Nevertheless, his work was closely observed by the military, which was ever vigilant in considering him and his colleagues to be dangerous to the national welfare.

By 1966 the nation was caught again in the dictatorship of General Juan Carlos Onganía (1966–9), who began the practice of 'black lists' that precluded many writers, musicians and other artists from working in any form of mass communication or in official theatres. Halac found that it was possible to deceive the Onganía dictatorship with pseudonyms that everyone knew. The Onganía period gave rise to armed organisations ('against the violence of the dictatorship it is necessary to respond with more violence'), thus creating the setting for Perón's return. Perón's return from exile in 1973 was clouded by an episode at Ezeiza, the international airport, just minutes before his plane was to land, when members of the right wing ambushed and killed several left-wing supporters on the speakers' platform. The episode was grimly prophetic of the deep divisions within Peronism which was, curiously, never a political party but rather a political movement.[7] The violence that erupted in Buenos Aires during the early 1970s, the radicalism of the Montonero guerrillas, the ineffectiveness of the government in dealing with terrorism and hyper-inflation, were but a few of the factors that set the stage for the disorder that ensued following Perón's death in 1974 and during the several disastrous months that Isabelita Perón, his wife and vice-president, managed to hold on after acceding to the presidency.

Ricardo Halac, disenchanted with the Communist Party because of its dogmatic stance, sought in Peronism an identity with the Argentine popular classes. The influence of Mao, Che Guevara and Castro incited the leftists to seek from Perón certain revolutionary concessions that he was not disposed to grant. Perón's decision to abandon the radical left in a public ceremony in the now-infamous Plaza de Mayo on May Day, 1974, in which he hurled insults at the chanting Montoneros,[8] set the stage for the violence to come. Perón's death just months later unleashed a blood-bath that was to culminate under Videla. Until then, except on sporadic occasions, the intellectuals and artists had not been attacked physically. When the ominous Triple A appeared, commanded by José López Rega, Perón's lackey and now the *eminence grise* of Isabelita, the new president, it carried out assassinations on the street and often sent ironic ultimatums to its victims. In April 1975, the Triple A threw out flyers downtown with a list of playwrights, directors and actors who were warned to leave the country within 48 hours, accused of a presumed 'Judeo-Marxist conspiracy'. If not, they would be assassinated. The event had enormous repercussions. On the list, among others, was the name of Ricardo Halac.

When he ignored the order, he received repeated death threats. At that point Halac had staged four original works, two very successful adaptations (Brendan Behan's *The Hostage* (1967) and *ShowBrecht* (1969) with fragments of Brecht's plays and a character, Brecht himself, who provided the transitions and spoke to the public), and some short theatre pieces that he had made for television, *A Night with the Great*, along with other writers such as Carlos Somigliana and Roberto Cossa. For the first time fully aware of the range of responses that a text can produce, Halac left the country for a time, and began to reflect seriously on the implications of violence.

Nevertheless, Halac returned in 1976, thinking 'ingenuously,' as he says, that the country would not end up in another dictatorship. But conditions were ripe for yet another military take-over, this one even more insidious and brutal than before. Between 1976 and the return of the democratic state in 1983, following the disastrous Falklands War (in Spanish, 'la Guerra de las Malvinas'), approximately 30,000 persons died and/or disappeared, victims of the witch-hunts of a psychotic and paranoid military establishment bent on brutalising, terrorising and exterminating anyone considered a threat to its control. During the worst years many of the intellectual class fled the country, seeking refuge, ironically, in Spain in the aftermath of the repressive Franco dictatorship which had finally ended in 1975.

Halac staged his new play, *Segundo tiempo* [*Second Time*], in 1976, a few months after the military coup. The lead actor, Luis Brandoni, was returning from forced exile in Mexico. *La Opinión*, then the most prestigious paper in Buenos Aires, carried two reviews of the play three days apart, an unprecedented action that revealed the confusion of the time. For the paper's regular critic, Halac had preferred 'not to explore the mythical essence of the Argentine couple – the only way to explain their problems and to bring them to an intuitive revelation – but rather to stay within national folklore'. The second critic, on the other hand, wrote: 'under the rubric of a matrimonial classic, *Segundo tiempo* is a political piece. In the debate over the role of man and woman in the nuclear family, there is a pathetic portrait of our political reality.' (*La Opinión*, 26 July 1976, carried both reviews in a weekly edition.) This dichotomy revealed the difficulties presented by a new theatrical vision.

Halac premiered *El destete* in 1978, a title that means 'weaning' in English and that has obvious social connotations.[9] The play smacks of an Alan Ayckbourn farce for its mistaken identities, games, stories and inventions (*à la Noises Off*). A crisis is precipitated when a frivolous afternoon turns into a comedy of errors. Two sets of parents descend unannounced on the room in an old house that two single fellows share, exactly when one of them has brought home a woman for some sexual playtime. The ensuing antics of dodging in and out of different rooms, inventing stories and situations and trying to disguise the escapade, has serious overtones with analogies to Argentina's political crisis. The two young men attempt to prove to the parents that they have settled down to a responsible life. The parents reveal their own frustrations and disappointments, as well as their illusions of establishing new relationships with the woman's baby, the 'grandchild' who for them represents a promise as yet unfulfilled.

Ironically the play depends on a homeless single mother to give the two young men the respectability and social approval they want and need from their parents. It is equally ironic that the older generation desperately seeks to salvage its own misguided parenting tactics by 'adopting' the infant. In the final analysis the young people play the stronger card as they attempt to handle their new *ménage-à-trois* relationship in a way that will provide for everyone's needs. In the disastrous years of the Proceso (Argentina's 'Dirty War'), the play shows the fragility of human relationships, the desperation of unsettled lives, the psychological introspection of people's needs and the extremes to which they will go in order to find satisfaction within a changing social fabric. Under the superficial guise of an outrageous farce, the play masks core problems within the country, expressing in humorous terms what it was not possible to say on stage during a period of repressive censorship.

In 1981 Osvaldo Dragún (*b.* 1929), an active supporter of the Cuban Revolution who has spent many years outside of Argentina, launched a bold experiment known as Teatro Abierto [Open Theatre]. The project involved twenty-one playwrights who wrote short plays and the twenty-one directors who staged them, three a night, seven nights a week, in the Picadero Theatre. When the theatre was soon mysteriously torched, it only inflamed the determination of the group to proceed, and within days the project resumed at the Teatro Tabaris. Although the experience was repeated in subsequent years, its momentum and its cause were lost when the country returned to democratic rule. This theatre project, openly critical of the Argentine government, served in a sense as a foretaste of the democracy to come.

Halac was in the vanguard of the Teatro Abierto movement with a play titled *Lejana tierra prometida* [*Far Promised Land*], the first Argentine play to feature the Mothers of the Plaza de Mayo.[10] This frontal attack on a system run amuck is a combination of biblical motifs, Argentine tango and national politics. Halac depends on haunting images of different generations to construct a vision of a troubled society. The play addresses the end of an illusion: the three central figures are the children of immigrants who want to escape, to cross the ocean in search of happiness and justice in another land. In addition, three strange *viejas*, women who have lost their sons to a remorseless society, commingle the compassion of grieving, desperate mothers with the surreal qualities of ethereal beings who hover, mostly unseen and in a timeless dimension, over and around the other figures whose lives have been irreparably damaged by this hostile society. As a potent political play with a strong message about the incivility of the military regime in Argentina during the Proceso, the text hides effectively behind an allegorical façade with biblical overtones. The three individuals appear as pilgrims, virtually in search of a holy mission to find their 'promised land'. During an indefinite time period, punctuated by occasional blackouts, they conjure up images of a place bordered by Switzerland, France and Italy that has mythical dimensions because no photographs or actual reports exist. Ana's pregnancy gives a tenor of hope and illusion for the future to their projected journey, although, as in the case of Jesus, the identity of the father is uncertain. The first reference to food on this allegorical journey is an apple, the symbol of mankind's fall from grace in the Garden of Eden. The sons of the three *viejas* are Francisco, Bertito and Abel, the last a name that resounds of biblical hatred, anger, jealousy and greed, characteristics of the military regime. The central theme of travel to the new land is itself subject to an element of chance, almost like casting lots, as they attempt to settle the privilege of going to the proverbial land of 'lette e miele' (milk and honey). The *viejas*, invisible throughout the early part of the play

while lamenting their own lost children, penetrate Ana's consciousness when she tries to kill her own child. They try to animate her when
she perceives her unborn son to be dead or dying, that is, without future
or hope in this condemned land. From that point forward, the *viejas*
take an active, committed role in defence of Ana and the promise she
carries for the future. Osvaldo's admonition that they must leave 'without looking back' echoes God's injunction to Lot to leave the condemned cities of Sodom and Gomorrah without concern for the past.
The metaphysical dimensions of the play, reinforced by selections from
Walt Whitman's poetry with their soaring qualities, are graphically
repeated in the toy glider that the two men take along as a diversion,
a referent of the longing for an unfettered spirit capable of transcend-
ing the vicissitudes of their daily existence. In his perceptive article,
Miguel Angel Giella explains the significance of the title as a fortuitous
combination of 'lejana tierra mía' (my far-away land), a venerable tango
of Alfredo Le Pera and Carlos Gardel, with 'tierra prometida' (promised
land), for its biblical and mythical qualities.

*Lejana tierra prometida* is one of the most significant plays
within the context of the Teatro Abierto, and the Argentine theatre of
the period, for Halac's perceptiveness in incorporating the Madres de la
Plaza de Mayo, a phenomenon that produced an international discourse
about the horrors of the Argentine Dirty War. As Diana Taylor has
noted in her book *Disappearing Acts*:

> The Madres, a group of nonpolitical women, organised one of
> the most visible and original resistance movements to a brutal
> dictatorship in the twentieth century . . . The terrifying
> scenario in which the Madres felt compelled to insert
> themselves was organised and maintained around a highly
> coercive definition of the feminine and motherhood which the
> women simultaneously exploited and attempted to subvert.
> The spectacular nature of their movement, which cast the
> 'Mother' in a central role, inspired and influenced numerous
> other political women's groups throughout Latin America, the
> United States, the Middle East, and Eastern Europe.[11]

This unique reference within the Teatro Abierto movement not only
recognised the stature and nature of the phenomenon taking place in

the Plaza de Mayo, but surely contributed as well to fostering its importance within artistic circles and to ensuring its dignity and its enduring
legacy. A good example of the horror of the time is the Pietà of the
Argentine sculptress Beatriz Orosco where the Holy Mother is holding
. . . nothing. She does not know if her son has died or not. He has simply
disappeared.

The Teatro Abierto struggled to survive in subsequent years, but
the movement had already begun to falter even before democracy was
restored. Osvaldo Dragún renewed the effort in 1982 with mediocre
results. For the 1983 project, Halac wrote *Ruido de rotas cadenas* [*The
Sound of Broken Chains*], a farce that provides an exquisite parody of
the justice system in Argentina.[12] The innocent trappings of the office
of a Justice of the Peace provide the setting for a walk through a surreal
encounter with marginalised people such as a pregnant bride, a prostitute, an incontinent grandfather, and other dysfunctional individuals.
The play sets up a dichotomy between people of different classes,
people in the mainstream and people on the fringe. Taken as a line from
the Argentine national anthem, the title exacerbates the irony of the
situation:

> Oíd mortales el grito sagrado
> 'libertad, libertad, libertad!'
> Oíd el ruido de rotas cadenas
> Ved el trono a la noble igualdad . . .
>
> (Hear, o mortals, the sacred cry
> 'Liberty, liberty, liberty!'
> Hear the sound of broken chains
> See the throne of noble equality . . . )

Halac's portrait of a society struggling with its marginalised element
continues to underscore the imbalances and the inequities that he personally found offensive and in need of redress. Far from having shaken
off its repressive chains, the people are still, in his dramatic vision, victims of an unjust state.

In 1983 Halac set off, unintentionally, a social panic. At that
moment the country was emerging from the Dirty War and people
were terrified that the military might return to power. In *Coup d'Etat*,
a made-for-TV show, Halac and his colleague Cernadas Lamadrid

imagined a new coup that was aborted through the combined efforts of a democratic citizenry. The show began with music and a voice that brought sad memories to the Argentines: a military march that interrupted radio and television programming with an official communiqué announcing the suspension of constitutional guarantees and the closing of Parliament. Given its importance, one of the radio stations in Buenos Aires recorded the beginning of the programme and broadcast it the next morning. Thousands of persons heard it in their homes and in their cars on the way to work, and nearly panicked because they did not realise it was fictitious. This South American version of the episode created by Orson Welles revealed once again Halac's constant effort to awaken and motivate a population gone astray.

Halac again challenged the system with another political action play, written after the return to democracy – *Viva la anarquía* [*Long live anarchy*].[13] Premièred in 1992 in the Enrique Santos Discépolo Theatre, it reveals the concerns that Halac had been expressing for years about the Argentine government. Without establishing an exact date, the play celebrates the legacy that the old anarchists passed to later generations. From a technical perspective it turns out to be one of Halac's most provocative plays because of the intervention of a dead man throughout the course of the dramatic action. The play considers the lasting question of the conditions imposed by parents on their children and the children's ubiquitous search for their own identity. As noted in the programme commentary, it is a question of 'las ideas de la utopía desacreditada y anacrónica y la distopía de la represión, el encierro y el racismo, casi como emblemas de esta época de asedio' (the ideas of a discredited utopia and the dystopia of repression, confinement and racism, almost as emblems of this age of siege).[14] The situation is bound up in the formation of the unions at the end of the nineteenth century following the models offered by, among others, Mikhail Aleksandrovich Bakunin (1814–76), a Russian revolutionary who strongly opposed Marx. His anarchist notions of opposition to capitalist systems gave rise to a turbulent dichotomy between the working classes and the imposing oligarchy of Argentina. Herein lay the seeds of the radical divisions within the governmental system of Argentina in subsequent years.

Bakunin found himself in a paradoxical situation. In order to implement abolishing the state, he had to create a secret organisation that was virtually tantamount to a repressive dictatorship. He believed passionately that a world in which the workers controlled the means of production and shared equally in the benefits was an ideal state. Besides, he recognised that the fertile ground for the implementation of these ideas was not to be found in the industrial states but rather in underdeveloped countries where the worker had nothing to lose. In contrast with Marx, who supported revolution among the industrial classes, Bakunin believed strongly in an investment strategy for the most dispossessed, marginal classes. If a man has a house and a job, however poor and miserable they are, they can temper his commitment to full involvement. Many of the urban terrorists of the twentieth century, especially in Latin America and the United States (as, for example, Patty Hearst, Eldridge Cleaver and others), found inspiration in the writings of Bakunin. Bakunin hated the Germans and also the Jews and therefore expressed his contempt for the opinions of Marx, who was both. Bakunin and his compatriot Kropotkin had an enormous influence during the years the unions were being formed, as the following note indicates:

> Tras las incipientes tentativas de organización gremial de los
> años 1870 (La Unión Tipográfica fue fundada en 1878 y a ese
> año pertenece también su primera huelga), se crea en 1885 la
> Internacional de Carpinteros y comienza a expandirse en el Río
> de la Plata el movimiento anarquista, que tiene especial arraigo
> entre los trabajadores de origen inmigratorio pero también entre
> los criollos. . . . En noviembre de 1902 se produce la primera
> gran huelga general, y como respuesta a las movilizaciones y
> acciones anarquistas el gobierno aprueba la Ley 4144, llamada
> 'de residencia', que permite la expulsión inmediata de los
> extranjeros considerados 'indeseables'. El anarquismo o
> libertarismo rioplatense, heredero en lo esencial de la línea
> colectivista inspirada por Bakunin y Kropotkin, proclamaba
> la anulación del Estado, la asociación libre de los trabajadores,
> la posesión colectiva de los medios de producción, y la

organización revolucionaria (destinada a concretar la utopía de la Revolución).

(In Argentina following the incipient efforts to organise the unions in the 1870s . . . , the International Carpenters Union was founded in 1885 and the anarchist movement, with its special appeal to the immigrant workers but also to the native population, began to expand in the River Plate area . . . In November 1902 the first great general strike took place, and as a response to the anarchist movement and action, the government approved Law 4144, called 'residency', which permitted the immediate expulsion of strangers considered 'undesirable'. The River Plate anarchism or libertarianism, heir essentially to the collective line inspired by Bakunin and Kropotkin, proclaimed the abolition of the State, the free association of the workers, collective possession of means of production and a revolutionary organisation destined to concretise the utopia of the Socialist Revolution . . . )[15]

The importance of Bakunin in Argentine politics is evident in the writing of Juan Domingo Perón, twice president of Argentina. Commenting on the national and international forces that impacted on Argentina while he was himself formulating his own doctrines, he summarised Bakunin's politics in the following words:

Miguel Bakunín (1814–1876), que fue durante más de cuarenta años jefe del anarquismo internacional, sostiene la necesidad de la desaparición del Estado y de la autoridad, ya que, por el solo hecho de ser impuesta, cuando ordena el bien, éste se convierte en mal, pues el bien no se hace porque se recibe una orden, sino porque se lo desea, porque se lo ama. En otra parte afirma que la autoridad es siempre despotismo, de ahí que el error de las revoluciones consista en destruir gobiernos para reemplazarlos por otros. La abolición del Estado y de la propiedad privada, sostiene Bakunín, abrirá las puertas a la constitución de federaciones de hombres libres e iguales, supremo ideal.

(Miguel Bakunin (1814–1876), who was for more than 40 years the head of the international anarchist movement, insists on the disappearance of the State and authority, since, merely because it is imposed, when it orders good, this becomes bad, since good is not done because one receives an order but because one desires it, because one loves it. In another place he affirms that authority is always despotism, from which the error of revolutions consists in destroying governments to replace them with others. The abolition of the State and of private property, Bakunin maintains, will open doors to the creation of federations of free and equal men, the supreme ideal.)

Perón immediately voiced his scepticism and took exception to these idealistic concepts of Bakunin and others by alleging as follows:

> Al pedir la abolición del Estado entran en el terreno de la fantasía, que no conduce a ninguna parte; mejor dicho, que conduce a cualquier parte. A los individualistas los condujo a convertirse en soportes del Estado totalitario; a los colectivistas, en sostén de la dictadura del proletariado, es decir, que ambos grupos pasaron de la negación del Estado a ser tributarios de las formas más violentas del mismo.

> (On asking for the abolition of the State they enter into a fantasy land which leads to nowhere; better said, which leads to everywhere. The individualists were led to convert to supporters of a totalitarian state; the collectivists, to support the dictatorship of the proletariat, that is, both groups went from denying the State to being contributors to the most violent forms of it.)[16]

In *Viva la anarquía* Halac incorporates a central character who believes fervently in the concepts of terrorism in order to carry out his plan to abolish the state. He believes that the end justifies the means, and he is capable of throwing bombs as a physical manifestation of his socio-political beliefs. While others keep trying to bury Simón, the old Russian Jew and proponent of anarchism, he insists on taking part in all the activities.

Halac feels no aesthetic obligation to explain the intervention of a dead person in the dramatic action. Instead of remaining silent, a cold and inanimate object at his own wake, the character participates actively with his friends/collaborators and with the members of his family in the creation of his own history. In a long act without marked scene divisions, the focus is on the walk to the cemetery interrupted by flashbacks. Although dead, Simón functions as a normal person, getting on and off the tram that carries him to Chacarita (the common cemetery in Buenos Aires, in contrast to the Recoleta, its more exclusive counterpart), at times obeying but generally ignoring the petitions of his son Nicolás who insists on burying him. They even play games with the father hiding behind the markers when the 'cosacos/policías' are looking for him. When at last they get permission to inter him, a fine snow falls – an unusual meteorological event in Buenos Aires – in homage to his native St Petersburg, while the old companions surround him singing 'children's songs that reveal different countries of origin' (18).

Simón arrived from Russia with preconceived concepts and attempted to impose his doctrines on Argentina, resorting to violence when it served his purposes. An unsavoury and abusive character, the wife-beating Simón caused his family to suffer physical deprivations – lack of food and heat – which mitigated the allure of anarchy as a way of life. His determination to tear the system apart left Simón and his family dependent on friends and neighbours to provide even basic creature and cultural comforts. In one sense, they appear committed to trying to 'avenge here what they suffered there' (10), a reference to the terrible conditions in Mother Russia that were duplicated in Argentina. In spite of everything, Simón keeps repeating throughout the play the familiar refrain, 'Viva la anarquía!' The one scene in which he shows his wife some tenderness and love stands in stark contrast to the standard portrayal of this rough and violent character. His strongly accented use of language opens up possible discriminatory attitudes among his circle of contacts.

The political legacy of the play is represented proportionately by Simón's two children: his daughter, who totally adopted her father's concepts: '. . . ahora vislumbro la vida que me espera. Una vida de lucha, de amarguras, de persecuciones, pero también de esperanzas. La vida que yo elegí. Que aprendí de vos, papá' (I glimpse the life that awaits me. A life of struggle, of bitterness, of persecutions, but also of hope. The life that I selected. Which I learned from you, papá) (18), *vis-à-vis* the son, who systematically rejected everything that his father represented, electing to become a lawyer and member of the bourgeoisie. Working and studying hard in order to accomplish his goals, persevering in the face of hardships, 'having burned my eyelashes' (14), his is a clear contrast to the path advocated by his father and his collaborator friends. The latter, in the final analysis, are few (notable by their absence from the wake) and function essentially as a Greek chorus, echoing the revolutionary and anarchical expressions. Only at the very end, when they bury Simón, does Nicolás admit a bit of pride in his father and he accepts the notion of 'putting a little anarchy into my life' (17). The 'making of America' or the 'making of a revolution' is ultimately a question of ethics on both sides; do the ends justify the means?

The work in its entirety is eloquent testimony to the incapacity of the Argentine people to cohere around a workable political system after more than a century of effort. The strongest aspects are the arbitrariness, the lack of unity, the divisions of opinion that produce factionalism and the constant tendency toward anarchy. In the play, when suddenly four uniformed men enter, it is not immediately clear whether they are 'cosacos' or Argentine police (14). Not only is this failure to recognise one's own reality symptomatic of personal and national objectives, but also it reflects the tendency to blame others instead of accepting responsibility for one's own actions. At times the play strikes a balance between destructive and constructive systems, between the anarchist viewpoint and that of the bourgeois capitalist. The bipolar legacy is, Halac contends, a characteristic of the Argentine political system which has driven it into confusion and ineptitude. Simón, for all his faults, is at times violent and other times compassionate, symbolic of the bifurcation in the state processes, but firmly committed to the destruction of the capitalist structure in order to achieve total freedom.

Halac's crusade to denounce injustice took yet another turn with *Mil años, un día* [*A Thousand Years, A Day*], a play with the alternate title of *La cabala y la cruz* [*The Cabala and The Cross*].[17] Commissioned in 1986 by the youth group of the Sociedad Hebraica Argentina, it was revived and published in 1992 as a part of the quincentennial celebrations in the Americas, with a view from the other side. In the late fifteenth century, Spain was the only multicultural and multiracial country in all of Europe. With the defeat of the Moors at Granada in January 1492, the final chapter was complete in the re-conquest of the Iberian peninsula after 800 years of Moorish occupation. Exulting in victory, Ferdinand and Isabella stepped up their campaign against the Jews, the other perceived threat to their Catholic kingdom. The Jews had served Spain and its monarchs well, providing an active commercial class and an educated elite for many administrative posts, but inevitably their wealth and power had created jealousy and hatred. The Spanish Inquisition under the inquisitor general Torquemada unleashed a reign of terror not dissimilar to the pogroms of later eras. By signing the order to expel the Jews from Spain in March of the same year, the Spanish monarchs not only set the stage for a period of tremendous suffering and pain to be inflicted on the long-time Jewish population within Spain but, ironically, they also set the stage for the commercial demise of the empire, in spite of the tremendous riches from the New World, as the country fell prey to German and Italian financiers.

The play investigates the question of what happens to a community when one sector of its population suffers discrimination because of an authoritarian decree. Halac's play focuses on Dr Isaac Levy, personal physician to Queen Isabel. A fictitious character, Dr Levy functions within this historical setting as the Queen's doctor and confidant, a position from which he was well situated to exercise influence over the decisions made by the royal court. Instead, in Halac's interpretation, he abdicated his responsibilities in key moments, which led to the catastrophic decree. Halac's own childhood memories include one that he relates as follows:

> En lo personal, el tema me corroe desde los diez años. Desde un día de 1945 en que viajaba en un tranvía junto a mi padre; que desplegó el diario para leelo, como era su costumbre, y descubrió atónito la información de que los aliados habían encontrado campos de concentración y crematorios en Alemania. La congoja de mi padre fue inmensa. Se puso a llorar en el tranvía, y tomando de la mano a ese desconcertado niño – su hijo – le dijo: 'Tenés que estar preparado, querido . . . a los judíos de pronto nos echan y nos tenemos que ir a vivir a otra parte'.

(Personally this is a theme that has been eating on me since
I was ten years old, ever since the day in 1945 in which I was
riding the streetcar with my father, who opened the newspaper,
as was his custom, and discovered to his horror the information
that the Allies had found concentration camps and crematoria
in Germany. My father was overcome by grief. He started to
cry on the streetcar, and taking the hand of this befuddled child
– his son – he said: 'You have to be prepared, my boy . . . all of a
sudden they throw us Jews out and we have to go live in another
place.')[18]

Halac himself confesses to having experienced anti-semitism
as a child in school when the Jewish children were obligated to study
'morals' during the time other children had classes in religion. The
military regime of the time was nationalistic, and many of the officials were pro-Nazi. One day when he could not go out because of the
weather, he heard the story of the passion of Christ in a version specially prepared for children which ascribed Jesus's death to the Jews.
Halac reports that 'todas las miradas de mis compañeros convergieron
hacia mí. Ese día tuve la vaga sensación de lo que es sentirse culpable
de un crimen' (all my classmates stared at me. That day I had a vague
feeling of what it is like to feel guilty of a crime).[19]

The action of *Mil años, un día* is located in three places: the
personal quarters of the Queen, the Levy house, and the cemetery.
Although there are moments of happiness, with hope for the future,
the play as a whole is deeply disturbing, dealing with feelings of loss and
mandatory separation. Dr Levy himself is a weak individual, incapable
of dealing with his family, unable to believe what is happening to his
people, and inept at changing the course of history. All the characters
have symbolic functions, especially in regard to the family dynamics
under the tension of supporting or opposing decisions to convert and
stay, or to depart with dignity. In contrast to the Christian cross, the
*cabala* imparts an air of magic and chance, of mystery and secrecy, as
those impugned seek answers in the cards marked with mystic signs,
the numbers and letters of the ancient and esoteric interpretation of the
Hebrew Scriptures. Ultimately, the search is for an answer to the ubiquitous persecution, the arbitrary decisions, the injustice and corruption

of the governing system that impacts directly, and often with deadly consequences, on the governed. The play is intimately connected, in a metaphorical dimension, with the terror and oppression that came to dominate the contemporary Argentine situation. Nora Glickman's excellent study that precedes the published edition gives special emphasis to the Jewish elements within the work, especially with comments on the function of the *shofar*, and others.

Considering Halac's trajectory within the Argentine theatre and his involvement with the political process, it is no surprise that his early works showed the same level of commitment to improving Argentine society. His first petit-bourgeois plays cannot be explained without reference to the intersection of the two myths mentioned earlier: making America, and making revolution. Halac was a product of the middle class, the same as his public. *Tentempié II* (the title refers to a puppet that bounces back to its feet when knocked down) for example, denounced the petit-bourgeois who claims to want change but nevertheless loves his luxuries.[20] While the earlier plays were less politicised, they provide excellent insights into Argentine character and ambiance of the period. *Segundo tiempo* [*The Second Time*, 1978][21] established a provocative early commentary on the women's rights movement in a country better known for its *machista* attitudes. The central female character who abandons her husband and the boredom of a sterile marriage where she feels trapped presage a woman who finds self-realisation and an ability to deal with her husband on new (her) terms. Even minimal employment outside the home provides a sense of self-value that transcends the 'sex-object cum domestic servant' image and provides the escape valve necessary to salvage the marriage. In this case family dynamics are bound up in sexual needs and satisfactions, an intervening and destructive mother-in-law, and societal pressures that militate against women's rights. That Halac, a male writer of Argentina, would select a theme that presents an enlightened and positive attitude toward equality for women at a relatively early date is yet another indication of his willingness to challenge the system, whether on political, social or gender issues.

Also antedating Teatro Abierto is *Un trabajo fabuloso* [*A Fabulous Job*, 1980], written during the fractious years of the military repression.[22] If transvestitism has become a commonplace in the theatre in recent years, it offered a challenge to an Argentine public at that point. While the play offers both situational and linguistic humour, typical of a cross-dressing situation, its basic premise is not at all humorous. The father in a conventional family, desperate for employment, 'becomes' a woman prostitute in order to cater to American tourists on holiday, and then he dies. In the venerable tradition of the Argentine grotesque, the extreme behaviour within extreme circumstances propel him, victimised by society, family and friends, into becoming a victim of his own delusions. Metaphorically emasculated, he struggles valiantly to maintain his dignity within a basically hopeless situation.

The play was not understood at the time of its première (1980) during the years of the repression, but in retrospect its meaning and function have become clear. The techniques of the play involve role switching, code switching, the grotesque, the characters' ability to deal with the unexpected and the factor of surprise. Although the play has many characters, and the purpose is not to develop them all, the focus on the central father figure underscores the irony of sacrificing his dignity (by becoming a woman) in order to salvage his dignity (of being the provider for his family). The suggestion of homosexuality in the cross-dressing falls to the counter-offensive of the son's Macho Bar, a site designed to idolise virility. The humour, though, is mitigated by the pathos of desperate characters, clinging to a shred of decency, struggling for some level of understanding. Even though the father dies at the end, the mother not only asserts his identity but she reaffirms his essence. During a time of ignominious change, it was difficult, both within this play and within the larger context of the society, to maintain one's sense of value as an individual. The exaggeration within the title, 'A Fabulous Job', underscores the use of parody in a postmodernist vein. It is significant that the officials of the influential Security Union who had been invited to see the performance contracted with Halac to give classes in one of their schools. Halac, who was blacklisted until 1982, found a way to earn a living and also to learn, from the inside, the workings of the powerful Argentine union that had grown from the time of the first Perón regime to become a part of the power structure.

In 1984 the by now nearly defunct Teatro Abierto called together fifteen authors to write very short plays (four pages) under the rubric, the 'Teatro Abierto Considers Freedom'. Although the works were completed, the project was suspended. Halac's entry was *El dúo Sosa-Echagüe* [*The Sosa-Echagüe Duo*] which was later staged in 1986.[23] The two characters (one a tango writer and the other a tango musician) are resonant of Don Quixote and Sancho Panza in their physical appearance, struggling to salvage their craft in the face of monumental cultural and political changes. With the military Proceso still fresh in mind, the ubiquitous references to the military 'cleansing' echo the government programme to eliminate the undesirables from society. The historical references to Irigoyen, replaced by General Uriburu in 1930, during the apogee of the tango culture, escalates this contemporary play to a similar level with its references to military assaults, exile and the contention that the Peronista period provided the best support ('Ask them if they remember back when they could really eat well', 213).

Halac has continued to agitate for political equality and justice in recent years. Although more at peace with himself and with his society than during the turbulent years of the 1960s and 1970s, he is still an intense individual who sees the problems and does not hesitate to take a stand against corruption, violence, decadence or, increasingly, the rampant loss of values, morals and ethics. His most recent plays, for example, include 'Frida' (1996) in which he searches for the essential values that inspire political and social action within artists.[24] Through a close examination of Frida Kahlo and her husband Diego Rivera in Mexico, he reformulates the commitment that every artist must make with his or her society 'by searching', in Halac's words, 'for the force in the past, in the indigenous, in all the thinkers and men of action that from their angle make the effort to create a better society. Just as Frida did.'

Halac served for two years as director of the National Cervantes Theatre (1989–91), during which he was harshly criticised, and since 1991 he has served as Director of the Chagall Cultural Center. Halac is committed to a better world, to a better society for all individuals, regardless of race, gender, class. Today, distanced from Peronismo, Halac lives and works as an independent writer in Buenos Aires. His theatre matters because of his constant search for new techniques to capture the story of this century in spite of production problems, a diminished public and the cultural impoverishment of a generation immersed in television. One of his great obsessions, before the première of *Mil años, un día*, was to know if the general public would attend a complex performance.

> I especially want to reach people's minds, massage them, caress them. Today we are more conscious of the fact that each and everyone is damaged . . . We are living through a time of great stress in a country that is changing, a country that has new owners and people who are demoralised. Everyone is searching for his or her place to see what to do. For that reason people go to see shows that tell them absolutely nothing.[25]

He maintains that 'faced with the banality of life, in a world such as today's that is devoid of ethical values, I do not regret having believed in the magic of words to reach the hearts of mankind. I am one more in the swarm of little people who resist the notion that consumerism is the god that will calm all our anxieties. The theatre must look for languages to tell the story.' In the final analysis, Ricardo Halac, a thoughtful and perceptive person, a playwright and a man of action, continues to be one of Argentina's most committed and forceful writers.

NOTES

1 John Simpson and Jana Bennett, *The Disappeared: Voices from a Secret War* (London: Robson Books, 1985), p. 47.

2 David William Foster, *The Argentine Teatro Independiente 1930–1955* (York, SC: Spanish Literature Publishing Company, 1986), pp. viii–ix.

3 Personal letter to the present writer, 14 January 1997. Unless otherwise stated, all subsequent quotations by Halac are from this source.

4 Ricardo Halac, *Soledad para cuatro*, in *Teatro*, vol. I (Buenos Aires: Corregidor, 1987). (*Soledad para cuatro, Segundo tiempo, Ruido de rotas cadenas, El dúo Sosa-Echagüe.*)

5 See, for example, Osvaldo Pellettieri, 'Ricardo Halac y sus veinticinco años de realismo', *Latin American Theatre Review* 20.2 (1987), 85–9.

6 See Miguel Angel Giella, 'Teatro Abierto 1981: De la desilusión a la alienación', *Latin American Theatre Review* 24.2 (1991), 69–77.

7 Simpson and Bennett, *The Disappeared*, p. 58.

8 *Ibid.*, p. 64.

9 Ricardo Halac, *El destete; Un trabajo fabuloso* (Buenos Aires: Paralelo 32, 1984).

10 See Miguel Angel Giella, 'Ricardo Halac: *Lejana tiera prometida*', in *Teatro Abierto 1981: Teatro argentino bajo vigilancia*, vol. i (Buenos Aires: Ediciones Corregidor, 1991), pp. 163–75.

11 Diana Taylor, *Disappearing Acts: Spectacles of Gender and Nationalism in Argentina's 'Dirty War'* (Durham and London: Duke University Press, 1997), p. 184.

12 Halac, *Ruido de rotas cadenas*, in *Teatro*, vol. i.

13 Ricardo Halac, 'Viva la anarquía', ms., 1992.

14 Quoted from a photocopied programme note supplied by Halac.

15 *Ibid.*

16 Juan Domingo Perón, *Filosofía peronista* (Buenos Aires: Editorial Freeland, 1973), pp. 166–7.

17 Ricardo Halac, *Mil años, un día*, in *Teatro*, vol. iii (Buenos Aires: Corregidor, 1993).

18 Quoted in Nora Glickman, 'Entrevista con Ricardo Halac', *Latin American Theatre Review* 23.2 (1990), 55.

19 *Ibid.*, p. 56.

20 Ricardo Halac, *Tentempié II* in *Teatro*, vol. ii (Buenos Aires: Corregidor, 1990). (*Estela de madrugada, Tentempié i, Tentempié ii.*)

21 Halac, *Segundo Tiempo*, in *Teatro*, vol. i.

22 Halac, *El destete; Un trabajo fabuloso.*

23 Halac, *El dúo Sosa Echagüe*, in *Teatro*, vol. i.

24 Ricardo Halac, 'Frida', ms., 1996.

25 *La Maga*, 12 November 1992.

OTHER WORKS CONSULTED INCLUDE

Geirola, Gustavo, 'Ricardo Halac' in Daniel B. Lockhart, ed., *Jewish Writers of Latin America: A Dictionary* (New York and London: Garland, 1997), pp. 255–60.

Gilbert, Helen and Joanne Tompkins, *Post-Colonial Drama: Theory, Practice, Politics* (London and New York: Routledge, 1996).

Graham-Jones, Jean, 'Myths, Masks and Machismo: *Un trabajo fabuloso* by Ricardo Halac and *Y a otra cosa mariposa* by Susana Torres Melina', *Gestos* 10.20 (1995), 91–106.

Pellettieri, Osvaldo, 'El destete de Ricardo Halac, o la simulación en la lucha por la vida', in *Teatro argentino contemporáneo (1980–1990): Crisis, transición y cambio* (Buenos Aires: Galerna, 1994), pp. 37–42. *Una historia interrumpida. Teatro argentino moderna (1949–1976)* (Buenos Aires: Galerna, 1997).

# Index

*Aadhunik Ramlila*, 142–3
Afewerki Abraha, 38–42, 43, 52; *If It Had Been Like This*, 38–42, 51, 52; *The Chains*, 39
Africa, 7, 20, 101, 106, 107, 109, 110, 112, 127, 164; constructions of, 7, 56–7, 60–1, 66, 67, 79–84
agit-prop, 38, 39, 114, 148
Aidoo, Ama Ata, 9
Alemseged Tesfai, 4, 5, 8, 42–7, 48, 49, 51, 52; *Luul*, 43; *Meningitis*, 43; *The Other War*, 8, 42–7, 48–9, 51, 52
Algeria, 79, 98, 113, 119
America, United States of, 7, 12, 36, 43, 49, 66, 77, 84, 99, 112, 170, 178, 179, 184, 187, 194
Andrey, Lúcio, 171–4
anti-apartheid theatre, 57
*antillanité*, 100, 111, 113, 117, 120
apartheid, 55, 56, 66, 67, 70
Appia, Kwame Anthony, 67, 68
'area boys', xii, xiv, xv, xvii–xviii; Area Boy Project, xiii, xiv, xvi; *Area Boy News*, xiv; sketches and songs, xvi–xvii
Arena Theatre, 156
Argentina, 4, 155, 177–98
*Aringindin and the Nightwatchmen*, 18
Axworthy, Geoffrey, xiv

Babangida, General, 18
Bakunin, Mikhail Aleksandrovich, 186–9
Bangladesh, 127
'Bar Beach Show', 19
Barletto, Léonidas, 178

*Barranca abajo*, 178
*Beatification of Area Boy, The*, xi–xvi
*Beau capitaine, Ton*, 97
Beaumarchais, 94; *The Marriage of Figaro*, 94
Beckett, Samuel, 80
Behan, Brendan, 181
Biafra, republic of, 13; war, 23
Biko, Steve, 59, 60–2, 65, 66
'Binglish', 126, 131, 133
black arts movement (South Africa), 58, 59, 67; in USA, 59–61
Black Consciousness Movement (BCM), 59, 60–3
Black Power, 84–5, 94
Boal, Augusto, 85, 154–9, 168, 174; *Games for Actors and Non-Actors*, 154; *Teatro Legislativo*, 155–7 *passim*, 168; *Theatre of the Oppressed*, 85, 154
'Bollywood', 130, 132, 133
*Border Connections*, xiv, xv, xvii
Boukman, Daniel, 4, 6–7, 97–100, 103–25; *Chants pour hâter la mort du temps des Orphée*, 98, 103, 107, 114, 121; *Délivrans!*, 6, 100, 103, 113–19; *Des voix dans un prison*, 98, 103, 107; *Et jusqu'à la dernière pulsation de nos veines*, 99, 103, 114; *La voix des sirènes*, 103, 107; *Les Négriers*, 98, 103, 107–12, 114, 119, 120; *Orphée nègre*, 98, 103–4, 105–7, 111
Brazil, 5, 154–76
Brecht, Bertolt, 5, 52, 93, 104, 107, 121, 129, 140, 156, 179, 181

*Cabala y la cruz, La*, 191–4
Canada, 76–8, 84–94
Canadian drama, 77
Canadian Indians, 77, 85, 94
Caribbean, The, 1, 6, 7, 76–84 *passim*;
    French-speaking, 97–125 *passim*
carnival, 76, 86, 155
censorship, 1, 179–80
Centre for the Theatre of the
    Oppressed (CTO-RIO), 156–60
Césaire, Aimé, 6, 80–1, 97–8, 100–6,
    109, 111–13, 120–2; *Et les chiens se
    taisaient*, 105; *Notebook of a Return
    to the Native Land*, 81, 101, 105,
    119; *The Tragedy of King
    Christophe*, 81, 110
*Chants pour hâter la mort du temps
    des Orphée*, 98, 103, 107, 114, 121
*Chains, The*, 39
*Chattering and the Song, The*, 18
Chekhov, Anton, 43, 129, 130
Christianity, 90–2
colonialism, 6, 8, 9, 50, 60, 79–80, 104,
    107; British colonialism, 7, 12, 43,
    76–7, 122, 126; Canadian
    colonialism, 77, 87; Ethiopian
    colonialism, 36–7, 46, 49, 52;
    European colonialism, 177–8;
    French colonialism, 6–7, 76–7,
    97–125 *passim*; Italian colonialism,
    37–8, 43; post-/neo-colonialism, 2, 7,
    8, 18, 50, 77, 87, 89, 117, 120
Company Ltd, The, xi, xiii, xiv
community theatre, xiii
Condé, Maryse, 97, 105; *Pension les
    Alizés*, 97
conscientisation, 61, 135, 137, 144, 152
*Coup d'Etat*, 185
Cree Indian, 78, 84, 86, 88, 92
Creole, 98, 100, 101, 103, 113–22
    *passim*
*créolité*, 100, 117–20 *passim*
Cuba, 98, 113

*Damnés de la terre, Les*, 116
*Délivrans!*, 6, 100, 103, 113–19
*Destete, El*, 182
diaspora, 61, 66–7, 68, 70, 100, 101,
    107, 110, 112, 127, 128

Dieupart, Robert, 98
Dragún, Osvaldo, 178, 182, 185
*Dream on Monkey Mountain*, 77–84,
    91
*Dry Lips Oughta Move to
    Kapuskasing*, 77, 84–94
*Dúo Sosa-Echagüe, El*, 196

*East is East*, 132
*Ecstasy of Rita Joe, The*, 77
*Egoli*, 69–70
*Encontros*, 163
England, 126–34 *passim*
Eritrea, 4, 7, 36–54
Eritrean Liberation Front (ELF), 36–7
Eritrean People's Liberation Front
    (EPLF), 36–54; cultural troupes,
    36–51 *passim*
*Et jusqu'à la dernière pulsation de nos
    veines*, 99, 103, 114
*Et les chiens se taisaient*, 105
Ethiopia, 36, 39, 44, 45

Fanon, Frantz, 6, 15, 59–61, 65, 67,
    79–80, 82, 97–8, 103, 105, 106,
    111–13, 116, 120–1; *Les damnés de
    la terre*, 116; *Peau noire, masques
    blancs*, 105
folk forms, 20–1, 86, 119, 137, 150–1
Forum Theatre, 157, 158
Fraga, Guti, 161–74 *passim*
France, 101, 107, 109, 112, 114, 119,
    121, 122, 183
'Frida', 196
Friere, Paulo, 136, 144, 146

*Games for Actors and Non-Actors*,
    154
Garvey, Marcus, 112
Gates, Henry Louis, 58
genocide, 8, 36
Glissant, Edouard, 97, 108, 111–12,
    113, 114, 118–22 *passim*; *Monsieur
    Toussaint*, 97
Glover Hall, xii, xiii
Gowon, General, 13, 18, 19, 31
*Government Inspector, The*, 129–30
Grotowski, Jerzy, 32
Guadeloupe, 97, 98, 102, 108

# Index

Haiti, 79, 81, 121
Halac, Ricardo, 3, 4, 178–98; *A Night with the Great*, 181; *Coup d'Etat*, 185; *El Destete*, 182; *El Dúo Sosa-Echagüe*, 196; 'Frida', 196; *La cabala y la cruz*, 191–4; *Lejana tierra prometida*, 183–4; *Mil años, un día*, 191–4, 197; *Segundo Tiempo*, 181, 194; *ShowBrecht*, 181; *Soledad para cuatro*, 179; *Tentempié II*, 194; *The Hostage*, (adapt. of Behan), 181; *Un trabajo fabuloso*, 194–5
*Hamlet*, 171–2
Highway, Tomson, 1, 6, 8, 77–9, 84–94; *Dry Lips Oughta Move to Kapuskasing*, 77, 84–94; *The Rez Sisters*, 86–9, 92
Hill, Errol, 120; *Man Better Man*, 120
Hondo, Med, 98, 119
*Hostage, The*, 181

Ibsen, Henrik, 43
*If It Had Been Like This*, 38–42, 51, 52
Image Theatre, 157
India, 1, 4, 127–34 *passim*, 135–53
*Indian*, 77
*Inglês maquinista, O*, 164
IPTA, 145
Irele, Abiola, 11
Irigoyen, President, 178, 196
Israel, 99
*It's All True!* 155

Jamaica, xi, xvi, xvii, 5, 84, 112
Jones, Errol, 82
Joyce, Joyce Ann, 58

*Kali Salwar*, 132–3
Kakaun Sela Kompany, 31–2
Kapur, Anuradha, 129
Kenya, 7, 126, 128
Kenyan-Asians, 8, 126–8
Kingston (Jamaica), xi–xviii *passim*

Lagos (Nigeria), xi, xii, xiii, 19, 33
Lapido, Duro, xiv
*Lejana tierra prometida*, 183–4
*Luul*, 43

*Machadiando*, 166–9 *passim*
*Man Better Man*, 120
Manaka, Matsemela, 55, 67, 69; *Egoli*, 69–70
Maponya, Maishe, 69; *Gangsters*, 69, *The Hungry Earth*, 69; *Umongikazi*, 69
Marie-Jeanne, Alfred, 102, 103
Marlowe, Christopher, 80
Martinique, 6–7, 97–125 *passim*
*Meningitis*, 43
Mehtaab, 129, 132–3; *Kali Salwar*, 132–3; *Not Just an Asian Babe*, 133
*Midnight Hotel*, 18
*Mil años, un día*, 191–4, 197
Miller, Arthur, 179; *Death of a Salesman*, 179
Mitterrand, François, 111
Molière, 121, 129; *Tartuffe* (adapt. Tara Arts), 130–1
*Monsieur Toussaint*, 97
*Morountodun*, 5
Mothers of the Plaza de Mayo, 183, 184

'nation', 16–17; 'national culture' (Canada and West Indies), 76; national identity, 77, 93, 100, 121; nationalism, 80, 102; nationalism (African), 55, 58, 66; nationhood, 8, 121
Native Earth, 84, 86, 92
*Natya Shastra*, 129
Neal, Larry, 58–62 *passim*
*Négriers, Les*, 98, 103, 107–12, 114, 119, 120
negritude, 81, 84, 101, 104, 105, 109, 122; *négritude*, 100
Nigeria, xi, xvii, 1, 3, 5, 7, 8, 11–35
*Night with the Great, A*, 181
*Nós do morro*, 160–74 *passim*; *Encontros*, 163; *Machadiando*, 166–7, 168, 169; *The 7 o'clock Show*, 165–6
*No' Xya'*, 85
*Not Just an Asian Babe*, 133
*Notebook of a Return to the Native Land*, 81, 101, 105, 119

Obasanjo-Murtala regime (Nigeria), 18,
    31
Ogunmola, xiv
*Once Upon Four Robbers*, 21–34
Onganía, Juan Carlos, 179–80
Orisun Theatre, xii, xiii, xv, xvii
*Orphée nègre*, 98, 103–4, 105–7, 111
Osofisan, Femi, 2–5 *passim*, 8,
    11–35; *Aringindin and the
    Nightwatchmen*, 18; *Midnight
    Hotel*, 18; *Morountodon*, 5; *Once
    Upon Four Robbers*, 21–34; *The
    Chattering and the Song*, 18; *Who's
    Afraid of Solarin?*, 18
*Other War, The*, 8, 42–7, 48–9, 51, 52
Oumwene, Tess, 9

Pakistan, 127, 128, 133, 134
*Peau noire, masques blancs*, 105
Pena, Martins, 164; *O inglês
    maquinista*, 164
*Pension les Alizés*, 97
Perón, Isabelita, 177, 180
Perón, Juan Domingo, 179, 180, 188–9
People's Experimental Theatre (PET),
    61–5 *passim*
*Plays for Dancers*, 83
Poulbwa, 98
propaganda, 4–5, 38
*Pula*, 55, 67, 69

racial discrimination, 55, 70, 127
racism, 56, 63, 68, 109, 111
*Rez Sisters, The*, 86–9, 92
Royal National Theatre, The, 130, 131
*Ruido de rotas cadenas*, 185
Rural Education and Development
    (READ), 141–3
Rushdie, Salman, 130, 134
Ryga, George, 77, 84–5; *Indian*, 77; *The
    Ecstasy of Rita Joe*, 77

Samudaya, 145
Sánchez, Florencio, 178; *Barranca
    abajo*, 178
Saro Wiwa, Ken, 1
Schwarz-Bart, Simone, 97; *Ton Beau
    capitaine*, 97
*Segundo Tiempo*, 181, 194

Serreau, Jean-Marie, 122–3
*Scenes in the Life Of . . .* , 128, 129
*7 o'clock Show, The*, 165–6
Shagari, Shehu, 18
Shakespeare, William, 80, 105, 129,
    130, 172, 179; *Hamlet*, 171–2
*Shanti*, 55, 61–5
Shezi, Mthuli ka, 55, 61–5; *Shanti*, 55,
    61–5
*ShowBrecht*, 181
slavery, 101, 109, 111, 164
Social Action Group (SAG) theatre,
    135–53
*Soledad para cuatro*, 179
South Africa, 1, 3, 4, 7, 8, 55–75, 134
Soyinka, Wole, xi–xviii, 2, 3, 4, 5, 9;
    *The Beatification of Area Boy*, xi–xvi
Sri Lanka, 127
Stoppard, Tom, 94
story-telling, 130, 151
street theatre, 135, 145, 152
Sutherland, Efua, 9

*tamasha*, 137
Tamasha, 129, 131–2; *East is East*,
    (Ayub Khan Din), 132; *Women of
    Dust*, (Ruth Carter), 131–2
Tara Arts, 128–31, 132; *Scenes in the
    Life Of . . .* , 128, 129; *Tartuffe* (adapt
    of Molière), 130–1; *The Government
    Inspector* (adapt. of Gogol), 129–30;
    *Yes, Memsahib*, 128
*Tartuffe*, 130–1
Tatata, Paulo, 169; *Abalou*, 169–71
Teatro Abierto, 182–3, 185, 194, 195–6
Teatro del Pueblo, 178
*Teatro Legislativo*, 155–7 *passim*, 168
*Tentempié II*, 194
Theatre for Development, 14–15, 137,
    149
Theatre of the Oppressed, 155–8
    *passim*
*Theatre of the Oppressed*, 85, 154
Theatre Passe Muraille, 84
Thiong'o, Ngugi wa, 6, 117
Third World, 9–10, 16, 60, 61, 99, 112,
    120, 121
*Ti-Jean and His Brothers*, 79, 120
*Trabajo fabuloso, Un*, 194–5

# Index

*Tragedy of King Christophe, The*, 81, 110

Trinidad, 8, 84, 112, 134

Trinidad Theatre Workshop (TTW), 76, 80, 82, 84

*Umongikazi*, 69

Unibadan Travelling Theatre, xiv

University of Ibadan Arts Theatre, 31

Union of Soviet Socialist Republics (USSR), 36, 39

Uriburu, José F, 178, 196

Vancouver Headlines Theatre, 85

*Ventres pleins, ventres creux*, 98, 103, 114, 121

Verma, Jatinder, 2, 6, 7, 8, 126–34

Virgin Islands, 84

*Viva la anarquía*, 186–91

*Voix des sirènes, La*, 103, 107

*Voix dans un prison, Des*, 98, 103, 107

Walcott, Derek, 6, 8, 76, 77–84, 85–97 *passim*, 120, 121; *Dream on Monkey Mountain*, 77–84, 91; *Ti-Jean and His Brothers*, 79, 120

Ward Theatre, xii–xv *passim*

Welles, Orson, 155, 186; *It's All True!*, 155

West Indies, 76–7, 78–84, 97–125

*West Indies, ou Les nègres marrons de la liberté*, 98, 119

West Yorkshire Playhouse, xi, xiii

*Who's Afraid of Solarin?*, 18

*Women of Dust*, 131–2

Yeats, WB, 80; *Plays for Dancers*, 83

*Yes, Memsahib*, 128